Finding
Gloria
Special Edition

MARIANNE CURTIS

Published by Emerald Publications

ISBN-10: 1481063928
ISBN-13: 978-1481063920

DEDICATION

This book is dedicated to my four amazing children and my grandchildren. You are my greatest achievements – you are my legacy. I hope this book brings understanding and I hope that you are never ashamed to call me "Mom."

To Dan, my editor, mentor and friend;
you taught me more than you will ever know.

To the many people who stood beside me throughout my life's journey – you all taught me something about myself and without your guidance and patience I would not be the person I am today.

To both my adoptive and birth families.
I am forever grateful.

The truth has set me free!

ACKNOWLEDGMENTS

Layout and design: Dan Guetre, One One Consultants Inc.,
Marianne Curtis, Emerald Publications
Proofreading and editing: Dan Guetre, Wilma Priebe, Dawn Hawkins and
Tom Hallick of Gorilla Cage Media Works

A very special thank you to all my volunteer readers;
your help, feedback and encouragement kept me motivated.

This story is based on actual events and depicted as accurately as possible.
While locations and situations are real, the names of people involved have
been omitted to protect their privacy.

"When a child has been abused – it changes their spirit.
It affects who they are and who they are meant to be."
Oprah Winfrey

PREFACE

Over the course of my life I have learned a simple truth - sometimes we have to hit rock bottom before we can claw our way desperately to the top. Unfortunately, like many lost souls, I had to learn this the hard way – one painful step at a time.

I realized something important one night after my third husband had just admitted he'd sexually assaulted me while I slept. It wasn't the first time, but it would be the last. It destroyed my spirit that someone I loved and trusted could hurt me in what I considered the most sacred of ways. He knew my past and when we married I believed his vow to love and protect me. Instead, he callously tossed those beliefs away and violated me for his own perverted pleasure. His sickening betrayal was just one more kick in the teeth after a lifetime of kicks.

Devastated, I locked myself in my bedroom; refusing to come out for three days. Emotionally spent I felt sucked into a whirlpool of internal agony – I was at my lowest point. Wrapped in utter despair, I felt trapped in victim mode. While I knew it was wrong, I carried the deeply rooted belief I deserved every rotten thing that happened to me in my life - this is what I'd been taught to believe about myself. My self-worth and self-esteem lay in shambles, and I couldn't find the glue to put it all back together again. I've spent much of my life unsuccessfully searching for unconditional love and acceptance - instead I received a lifetime of pain and disappointment. The only thing I was positive about was how tired of being hurt I was; especially by those I loved and those who claimed to love me.

During my self-imposed exile I realized I had somehow allowed myself to become a shell instead of what I was meant to be. I was feeling miserable with my heart filled with self-loathing. I hated that I was weak and scared so I picked up my pen and started to write. I wrote to clear my head, to clear my heart but mostly to understand how I arrived at this crucial breaking point. Ultimately, I was writing to save my soul and my life!

Since putting my life story on paper, I have learned I am not an empty shell as I once assumed. I have learned I am strong; I am a fighter and I was meant to be here and write this book. Baring my soul and being vulnerable, I have disclosed my truth for everyone to see and in the process I found myself. Through the creative process, I have come to realize I have finally faced my demons and risen above them.

Before diving deeper into this story, it is important for the reader to note the many players in the story of my life – some good and some bad. Regardless of status, the characters remain nameless in this tale of woe for a reason.

I am eternally grateful to the nameless heroes and heroines who've played a role in the story of my life. Their names are tattooed forever on my once tattered heart. Their simple kindnesses gave me hope when I thought all hope was lost. These courageous people can rejoice in knowing they played a significant role in this woman's healing.

As for the villains, they also remain anonymous on these pages, but they are never forgotten. Their names are branded in every scar I bear - seen and unseen. These people need to know how they affected my life, but they do not deserve condemnation – not even from me. I forgave them long ago because I refuse to allow bitterness to destroy the wholeness I have finally achieved.

This may be a difficult story to read but it is my healing process. As each page poured out of my soul, I slowly came to realize I have been blessed in many ways. Finally, I have learned that this entire time I had everything I needed in life to be happy. I just needed to find faith and believe my life was full of wonderful things instead of dwelling on the horrors of the past. Most of all, I had to believe I deserved true happiness. Without this belief, my life would continue to spin out of control. Writing my story has allowed me to find all the pieces of the puzzle called "my life". Now I see a beautiful tapestry instead of a pile of worthless rags.

With forgiveness comes freedom.

CHAPTER ONE

I have always dreamed about being a writer, but it wasn't until about fourteen years ago I began to focus on writing as a career. Since then I have had more than seven thousand articles published in a monthly newspaper called the *Dawson Trail Dispatch*.

While I spent most of my life without a voice, when I write for the paper people pay attention to what I have to say. As a reporter I have written articles that have turned municipalities upside down or raised eyebrows and panic at provincial legislative levels. Articles I've written have helped organizations; whether to buy medical equipment for individuals or raising money for organizations and foundations. Over the years, I've helped raise awareness for countless causes and groups. It is a thankless profession, but it makes me feel good knowing I was doing what I love – writing - while making a real difference in lives and communities. One of my favourite stories was how the Richer School collected thousands of pennies for a two year old who needed a heart transplant because they saw the story I wrote about her and her family. Most of the time I don't get a "thank you" but when I see the results from my articles, I know I am making a difference. For me, that was all the reward I needed.

When working a story, the public would see a confident woman who asked tough questions using both humour and empathy. In a region notoriously conservative and stiff, there was never a doubt: I was different, and I stood out in a crowd. At first, it was difficult to earn respect in my field because I was considered an "outsider." Years earlier I'd learned the hard way that unless you subscribe to the culture of this area, it is difficult to fit in. True acceptance was nearly impossible. Yet, I persevered and fought hard to earn and uphold a fair, unbiased reputation as a journalist – mostly with success.

Meanwhile, behind the scenes, my life was an unhealthy mixture of joy and turmoil. I was living on an emotional roller coaster. Many of my personal struggles occurred within my heart and behind closed doors. My public side and private life were contradictory - only those close to me knew how conflicted I was. Privately, my heart was torn in pieces and my personal life was in shambles.

I struggled daily to raise four children, mostly on my own, to the best of my ability. Immature and inexperienced, I believed I was failing miserably. I lost count of the numerous times I would ask myself, "What is the purpose to my life?" I was like a hamster, spinning on a rusty wheel – making a lot of noise but void of destination. No matter what I said and did, I constantly felt like a failure and disappointment. I just couldn't wrap my head around how I was helping countless strangers when I couldn't help my own family or myself.

I felt like a constant victim and I hated it. I knew I could be better and I knew I was a good person but years of abuse filled me with doubt and self loathing, leaving me to believe I was not worth a good life. Then one day I said enough was enough – I was tired of being on the outside of life looking in. I realized I could not keep living like this and something had to give. I needed to find the answer to why I always felt this way so I started to delve deeper into where I came from and what I had been through.

Slowly a big picture began to emerge. The truth was: as a child and teenager, I was a victim of emotional, verbal and physical abuse. This dysfunction did not give me the stable and secure foundation I needed so as an adult I made many mistakes - some I am too ashamed to admit even to myself. Thankfully I realize now, all these experiences, good and bad, played a significant role in making me the woman I am today.

Without strength, determination and stubbornness I would not be here. I would not be able to share this sometimes heartbreaking story. I would not be able to take responsibility for my mistakes. Nor would I have finally realized I am not completely at fault. You can't blame a child for not learning to run, if you don't teach them how to walk in the first place. Without these traits I would not be able to wake up smiling in the morning, determined to make each new day a chance at a fresh start. Most of all, I never have been able to fully forgive those who wronged me throughout life.

Someone once told me the past is in the past and people need to stop using their upbringing as a crutch. People need to take responsibility for their lives and make the best of it, he said. This may be true and there are many people who blame their history but I'd like to believe I am different - that for once I am special. I sometimes linger on the past but only to learn from it – the cycle was going to end here and it was in my power to make it happen. Reflecting gives me an opportunity to find answers to questions I've been afraid to ask. It gave me an opportunity to search for the elusive piece of myself that has been lost for so long.

I discovered with research that many people who suffer severe abuse in their lives lose their true selves. Like being brainwashed, you are not even aware it is happening. Unless you have travelled that horrific road, it can be difficult to understand how lost one can get. When you are told the same things constantly, it becomes a subconscious mantra you never shake. It stays buried deep within only to rear its ugly head when you least expect it until you correct what is steering you off track. Only then can one make the right choices and return to the correct path which will eventually lead you to becoming the person you were always meant to be.

My life's path veered off course drastically during childhood. I have always believed a mother's love should be unconditional. It wasn't until I became a mother myself I finally understood what unconditional love really meant. I concluded that no matter what we do in life, the warmth of a mother's loving heart should always welcome one home. This was the acceptance and love I never received and without realizing it, this has affected my entire existence.

In my head and heart, it is very difficult to find self-worth when I'd been rejected by not one, but two mothers. The first rejection occurred when my birth mother signed my adoption papers. The second came when my adoptive mother started saying she wished she'd never laid eyes on me. I grew up believing I was the ugliest, dirtiest, most horrible person on earth and that no one would or could ever love me.

Subsequently, I've spent my entire life coming to grips that this was not reality. I've come to realize there was a reason my birth mother gave me up. There was also a reason why my adoptive mother was so cruel to me. These reasons had nothing to do with me as a person — that is the reality. However, years of brainwashing and abuse left deep scars on my heart and spirit. I cannot deny or run from this and trust me - I have tried.

Four decades after taking my first breath, I finally discovered the truth about my birth. With that came true understanding that my past may have been traumatic in many ways, but it also helped create the uniquely wonderful woman I am today. I could have grown up bitter and unemotional. I could have abused like I was abused; and hated like I was hated. Instead, I dedicated my life to loving those close to me and making sure they feel that love every single day of their lives.

My name is Gloria and this is my story.

CHAPTER TWO

There are things I am going to share that some readers may find disturbing and difficult to swallow. This story is an honest retelling of my life as I lived it and if you are expecting an easy read, you will not find it within these pages. This may be a disturbing tale to read, but remember it was a difficult life to live. There is one thing I can promise – it has a happy ending.

Admittedly there are parts of my life I would erase in a heartbeat. Yet, I sit here knowing each experience has shaped and moulded me over the years. It has taken me half a lifetime to realize and appreciate this simple truth. There was a time I could not believe my past was ever good and I am grateful my eyes and heart are finally open to the truth. Unfortunately it took me awhile to get to this point and committing my colourful story to paper was all part of my healing process.

I guess the beginning is the most ideal place to start. Although I am not sure which beginning I should focus on - there have been many in my life. Ultimately, it doesn't matter because eventually all these beginnings lead to the same thing – me.

My life's journey began during the early hours of May 3, 1968 at the Royal Alexandria Hospital in Edmonton, Alberta. After hours of labour, my mother pushed me into the world into a room filled with silence instead of the joy that normally comes from giving birth. There was a doctor and a few nurses involved, but no loving husband or celebratory congratulations. Before she could see me, I was quickly whisked away to the nursery. My fate was already decided - I would not be spending my life in her loving arms.

My birth mother was nineteen when I was conceived and it should have been the happiest day of her adult life. My birth mom was young, smart and beautiful - she had the world at her fingertips. Just graduated from high school, she was eagerly looking forward to university where she yearned to study to become a teacher. Then she met my father. He was forty-four when I was born and worked as a cab driver. They started seeing each other regularly and eventually she fell in love with him. Seduced by his magnetic personality, the pair planned to get married. Not long after he proposed she excitedly announced that she was going to have a baby.

Her excitement was short-lived. When she told her family, instead of celebrating my upcoming arrival, my grandfather rejected my mother and her delicate condition. Instead of being excited to be a grandfather, he responded negatively. *What will the neighbours think?* He demanded.

It was the late sixties and an unwed teenage mother was considered one of the worst things that could happen to any Catholic family. As a devote Catholic and the king of his castle, my grandfather refused to accept an unwed daughter. It was shameful and unacceptable. Accepting her condition would have meant condoning her choice to have premarital sex – a huge no-no in the Catholic doctrine. Yet very little could be done once the "seed was sown". Abortion was not even a consideration. It was too new of a medical procedure plus it was against everything my mother's family believed. Good thing too, otherwise I wouldn't be here to share my story.

My grandfather decided to confront my father and demand he make an honest woman of my mother. Over the summer the pair had already become friends and golf partners – it was easy for the two men to become companions because not only were they going to be family, but they were both the same age. Under the circumstances it seemed natural my grandfather approach his soon to be son-in-law and demand a wedding take place immediately.

However, with this epiphany in hand my grandfather arrived on the doorstep of his future son-in-law, where the door was opened by another woman. My grandfather soon learned she was my father's wife. This came as a huge shock for everyone – especially my mother.

She was a young woman excited about the future and meanwhile she was the other woman. Everything my father told her during their courtship turned out to be lies. The scoundrel led her to believe he loved her and they would wed while in reality he was already married with two young daughters.

With a heavy heart, my grandfather returned home and reluctantly told my mother the sordid truth. There would be no wedding and there would be no happily-ever-after. Devastated and heartbroken, my birth mother never spoke to my father again.

Technically even though my mother was nineteen, she was still a minor - at the time, the age of majority was twenty-one. Questioning my mother's judgement my grandfather took charge what he considered his wayward daughter's "unfortunate situation". He was adamant he would not support us – the pregnancy, after the birth or anything. My birth mother was told in no uncertain terms if she decided to raise me, he would not support her financially and we would end up on the streets. It wasn't like today when teenagers get pregnant and they can collect welfare, get an apartment and a free leg up in life until their child is six. In those days, if family cut you off, you lived on the streets or starved.

In the end, I guess my mother could have stood up for me. But I can also see how she would have been intimidated by her domineering father. He would constantly remind her that she was underage and he had full control of her life. Because of her age, even if she rebelled, my grandfather could make decisions on her behalf without her knowledge. Backed into a corner she did what she felt was the right thing for me. Once she gave birth, she would give me up for adoption. She was given no choice.

The toughest decision of her life made for her, my grandparents allowed my mother to stay with them until she started to show. Until now, as the only girl in the family, my mother got everything she wanted – she was her daddy's girl. Now, for the first time in her life she was shunned by family and isolated from friends. She was sworn to secrecy and forbidden to share her experience even with her best friend. How her heart must have broken – such a heavy burden for one so young.

When she could no longer hide her pregnancy, my birth mother was placed in a home for unwed mothers in Edmonton. There she spent the remainder of her pregnancy sequestered with other unfortunate girls, knowing the outcome was already decided for her. There was nothing she could do but abide by what her parents dictated or her life would be ruined. She remained in that home until I was born, predestined for adoption. As a mother, I cannot imagine the pain she must have felt knowing she would never be a part of my life.

After my birth, we both stayed at the hospital for six days. During that time my mother would sneak down to the nursery often despite the rules, to watch me sleep in my hospital bassinet. The rules were very strict. Once a mother decided to give up their child physical contact was discouraged. This strongly enforced rule was expected to prevent bonding and keep the birth mother from changing her mind. She was not always alone in defying the rules during the secretive visits to the nursery window - my grandmother was also a regular fixture.

Finally, on the day of her hospital discharge, my birth mother begged a nurse to allow her to hold me. My mother didn't care about the rules. She wanted – no, she needed to cradle me just once before she was forced to say goodbye forever. A reluctant decision to bend the rules was made by staff and with my grandmother at her side, my birth mother cradled me close to her heart; kissing me from head to toe.

"I loved you so much and I couldn't send you off without telling you," she told me four decades later. "I inspected your fingers and toes, trying to memorize everything about you. I sent you away with hundreds of hugs and kisses. I wanted you to know that I loved you and I always would love you."

Heartbroken and defeated, my mother held me close to her heart for as long as possible until the nurse finally returned and "tore" me away from her arms forever. Before she was discharged, pages of paperwork were placed before her and she slowly signed each one on the dotted line. At the bottom of the Application to Surrender she painfully penned her reason for relinquishing custody of her newborn daughter.

"I feel that I would not be able to give her a proper home as my life is still unsettled. This way I know that if she is adopted she will receive the proper love and care due her by two parents who will love her and want her," she wrote.

With tears pouring down her face, she signed the last page and sadly pushed them aside. The walk down the hall and out of the hospital was the longest in her life. Her only solace in leaving me behind, even though it broke her heart, was the knowledge she'd done the best that she could. It gave her small comfort.

Before walking out of my life forever, my birth mother gave me one final gift. She named me Gloria Jean. It was a name she'd chosen years earlier when she was a little girl, playing house and imagining life as an adult. Unfortunately, this was nothing like her childhood fantasies.

CHAPTER THREE

November 8, 2003

Tonight I discovered my adoptive mother had been admitted into a nearby hospital. My adoptive mother is on her deathbed! Or at least that was what I was told. Not only was she in the hospital, but she'd been a patient for almost two months. My heart sank as my third husband repeated to me the message he'd heard from my nine-year-old son. After coming home from a weekend with his dad, my son told his stepfather he'd overheard a mutual friend say he'd seen my mother in the hospital.

My stomach did flip-flops as I grabbed the phone and dialled the number for Bethesda Hospital in Steinbach. It was answered by a nurse stationed in the emergency room. I had forgotten all calls were automatically dispatched there after midnight. Knowing I sounded like an idiot I quickly explained I'd heard my mother was hospitalized and I was looking for information. The nurse was able to confirm the rumor but that was all. I waited impatiently as she transferred my call to the correct ward.

Clutching the phone, I trembled uncontrollably as I waited for someone to pick up the line. I looked at the clock. It was three o'clock in the morning. I felt ridiculous calling but I had to know what was going on. I wouldn't sleep until I knew the truth. It angered me that I was making this call when I should have been told this news by someone in my family. How could I ever explain to a stranger I had just found out this terrible news? I felt ashamed my family cut me from their lives so completely they could not even call me to tell me Mother was in the hospital.

"Hello, nurses station," a new voice finally answered the phone. Swallowing my pride I tried to stifle my raging emotions as I inquired on my mother's condition. I didn't get an answer right away. Instead of answering me, the nurse asked me a few questions of her own. As expected, the nurse's voice betrayed disbelief as I explained to her I had just found out about my mother's dilemma. Sympathetically, she confirmed Mom had been admitted on September 10. She added, according to my mother's chart, I was listed as an emergency contact if something serious happened to my mother. This came as a surprise, considering no one had told me Mom was admitted.

My next question was: who had admitted my mom? In my heart I already knew the answer. I already suspected that once again my sister and brother-in-law had taken control of the situation and deliberately excluded me but I had to know for sure.

"Your brother-in-law brought your mom in one night after she was found wandering outside and confused." explained the nurse. This was news to me. I didn't realize she was having memory problems. It was explained that on my mother's first night in the hospital, she walked out the front door unnoticed, and the local police launched an extensive search. The incident ended well a few hours later; my mom was found only a couple miles out of Steinbach. Apparently she was trying to walk home – back to the farm. A farm, she left in the fall of 1997, the year my father died. It was a farm she always seemed to hate, yet suddenly it was the only place in the world she wanted to be.

After placing the phone back onto the hook, I sank into my husband's waiting arms. I curled up like a scared little girl and cried like my heart was breaking. I felt so betrayed by my family and sick with worry about my mother.

The last time I had seen her was only a few months earlier. I had run into her at the local mall while shopping one afternoon. My daughter, husband and I walked right up to her and she did not recognize me at first. We talked for a few minutes - she told me she was grocery shopping with my sister so I didn't stick around. Unfortunately, I was in a hurry and while I thought it was odd that she didn't recognize us at first I didn't red-flag the situation at the time. Before that incident, it had been over a year since I visited her at home. I had my reasons for staying away but suddenly they were meaningless.

Feelings of guilt, fear, pain and remorse flooded me as I thought back to the last few years. I sobbed for my mother. I sobbed for me. I sobbed for what might have been and what never was. It is difficult to think of Mom with only one emotion. I remembered all the times I tried to be the daughter she seemed to always want. Yet, I hurt so deeply because I failed miserably with every attempt. My sister was always "The One"; the perfect daughter in my mother's eyes. I was forever the unlovable outcast, the butt of every joke and humiliated constantly.

But with that simple phone call to the hospital all the reasons for keeping my distance no longer mattered.

The following day I drove to Steinbach to see her for myself. Even though I was worried sick, I couldn't help but be angry with my family for not telling me. In recent weeks, my oldest daughter had been a fixture in the emergency room while we tried to diagnose a stomach problem she was having. If I had known my mother was just down the hall, I would have been spending time with her instead of wasting it sitting in a waiting room. Despite everything, I would never have ignored her and her condition.

The next morning my husband and I walked through the front doors of the hospital. I was grateful the nursing station was empty when I first arrived. It gave me a chance to catch my breath and gather my composure. Like every visit with my mother, I had to prepare myself mentally and emotionally. These encounters were never easy even under ideal circumstances.

When I was finally noticed, a nurse wandered over and I explained who I was and why I was there. My first query was to ask about my mother's condition. My relief was instant when I heard she was not dying - she was just mentally confused. I had worked for three years as a health care aid in a nursing home, so I understood my mother was at the age where memory would naturally start leaving her. I mentally prepared myself but I was still shocked when I entered her hospital room.

The first thing I noticed was my mother was in there with two other elderly women. Being the anti-social woman she was, I could not imagine how she could possibly tolerate the lack of privacy and space. She was not the mom who went shopping, hung out with friends, went on coffee dates or played bingo. She was a hardworking, devoted farmer's wife. She did talk to various women from church, but she was not one to foster close enough bonds to form friendships. They always remained more like acquaintances. After my dad passed away, my mother literally locked herself in her home. She even refused to answer the phone unless she recognized the phone number on her call display. Honestly the real world terrified my mother and she kept herself safely locked away from harm and ultimately from life.

Glancing toward her bed, I recognized one of my mother's hand-crocheted afghan blankets. I remember watching her make it, her nimble fingers working the soft yarn with skill and speed. I found comfort in the familiarity of that simple blanket but it also reflected the permanency of her situation. Underneath its woolen weight lay my mother, all curled up and alone. The woman I saw was nearly unrecognizable. The waist length dark hair that had greyed over the years was now shortly cropped and white. It also looked like as if it not been combed for a few days.

After a slight hesitation, I continued into the room. Hearing my footsteps, she looked up curiously. My heart quivered in relief when Mom's face lit up with a huge smile. Despite warnings from hospital staff she might not recognize me, I could tell she did. I could see it in her beautiful brown eyes. To my even greater surprise, she sat up instantly, opened her arms and reached out for me. In tears, I allowed myself to be pulled into her arms and let her hold me.

I was transported back to when I was a little girl, to a time before when her comforting embrace could make the world seem better. I found myself gladly embracing her, clinging to her now frail body. I did not want to let go and neither did she. I anticipated painful rejection; instead there was a welcoming acceptance in her arms that I never expected. She kept pulling back to look lovingly into my tear-filled eyes then she'd gently pull me back into her arms. This lasted nearly ten minutes.

When I could finally speak I asked if she knew who I was - I had to know if she knew who she was holding. I had to know it was real; not an illusion of my love starved soul. Without hesitation, she responded "Marianne". She has admitted in my teenage years she hated the name Gloria so she'd changed my given name when I was first adopted.

I felt instant relief but there was also a deep seeded fear and suspicion. Just to make sure, I asked her again if she knew me. This time, she looked at me with puzzled eyes and stated emphatically, "You are my daughter!" Her tone of voice changed when she responded to my repetitive questioning. It was like she was saying, "How dare you even ask me that question again."

I sat there; choking back uncontrollable tears I couldn't bear it a moment longer. Overwhelmed with emotion, I stepped out of the room where my husband patiently waited in the hallway. As he held me, I let my tears flow unchecked. When I was finally able to compose myself long enough, I stammered, "That woman is not my mother – where was this person twenty years ago?"

I was ashamed as soon as the words left my lips but I could not contain them. For years I had craved a mothers' loving touch. It was there when I was a little girl, but as I grew up, it became non-existent and I was turned into a puppy, waiting to be patted on the head. But even that simple act of tenderness never came, especially when I needed it the most. I was used to being pushed aside and belittled. For her to reach for me willingly and pull me into her arms such as it was in the hospital room was simply overpowering.

From inside her room, I could hear Mom fiddling around with the few personal items she had from home. Not wanting her to think I had snuck out, I quickly composed myself and re-entered the room. Smiling happily, she invited me to sit beside her again. It felt odd to be sitting on the edge of her bed. That simple act was a sad reminder of one more thing that I was never allowed to do when I was younger. It seemed ironic that all I had wanted as a child was suddenly before me. But in reality, it was too little, too late.

Don't get me wrong - it was wonderful to feel the warmth of her arms around me but at the same time in my heart I knew with her diminished mental faculties we'd run out of chances to make things right. As sad as it sounds, I wished my mother was still the bitter, worried person I'd grown to know. I knew that side of her and could understand it. To see her so happy at the sight of me should have brought me peace, but instead, it broke my heart. It was a side of her I barely remembered and it confused the hell out of me.

It was then I realized I had never seen her look so happy and relaxed. Her eyes were even sparkling with genuine joy at seeing me and even more surprising - love. Try as I might, for the life of me I cannot remember seeing my mother's eyes impart with happiness - especially when she was looking at me.

Realizing it was getting late in the afternoon, I knew it was time for me to say my goodbyes. After promising my mother I would come back, I gave her another hug and left the room. As I walked down the hall I looked back. Mom was standing outside her room, jacket in hand and a puzzled look on her face as she watched me walk away.

Climbing into the car, I thought back to that sight and burst into tears all over again. It was so hard to leave her. She was like a lost child watching her parents leave her behind without the ability to grasp why she must stay. It was shocking for me to realize my mother was indeed childlike in her own way. It broke my heart to know she would never be the same again.

CHAPTER FOUR

When I started writing this book, I could not remember much about the first few years of my life. I had blocked a lot out. Some memories I blocked intentionally because of the pain they caused and others have been blocked because I was too young to consciously remember. Little snippets of my life come back as flashbacks now and again, but for the most part vivid memories are few and far between. Thankfully, through completing this project I have remembered a lot about myself, my life and my family. Some of what I've learned has been good and some of it bad. But that is okay; what matters is the result and it has all been part of my journey towards healing.

When I was a child, we lived in a three-bedroom bungalow on Montrose Road in Niagara Falls, Ontario. Our home was in a newer part of the city with an open field behind that was farmed until a few years before we moved out. My mother loved the house because it was made of brick and had hardwood floors, in her perspective it was strong and could last forever. It was a physical symbol-of-stability which I believe she needed more than anything.

When you walked through the side door, which faced the street, you entered the kitchen through a doorway to the left. This was my mother's domain. She was an old-fashioned homemaker who prided herself in keeping a tidy home, sewing clothes for everyone, knitting and cooking. Her Ukrainian cuisine was sure to make any mouth water and in many ways we were spoiled during those days. She took good care of us. It was a ritual that no matter how busy everyone was, we would sit down and have dinner together in the dining room. There were no exceptions. A homemade meal was always on the table shortly after my father walked through the door at the end of a hard day of work.

My father was a tall thin man, with jet black hair and hazel eyes. I always thought he resembled Ronald Reagan. Dad worked at Ontario's Ohio Brass, which manufactured insulation and surge arresters for high-voltage electrical equipment as well as mining equipment. When he wasn't working, he loved bird-watching and photography. He also enjoyed woodworking and remodelled our unfinished basement into a pine recreation room - a favourite place for me to play.

Many years later I discovered my parents met through a newspaper ad. My mother was the youngest daughter of a poor Ukrainian farmer from Wishart, Saskatchewan, a tiny hamlet about 168 kilometers north of Regina. Her parents emigrated from the Ukraine and settled in the area within the municipality of Emerald. Life was difficult for them, especially during the Great Depression when my mother was born. I later found out that her father was an alcoholic who took out his anger on his timid wife and family. My mother adored her mother, and always mourned she'd left home and moved so far away to be with my father.

When I was a little girl I loved looking at photographs of my mother when she was younger. I thought she was extraordinarily beautiful with her long, chestnut hair and big, sad brown eyes. One day she confided that when she was in her late teens she had fallen in love with a local boy, a fellow classmate. They were planning to get married when he suddenly died tragically – he drowned in a local swimming hole. My mother was inconsolable. When she turned eighteen she left home and moved to nearby Yorkton, Saskatchewan where she worked at a nursing home until she met my father.

At the urging of my aunt, who was convinced my mother would become an old spinster, Mom placed a personal ad in a Winnipeg newspaper in hopes to find a husband. She was surprised to receive many letters from eligible bachelors, but did not open a single one. It wasn't until her sister pestered her to take a chance she finally opened the last one. It was from my father.

While my mother was a poor farm girl, my father was a city boy from Welland, Ontario. How my father laid his hands on a personal ad placed in a Winnipeg paper is lost to history.

His parents initially had a small beef farm, but his father was forced to dispose of the operation after he lost the use of his legs. Just like my mother's father, he loved to drink and after a bender, crashed his car and never drove again. He remained bound to a wheelchair the rest of his life. To help his family out, my father and his only brother started a trucking business together. My dad loved to drive and as a truck driver, spent many hours happily bouncing around in a cab-over transport truck.

The budding lovebirds started writing back and forth for a few months. Eventually my father sent her a train ticket and she made the trip to Ontario to meet him and his family. When they finally met everything seemed perfect and they fell in love. The couple married soon afterwards and settled in Welland. Once they married, my mother convinced my father to come off the road – she did not want to be married to a truck driver. So he gave up his dream and the life he loved and settled into a factory job as a machinist at Page-Hursey in St. Catherines. While they saved money for their own home, the newlyweds settled in with my father's parents and started their own family. My brother was born within the first year of their marriage.

When I think back to the few things my mother shared about her past, it was about this time that she started to show signs of irrational behaviour. Now I realize, it may have been postpartum depression, but at the time, the disorder was not something doctors really recognized. But in her mind, life had changed drastically. She was a new mother living with in-laws she was convinced despised her. She started to accuse my father's family of involvement in witchcraft and she became obsessed with irrational fear. She was even convinced that her in-laws were trying to kill her.

One story she often told about those 'dark days' was how my father's only sister had died. My aunt was killed in a car crash while my mother was pregnant with my brother. The way my mother told it, I had an uncle she felt was involved with Satanism. As the family gathered to discuss the tragedy, this uncle pointed out it wasn't supposed to have been my aunt who was killed and implied that it should have been my mother. In her increasingly fragile and paranoid state, this was another chink in her rusty armour. Horrified, rational or not, my mother started to fear for her life. Looking for help, she went to the family doctor and was prescribed various medications and even shock treatment therapy. In those days, shock therapy was used to treat depression, and I remember her admitting to me in a later conversation that was her diagnosis. She never stayed in treatment for long.

As my brother grew over the next couple years, my mother seemed to garner emotional strength. She was setting in motion becoming the matriarch of her own domain while living in the basement of her in-laws. My parents decided to have another baby. But it was not an easy process. My mother had lost an ovary after having my brother so this made conceiving more difficult the second time around. My sister finally arrived about two and a half years after my brother. When my sister was born my mother was elated. She had a son and a daughter. Everything was finally perfect - or so it seemed.

After my sister's birth, my mother's mental state was once again in decline. She grew restless and determined to put as much distance between her in-laws and her growing family as possible. Because he loved her and his family, my father indulged her. I am not clear on what happened after this point other than my family left Welland and headed west. My father eventually landed a job near Camrose, Alberta. I am not sure what he did for a living at this point but he earned enough to build my mother her dream home on newly-purchased property.

My mother should have thrived in Alberta. She was finally away from the in-laws she was convinced despised her, my dad was building her a house and it was a new start for the little family. Either way, she should have been happy but deep down she harboured her own painful burden. When I was little, I'd devour the many black and white photographs from that time frame. My father loved taking pictures so there were many snapshots of Mom standing by the house or posing near a new car my dad had bought. There are also many photographs of my brother and sister concurrently and life appeared picture perfect. But the pictures of my parents betrayed another story. In each photo my father was beaming from ear to ear while my Mom's eyes betrayed a sadness I never understood.

It wasn't until recently I learned the true scope of how tortured my mother was in those days. My sister surprised me by recalling how her memories of childhood included sitting in the backseat of my parent's car while my father desperately reached over my mom's lap trying to hold the car door shut to prevent her from leaping from the moving vehicle. I had no idea my mother was so tormented she wanted to end her life.

Her own recollection stirred my memories of how my mother got so bad at times my father was afraid when she drove anywhere alone with the car. If she wasn't home on time, he always feared the worst. How she got past that point, I don't know – based on the story I am trying to tell, maybe she never really did. I do know that she was determined to have another baby. Unfortunately things do not always turn out as planned.

This time, ongoing medical issues left my mother unable to carry a baby to term. She told me once she had several miscarriages before they finally gave up trying. While most of the losses happened the first few weeks after conception, some of the babies were carried halfway to term. She admitted once that with each pregnancy she lost, a piece of her already fragile heart died.

Unable to bear any more losses my parents decided to look at other options to add to their family. Adoption seemed a valid solution so my parents looked into it further and eventually proceeded. They filled out the application and started the screening process with the Child Welfare Branch of Alberta. There were several home visits including one-on-one time with each family member. This hurdle complete, it was determined that my parents were suitable candidates for adopting. They were now taken to meet new babies. My parents decided they wanted a little girl born of a Ukrainian Catholic mother – something that never wavered.

"We wanted a blue-eyed, redheaded baby girl," my mother once told me. She was always partial to red hair because her own mother was a natural redhead. I was a blonde, brown-eyed baby. "But when we saw you, we fell in love with you," she confided in me on one of her good days.

When I was much older, my mother cruelly told me that I was not their first choice. These words are as painful today as they were when I first heard them when I was about ten years old. I was six months old when I finally went to my new home. I had spent half of my first year of life in a foster home with several other babies. My mother was thirty-six and my father was thirty-seven when I finally came home.

We lived in Camrose for another year while my adoption was finalized. One of the conditions for my adoption was my family had to remain in the general area until I'd lived with them for a year so Child Welfare could conduct surprise home visits regularly to ensure the adoption was a good fit. Social workers had the authority to drop in at any time they pleased. With any hint that I was not thriving, I could have been removed from my new family forever. Until I became a mother myself, I could never understand how stressful and intrusive this would have been for my very paranoid mother.

It is easy for me to believe that because of my mother's was constant fear that someone could come into their home and take me away my family pulled up their roots and headed back to Ontario. Her constant paranoia fed that fear.

But, instead of moving back to Welland, close to my father's family, they bought the bungalow in Niagara Falls. It was here I would spend the next eight-and-a half years of my life.

CHAPTER FIVE

My entire life, I have looked back at the years we lived in Niagara Falls as the best years of my childhood.

Until I was about two and a half, my mother and I were close. We were inseparable and I would freak out if anyone tried to take me away from her. She was my entire world and at this point, I knew she adored me. I remember walking downtown to the bank with my mother, rain or shine. Sometimes she'd pull me in a sled, other times I would stumble along, scuffing my shoes.

I was always with my mother. My brother and sister were thirteen and ten years older than me, so they did not spend as much time with me as I would have liked, unless they were forced to. But this truth could be said for sibling relationships in many families.

My mother was very protective of me to the point of being suffocating. I sometimes wonder if she still worried someone would come into our house and take me away from her. Because of this paranoia, I was not allowed to leave the house or yard without someone going with me. Leaving me with a babysitter was out of the question as my mother had little trust for anyone outside our house.

I am not sure what happened, but she was convinced that while I was in the care of an extended family member something happened. Just before giving birth to my first child, she suggested that I was sexually molested by this family member – but I have no memory of anything inappropriate happening so I personally have my doubts. All I know is that suddenly I was no longer mommy's angel. Initially shy and clingy, I started to go to almost anyone having replaced my shyness with a seemingly new extrovert attitude. I think my mother was displeased with my conjured independence. She reacted badly; in her mind she was losing her little girl.

Many parents would fight to regain their importance in their child's eyes. My mother reacted to the contrary, she herself withdrew. Sensing my mother's rejection, I gravitated to the next available adult – my dad. I adored him and everything about him. While I spent my days with my mother and knew everything about her (at least in my child's mind), my father remained an elusive mystery.

Each morning he would leave for work before I was awake, and I'd wait eagerly for him to come home at the end of the day. His return never failed – he was never late. Within minutes of walking through the door, he'd find his favorite chair in the living room and I was soon crawling uninvited into his lap. We'd sit there and I'd babble incessantly about my day. Then I'd just cuddle in his arms while he watched television until supper was ready. While I loved the time we spent together, my mother seethed with unreasonable jealousy.

Until I started school I had few friends. I followed my brother and sister around like a lost puppy. I adored my big brother, who strongly resembled my father but he was taller even as a teenager – a bean pole actually. He was thirteen years older than me and seemed to love the undivided attention and endless giggling from his little sister. The older I got, the less I seemed to annoy my older brother. He got past the point of accepting me as an interloper and became an actual caring sibling.

He would make me howl with laughter doing crazy imitations. He was the only person that I knew who could watch cartoons and mimic the voices of the critters. His favourites were Donald Duck and Porky Pig. Even our cats owned a voice complements of my brother. We would laugh to tears at his conversations with Rossi, a white cat we'd smuggled from Saskatchewan one summer.

My brother also had an awesome bedroom in the basement where I liked to play in even though it was off-limits to me. I would crawl onto his bed and watch him work on his projects. He loved to tear electronics apart so the smell of solder is something I will always associate with him. My mother's brother got him hooked with tearing apart radios, televisions and anything else that was electronic. He would dismantle them and put them back together – sometimes working better than before. Other times, parts would end up in a box at the back of his closet. When he wasn't working on electronics, he was building model airplanes or model cars.

My brother also loved music. There was a great hiding spot under the basement stairs in his closet where I would crawl into the back and listen to him play his guitar, sometimes falling asleep amid his dirty laundry. I would spend countless hours somewhere in the vicinity of his playing. It wasn't until I was older and became a music lover I recognized songs he played from bands like the Beatles, Simon and Garfunkel, Led Zeppelin and Aerosmith. He could play any song by ear and that made him spectacular in my child's eyes. I always hoped he would teach me how to play but it never seemed a priority in his eyes.

When I wasn't being the annoying baby sister, he seemed to enjoy spending time with me. I'd like to think now it is typical for a teenage sibling to outwardly protest entertaining any sibling more than ten years their junior but inwardly thrive on the "hero worship".

One of my fondest memories was how he'd perch me in front of him, on the bar of his 10-speed bike. Mom would send him to the corner store for milk or bread and I would feel lucky to tag along. Instead of walking, the crossbar would become my domain and off we would go. He was always careful I wouldn't fall off as he sped down the street with me squealing in delight.

I remember losing a tooth one day and placing it carefully under my pillow for the tooth fairy. I woke up in the middle of the night to catch my brother sneaking out of my room. The next morning I found a five-pack of bubblegum balls under my pillow instead of my tooth. I wandered into the kitchen showing off my treasure and everyone acted surprised. I don't think he ever figured out I suspected how it got there.

My brother was also obsessed with cars and would haul old jalopies home with plans to turn them into sleek hotrods. This hobby drove my mother nuts because our driveway always contained the carcass of at least one old "project car". All the hours I spent watching him work gave me a love and appreciation for classic cars and trucks. I drove him crazy with my endless questions, but over the years, I learned enough from watching him that I can now confidently care for my own vehicles. He never knew how much of an impression he made on me and how much I adored him.

While my brother didn't mind me for the most part, my sister seemed to consider me a royal pain. Even though she was always colder, she always fascinated me. She was in high school and loved her clothes and shoes. With long auburn hair, I always thought she was so beautiful. I would watch her get dressed up and put makeup on with awe until she would finally get annoyed and kick me out of her room.

She was also an amazing artist, and would create amazing pencil sketches. Her artistic talents knew no boundaries. She would later turn her talents to painting with oil on canvas. If we were blood siblings, I'd say this was from where my oldest two daughters get their artistic talents.

I remember fondly a rare afternoon where she got down to my level and crawled under the hedge by the front steps and played cars with me. My mother had bought me a bag of red, yellow and green plastic cars at the local general store. I loved playing with them because they required a lot of imagination – there were no opening door or turning wheels and imagination was something I never lacked. My sister painstakingly created roads in the dirt until we had a complete city. It was one of the few pleasant memories I have of her spending time with me. I also remember how mad she was when we were done playing and I just 'wiped' her work away. I was just a little kid, done with playing for the day but I think she took it personally because she got angry with me and refused to play with me ever again.

When I was really lucky, I got to play Barbie dolls with her. I was still too young to have my own because of all the small parts, but once in awhile she would bring her collection out to play. My mother would sew her tons of clothes for the dolls, so it was always fun to dress them up. She would eventually get angry with me and hide them all because for some odd reason, I would cut off all their hair, never grasping it wouldn't grow back. I think my sister just assumed I was out to wreck her stuff.

While I do have some great memories of growing up with my siblings, for the most part, my mother was insistent we keep to ourselves. I had gotten used to being the baby and the center of everyone's universe. As I got older and my brother and sister became busier with high school, looking for jobs and their budding social lives, I grew lonely at home entertaining myself. I'll admit, I was starved for attention and would do almost anything to get it, even if it frustrated everyone else.

A little girl moved in across the street from our house when I was about three or four years old. I felt like I had won the lottery. She came from a big family and she was the only girl in a gaggle of older brothers. We became playmates and best friends even though she was a year younger than me. Her family was more progressive than our family. They were more open to the traditional 70's family ideals. Changing technology, lifestyle and culture did not scare them. They even had a little pet monkey.

My parents did not approve of their lifestyle so I was never allowed play at her house but she would spend hours at mine. We would play together for hours and then start fighting as only best friends do. She'd get mad, take her toys and go home, then a few hours later, she'd come back and we'd start playing again. We used to drive my mother batty because she would often have to referee our disputes. Most of our squabbles stemmed from me constantly demanding to have my own way. My lack of social skills stemmed from isolation. Despite everything, we were inseparable and the best of friends until I started kindergarten.

When I was about four, a boy my age moved in next door. I suddenly had two playmates, which made the days even more fun. He brought out the adventurous side in us, as only a boy could do. He tried teaching us to climb trees, hang upside down on the swings, and explore the hundred acres of vacant field behind our homes. The more time I spent with my friends, the less I spent with my mother and she didn't take it very well. It wasn't the mother-daughter closeness that she felt she was losing as she had already started stepping away from that path. But the inability to maintain control over my world was a real threat to her psyche.

While I was enjoying life with my newfound playmates, my mother's behavior started to change. She grew increasingly paranoid. She'd spy on us through the basement windows and accused us of being inappropriate. I remember one afternoon, playing house with my two friends. We loved playing house. We were all cuddled in the basement bed, when my mom peeked in on us. The next thing I knew, she was downstairs, screaming at all of us. She sent them both home crying after freaking out on us because we were playing in bed together. It was innocent and I never understood her overreaction. Neither did my friends. This occurred many times to the point that my friends did not want to come over to play anymore.

It wouldn't matter though, because once I started school our friendships changed. I was older than both of them, so once I started Kindergarten, they stayed friends with each other and I moved on.

I was one of the youngest students in my class when I started school at Greendale Elementary. The school was about seven blocks from home and I would have to walk it daily, rain or shine. At first my mother walked it with me. I remember many times following her, trying to make my short little legs keep up with her longer steps. If I lagged in my step she was quick to get angry, scolding me, sometimes not waiting or giving me a yank on the ear.

By Grade two, I was on my own. After two years of walking to school with me, my mother had timed the route down to the last minute. Once she trusted I could cross the street without getting hit by a car, she let me walk the few blocks to school alone. For me, this was exciting. I could dawdle and enjoy the view. However with this extra freedom came caveats. I was given strict rules – I had a certain time period to get home and if I was one minute late, my mother would be angry. There were no exceptions.

I recall one winter, a nasty snowstorm kicked up during the school day and classes were dismissed early. My mother did not have a vehicle so there was no choice: I had to walk home. I remember stumbling through waist deep snowdrifts, blinded by the blowing snow. My only guide was the occasional hedge or break for driveways or streets. At one point, I heard yelling but I remained steadfast on my goal – I had to make it home. Suddenly I was snatched out of the storm and quickly found myself being pulled into a heated truck with several construction workers.

The workers had seen me blindly tracking my way and grabbed me just before I tumbled into a deep hole they'd been digging in the street. If they hadn't grabbed me, I would have fallen more than ten feet. They kindly drove me home and handed me over to my mother. She politely thanked them but as soon as the door was closed, her attitude quickly changed. Soon I was whipped for getting into a vehicle with strangers, spanked for leaving the school early (she never asked if we had been dismissed) and then sent to bed without dinner for scaring the living hell out of her.

After that, I was always worried about making her angry, yet there was never any consistency to what set her off. Many times I'd be sent to bed without dinner or I would get a spanking. To make things worse, I was so scared to be late, I'd forget to visit the bathroom before leaving school and by the time I'd get home I'd have peed my pants. In retrospect I look back and try to retrace the thought process I made. It was easier to hide my humiliation in the bottom of a laundry hamper and postpone punishment than to face the instant condemnation I'd get for breaking my mother's rules.

Things were complicated at home and not any easier at school. It was not as easy for me to make friends in school as I thought it would be. I made it difficult for myself because I aggressively sought approval at every turn. I had an overactive imagination so I would invent stories about my life. I was told so many times, by my mother that I could not speak about what happened at home, that I would make up things. When I did tell the truth, I was always called a liar. How I wished my life was like everyone else's.

It was frustrating because all my classmates seemed to have the best of everything and I had to remain content with what I had. My mother firmly believed that if she gave us everything we wanted, we would become spoiled and unappreciative so she was rarely generous. Most of my classmates played together outside school or went to birthday parties and I wanted to be included. At first I would get invitations to parties, but because I never went, they eventually stopped. All I wanted was to fit in but my mother made it impossible. I know I resented it.

It was around grade two I began to realize that many things happening at home were unusual. While classmates boasted about spending holidays with extended families, including grandparents, it became painfully obvious that my mother could not stand her in-laws. Visits were always preceded by arguments between my parents. Finally, out of duty and obligation, my mother would concede defeat and we would go to Welland to see my dad's family.

I loved it there – my grandmother or Baba as we called her, only spoke Ukrainian. While I didn't understand her, I knew she loved me.

Even my grandfather fascinated me. At this age, life was still strange and unique even if it was in the form of a wheelchair-bound grandfather and a grandmother who spoke a language that was both poetic and exotic. I also had two cousins slightly younger than me. Their parents (my dad's brother and his wife) doted on them and I was often jealous of their many toys and fashionable clothing. Moreover, I was jealous of their life. They had parents who outwardly showed their love and affection – something that was stolen from me. My mother preferred to keep things simple and I rarely had fancy dresses filled with lace and ribbon like my adorable cousin had.

Christmas was always exciting when we gathered at Baba's but at the same time, it was heartbreaking. I would open all my gifts with excitement – my father's family was always generous and they spoiled all of us. The car was always overflowing with toys when we went home. Unfortunately, my sudden wealth of wonderful playthings never lasted. I knew when we got home, my mother would go through everything and eventually my treasures would disappear, never to be seen again. It was like she expected anything brought home was cursed and bringing it in would be allowing that dark cloud to affect our household. It may have been logical to my mother but to me it was just mean.

When classes would start again after holidays I would go to school and tell all my classmates what I got for Christmas. I always looked forward to "show and tell" because it was nice to have the spotlight on me. Unfortunately, while I would "tell" I could never show the wonderful things I had received because my mother had already thrown them out or stashed them in places unknown. Subsequently the kids never believed me, making me look like an even bigger liar. I would try to explain to my classmates but only succeeded in making things worse. No one understood what was going on – how could they?

My life was unusual. Classmates noticed and picked on me because of it. I was constantly bullied because of my "tall tales". They were unsubstantiated truths but to the outside world, they were seen as lies. Out of pure desperation to be liked and accepted, in grade three I announced I was having a birthday party and invited my entire class. I'd never had a birthday party before and I wanted to be liked so badly. When my classmates showed up on my doorstep, I assumed wrongly that my mother would instantly cave and allow me to have the impromptu party. Instead, she banished everyone from the property and turned her anger on me. I got a licking that I never forgot. When she said she would make sure I couldn't sit for a week, she did exactly that. This was one of the first times her anger overcame her. I would never try that stunt again.

Not only did I get a spanking, but the cake she had baked and decorated earlier that day, along with all the presents my family had bought disappeared. I didn't have a birthday celebration that year at all. To add insult to injury, I was beaten up after school the next day by a girl that lived down my street. She didn't like the fact she had been invited to a party that was not even scheduled. From that day on, whenever she found me, she would push me around until I could escape. Eventually I got smart enough to either leave school quickly or hide on the way home so I wouldn't meet up with her. I remained terrified of her until we moved from Niagara Falls.

All I wanted was some sense of normalcy even though I was not quite sure what 'normal' was. I knew my friends were having fun, doing things as a family, and learning new things while I dreamed of having a life just like them. Meanwhile, for me, home was becoming an unhappy little prison.

Little did I know, things could and would get even worse – and they did.

CHAPTER SIX

The one thing I learned young was that my mother was a deeply religious woman and her faith was strong. For as long as I can remember she was a devoted Catholic and as such our family never missed Sunday mass. While most kids were learning how to talk, we learned how to pray. Not the standard "God bless my family" prayers, but rosaries, novenas and other Catholic litanies. When we were sick, we still did not miss a service. I went to Catechism, received the Sacraments and even enjoyed going to church at first. I loved the architecture, the candles, incense and music. This was normal in our house and bearable until my mother's faith took an extreme right turn.

Mom became a fanatic. She started changing around the time that she discovered a new cult-like religion. She came across a free newspaper one day that originated from Bayside, New York. The paper, a propaganda piece published by a religious sect, claimed a woman named Veronica Lueken received visits from the Virgin Mary and her son Jesus regularly. Hundreds of believers would gather on Catholic feast days at the Vatican Pavilion at the old World's Fairgrounds in Flushing Meadows-Corona Park in New York to see the seer and witness "miracles". By 1975, the site was known as the "Lourdes of America."

The messages supposedly received by Veronica revealed the general state of evil in the world, the state of corruption within the Catholic Church, the evil within the Vatican itself, and the need for worldwide atonement to God to avoid chastisements. Believers were told that if this was not done, there would be terrible consequences. More specifically, the messages warned that a worldwide warning and fiery chastisement in the form of a "Ball of Redemption" or comet which would strike the earth. They also predicted World War III and other disasters that would allegedly remove three-quarters of the world's population. To prove that there was truth to these messages, every day news items were twisted into "signs" the predictions were coming to pass. This gave believers a sense of urgency - including my mother.

Desperate for something to believe, my mother fell for the apocalyptic message hook, line and sinker; our lives began changing to meet the specifications of her new beliefs. She became obsessed with the end of the world and saving our immortal souls. Her belief in this cult's teachings was so viral, that it affected her deeply until the day her mind finally shut down and she slipped into dementia five years before she died.

Soon our much-enjoyed family camping trips were put aside so the money could instead be used to take bus trips to New York to attend vigils which never started until just before midnight.

Until I started school, my life revolved around my family and the house, so when we'd pack up the car and hit the open road, I was elated. We didn't spend any time socializing with the outside world but my parents loved to travel. Maybe it was because my dad had the heart of a long-haul trucker, but he didn't like to sit still for long. When he wasn't working on improving our house, we would enjoy road trips and Sunday drives.

During the summer months, my mother and father would spend his two-week vacation traveling. When I was too little to be left with a baby-sitter, we took many family road trips where we eventually visited nearly every province and many of the American states. Occasionally we'd even head to Saskatchewan to spend time with my mother's family. Most of these road trips I was too young to remember, but I knew we'd been many places because my mother collected spoons and stickers as souvenirs of landmarks and cities we visited. These were placed fondly on an old green metal cooler that made every single trip with us.

On one of these trips my dad picked up his prized possession – a handcrafted fibreglass birch canoe. I remember sleeping in the bottom of that boat while my parents paddled along Black Creek,

Ontario on lazy Sunday afternoons. We'd paddle silently along the river, stopping occasionally to take pictures or to just enjoy the sounds of nature. Eventually, I would tire and curl up on the bottom of the canoe while my parents spoke in muted voices in an attempt to not bother the wildlife or me. Those were glorious days.

When I got older and could be left with my siblings, my parents would pack up for a weeklong adventure on their own. They'd head out into the wilderness so they could canoe, fish, and pick blueberries. I was never lucky enough to go on those trips although I remember my brother and sister taking turns going with them. I was always upset to be left behind. Most of all, I was afraid I was missing something exciting and I was afraid they were having so much fun while they were gone they wouldn't want to come back. Maybe some of my mother's paranoia was rubbing off on me.

Either way, all this seemed to stop once my mother discovered Bayside. Instead of enjoying the simple pleasures of life, my mother became focused on suffering and penance.

The vigils in New York were always greeted with mixed emotions for me. On one hand, it was exciting to be on a huge tour bus full of singing and praying Catholics. I loved watching the candlelit crowd. I enjoyed these trips even though I didn't fully understand their meaning because it was important to my Mom. She seemed to glow when she participated in these things. I yearned to have her love me like she loved God. I was just a little kid but I remember kneeling in the snow, freezing while everyone around me prayed and sang. Child and Family Services would have had a field day with that if they'd known.

After finding this new faith, one of the first drastic changes she made was to destroy our television. Thanks to Bayside, my mother believed it was a tool of the devil. One Sunday afternoon my brother, mother and father disappeared for a couple of hours, along with the family television. I found out later that they went to the Niagara Gorge and tossed it into the Niagara River. There would be no more *Walt Disney*, *The Waltons*, *Wild Kingdom* and other family shows that my dad and I enjoyed watching together. Soon our evenings were spent praying, and reading religious books that my mother was suddenly buying as money allowed.

Her next step was to change how we dressed. All my comfortable clothes were destroyed to be replaced with long skirts, and turtle necks. My sister's wardrobe suffered the same fate. Her modern bellbottoms and platform shoes were replaced with a new wardrobe mostly created by my mother. The more conservative the clothing, the better – slacks were no longer allowed. I think this affected my sister most because she was in Grade 12 and fashion is important to any teenager girl. But no one dared argue or stand up to Mom. We just followed her lead like sheep.

Soon she was buying statues of Mary and Jesus and many Catholic saints. These religious icons replaced the much loved family pictures and knickknacks my mother used to have around the house.

Every single night we would surround my parents' bed on our knees and say three rosaries before bedtime. Bored and tired, I would fall asleep; drooling on the bed by the time we hit the second set of beads. Exhausted from his day at work, my dad would soon be snoring beside me. Eventually my mother converted my sister's main floor bedroom into a chapel and my father was allowed to go to bed instead of joining us but never without an argument with my mother. This was a difficult time for me as I didn't understand what was really going on – I was only about seven. I overheard the conversations my mother had with the rest of the family and the entire apocalyptic concept scared me. A child's already overactive mind suffered when hearing daily discussions about the end of the world, war, and death. As a result, I lived in constant fear of being judged and found wanting. I didn't want to be punished that way. I tried to be virtuous but I was a typical child. I was curious and mischievous but I was never what I would consider as "bad" – a term my mother used regularly towards me along with "possessed" and other terms I didn't understand.

With my soul now in jeopardy, I was now old enough for the real discipline to start. My mother was no longer afraid to spank me or discipline me in any way she saw fit. Many Saturday mornings, I could be found on my knees in the middle of my parents' bed praying before pictures of the Sacred Heart of Jesus and the Immaculate Conception which hung above their headboard. The more mischievous I was during the week, the more prayers I'd have to say. I would have preferred to be playing in my room or having breakfast. Instead I had to wait until my punishment was done before I was able to eat and begin the rest of my day. I was so afraid of spending my days like this, even though I tried to be extra good, according to my mom I failed – I was forced to pray many rosaries.

Over time I began to believe that I really was an evil child. It seemed like I was always being punished. If I thought this was unfair, I was reminded how when my brother was younger, Mom would make him kneel on rocks to pray so I should be grateful I got to kneel on her bed. Life got to the point where I was afraid to move for fear that what I would do, would land me in bed without supper, or on my knees praying for hours on end.

With my overactive imagination, it was easy for my mother's obsession to contaminate my dreams. I started suffering horrible nightmares. I'd dream I would die, go up to heaven, God would look at me with contempt, decide I wasn't good enough and send me plummeting to hell. I'd wake up terrified and more determined that I would try to be a better child so I wouldn't suffer such a horrific rejection.

Instead of being comforted, I was mocked. My fear of rejection and abandonment intensified. I started dreaming my family would take me shopping at some store or the mall and leave me there. At first my family would be close, my mother even holding my hand. Then suddenly they'd be gone, the store would be closed and I'd be left alone. I was constantly worried that if I was a bad girl I would be left behind anytime we went shopping once those dreams started. Instead of feeling secure and loved as a child, I lived in constant fear of abandonment.

My dreams were so real that I would wake up petrified and screaming. It would take my entire family to get me back into my bedroom at night. My mother would say it was like I was possessed at bedtime. My entire family would grasp whatever flailing limb they could and they would all try to take me down the hall to my bedroom, while I kicked and screamed until I was hoarse. I am amazed no one heard my terrified screams and called the police. Sometimes I'd wake up in the middle of the night and escape my room but this was eventually stopped when my mother installed a lock on the door from the outside, and I'd get locked in at night.

Knowing I'd eventually get locked into my room, as the clock ticked towards bedtime, the anxiety started to build. The only person who could ever calm me down was my father. It became a nightly routine that he would come into my room and would tuck me in for the night. He was always so loving and sweet. He'd only leave when my mother would start yelling at him, asking what was taking so long. I loved how he'd make sure my closet doors were closed, and make sure there was nothing under the bed. Then he'd lean over, brush my hair out of my face, kiss my forehead and slip from the room. This innocent nightly ritual was eventually squelched, thanks to my mother. She started to get upset my father would spend so much time alone with me. She used to scream at him that it was not proper he be alone with his young daughter. He would answer her with silence.

I didn't understand what the accusations were until I was much older, but she was convinced that he was molesting me during these nightly rituals. Once I was older and a mother myself, she admitted she overreacted because of her own experiences. She later told me she was just trying to protect me from what her father had done to her.

I never needed to be protected from my father – but I would eventually need to be protected from my mother

CHAPTER SEVEN

In 1977 life as I knew it took another drastic and unexpected turn. I was turning nine and just finishing grade three.

The year before, my brother finished school and was having a hard time getting a good paying job. The only jobs he could find locally were at places like McDonald's and Pizza Hut but they never lasted. He was a genius with electronics, and even went to Niagara College to improve his education, but at the time jobs in the field were still few and far between. While jobs were getting scarce in southern Ontario there was an employment boom to the West so he decided he would set off in that direction to seek his fortune and future.

Meanwhile, the company where my father worked as long as I can remember was also on the verge of closing its doors. Knowing he would soon be laid off, my father decided to tag along, to both support my brother, and to find something for himself. While they intended on finishing their trip in Alberta, they never made it. Somehow along the way they stopped in Steinbach, Manitoba.

I still remember how upset my mother was when she received the phone call from my father saying that he and my brother had bought a farm in southern Manitoba. Not a simple hobby farm but a full fledged dairy farm. Neither man had any experience with farming other than from the small beef operation my grandparents once operated. My dad told Mom to put the house up for sale and he would be back at the end of June to pick us up so we could all head west. The timing for the move was perfect for my sister because she was in her final year of high school; she was able to graduate before we moved.

To say my mother was upset is an understatement. She was furious and hurt that my father and brother made the decision to change all our lives without first consulting her. But she was obedient. Mom listed the house for sale and started packing up the only home I had ever known. She grew bitter and a personality change took over her spirit while she prepared for the move.

It was a stressful time, and I wouldn't know until I was grown up how hard that move was for my mom. After growing up on a farm in Saskatchewan during the Great Depression, farming was not the lifestyle she wanted for her family. It was a hard life, full of sacrifice and it was something she didn't want to relive. Yet, my mother tried to make the best of the situation and raved about how we would be living along a dirt road and how I'd have to take a school bus to school every day.

For me, moving was exciting. While I would be saying goodbye to my few friends and my school, it was also an adventure. For years, my family watched *Little House on the Prairie* so I had an unrealistic fantasy about what life on a farm would be like. The weekly series depicted farming as a simple life, full of old fashioned values. It also accurately reflected the new simpler life my mother wanted us to live. It was the only show we watched on a regular basis until the television met its demise at the bottom of the gorge. I was thrilled at the prospect to be like Laura Ingalls, the little pioneer girl who was the apple of her father's eye. My father even nicknamed me 'Half-Pint' just like Laura's father did in the show which made me feel special. I was more than ready to be the happy little country girl, running free in the prairies.

While my mom and sister packed the house and readied it for sale, I tried to keep out of the way as much as possible. I was too little to actually be of any use packing so I kept busy preparing for the big move in my own way. I missed my dad terribly and I was ecstatic to finally know that I would be seeing him again at the end of June. My mother dug out her old bike and decided it was finally time for me to learn how to ride a two-wheeler. After all, if we were on a farm surrounded by fields along a dirt road, I would be safe. There was plenty of frustrating moments but eventually both my mom and sister taught me to ride in the backyard so when Dad returned I could surprise him for Father's Day. His face beamed when I showed off my new skills pedalling my mother's ancient bike up and down the driveway. His prideful smile made every bruise and bump I earned while learning to ride worthwhile – and there were a lot, since the bike I learned to ride was my mother's and way too big for my stubby little legs.

Learning to ride a bike fostered my independence. Even I could see that I was starting to grow up. I'd wanted to learn how to ride a bike for years, but my overprotective mother was convinced if I did while we lived in the city, I'd get killed. We lived along a busy street so she was probably right. In my search for adventure, I tended to be careless and got myself into situations that I should have avoided.

A good example was earlier that spring, when my curiosity saw me stuck in a puddle of boot-sucking mud. The field behind our house was being developed into a new subdivision, and construction crews were busy building roads and installing culverts. One afternoon, I was playing in the back yard when I heard water dripping. Curiously I wandered off on a quest to find the source only to get stuck in the mud - badly.

Instead of calling for help, I struggled for what seemed like hours, trying to tug my rubber boots out of the mud. Eventually my knuckles were raw and bleeding from my many failed efforts. I was caught between a rock and a hard place. My boots were new so I couldn't just leave them behind and if I took them off, I'd have to step into the mud which would make me dirty. I was terrified of being caught in this situation by my mother so I fought to get free with no success, while sobbing in frustration. Eventually my brother heard sobbing and he came to investigate. When he finally spotted me and assessed the situation, he laughed his head off, before fetching a broom to pull me out with while my family tagged along. With them all laughing, I assumed everything was okay. However, after I got a comforting hug from my mom to settle my terrified mind, I was then given a sound licking for leaving the yard and putting myself into danger.

Now that the backfield was filling up with new homes, I was more than ready to move somewhere I could explore to my heart's content without worrying about having my wings clipped. The farm promised the freedom that I so desperately wanted. At the end of June, my mother, father, sister, a five-gallon pail of guppies and angelfish; and three cats made the trek through southern Ontario into Manitoba. The van was as full as we dared and we added a U-haul trailer packed with our personal belongings. The rest of the furniture had already been loaded into a big moving truck and would arrive at our destination at a later time.

It was the beginning of summer and starting to get steaming hot; and we were packed like sardines in the ancient blue cargo van. My dad had purchased the van a few years ago specifically for our family camping trips. It was only a two-seater, so my brother had taken a pair of bucket-seats from one of his cars and bolted them to a sheet of plywood so it would be semi-comfortable. My dad had also designed and built a bunk in the back so we could sleep on the road. In those days, it seemed safety was only an option.

It took us three days of travelling to get through southern Ontario. It would have been shorter going through the United States, but with a trailer full of personal belongings and the pets, my parents did not want to go through customs at the border. The trip seemed to take forever but I had tons of books and puzzles to keep me occupied, along with the added bonus of antagonizing my big sister. By the time we arrived in Steinbach, everyone's nerves were frayed.

I remember pulling into Steinbach for the first time. Always on the lookout for landmarks, the first thing we spotted was the old windmill at the local museum north of town. Having never seen a real working windmill before, I wanted to stop but I was told we had to grab a few things and head out to our new home. It had been a long journey and my mother was looking forward to cooking a real meal for her family. With that in mind we went down Main Street in search of a grocery store and settled on Penner Foods. I waited with excited impatience as my mother grabbed a few things before we hit the road for the last six miles.

My first impression of the farm was it was paradise. It was a dairy farm, so there were cows and calves everywhere. The older two-story farm house was surrounded by stately pines making the yard nearly invisible from the road. There was a machine shop in the yard, and several other buildings including a horse barn, hay shed and several wood and steel grainaries. The paddocks were surrounded by tamarack rail fences, and animals were scattered everywhere including several racehorses which I instantly loved. The animals on the farm came with the sale so they were all ours, except for the horses. This was very different from our little lot in the city.

The farm was a paradise in my innocent eyes but to my parents, the reality was very different. Upon our arrival, we were shocked to discover the previous owner and his family had yet to vacate the premises. Until the paperwork for the sale was complete, they planned to stay and teach my father and brother how to be successful farmers. This was an unexpected and unpleasant surprise for our family. My parents thought we would be moving straight into the house. Instead we were forced to set up camp in the yard, literally.

Our belongings were unloaded and stacked in a tiny single car garage complete with dirt floor. My parents pitched a big canvas tent in the side yard for my sister and I to share. Mom and Dad set up their home in the van because it had a real bed. A makeshift kitchen was set up in the garage; at first we barbequed or used the old Coleman stove. Later when our furniture arrived, the fridge and stove were installed in the garage so my mom could start cooking again. That entire summer, family meals took place on a picnic table in the yard. We spent the next few months living like vagabonds on the property of our new home. For me it was an adventure, we were camping after all. But I can see how difficult it was for my family. We were all affected except my brother. When my father returned to gather us up, my brother moved into the house and that is where he stayed while we lived outside like gypsies.

My mother was not happy with this arrangement. Before the move, I am convinced my parents loved each other and had a great relationship. In Ontario, I would be comforted by the sounds of them whispering on the other side of the wall, sharing their private thoughts behind closed doors. Now my mother seemed constantly disappointed or angry with my father and I didn't understand it.

I learned much later that some of my mother's bitterness stemmed from the purchase of the farm. When my dad and brother originally bought the place, they had agreed to be equal partners. They purchased the land, homestead, animals and machinery, and my parents paid a good price for the property. But when Dad returned to Ontario to retrieve us, the previous owner of the farm pulled a fast one. My parents accused him of selling off the herd and replacing it with an old, dried up bunch of cows. The implements were also allegedly sold, and replaced with ancient machinery, some had been modified from their original horse-drawn design. This is not how my mother expected her new life to begin, but there was not much we could do. If my parents had backed out of the sale, we would have been homeless.

We tried to make the most of our first summer in Manitoba despite our sparse living conditions. The farm including the yard was eighty acres of field, pasture and bush. In addition, my father leased a hundred acres across the road so he would have crop land until it was sold a few years later. I loved that piece of property because it had a dugout way in the back. I spent many summers reading on the banks of the pond, watching wild ducks and listening to crickets. The path to the watering hole was a dirty trail worn into the ground from the constant meandering of a tractor. It was the perfect place for me to safely practice riding my bike.

In the fall, just before school started, we were finally able to move into the old farmhouse. The two story house was roomy but the upstairs space was limited. My brother had already taken up half the second floor so my sister and I ended up sharing a smaller room facing the driveway and main farm yard. Until now, my sister always had her own room so she did not like being forced to share her room with me. She was a lot older than I and having a bratty little sister going through her things was not her idea of a good time. I must admit though that I enjoyed snooping through her stuff. She had great things, especially once she got a job at the local printers.

We may have left the big city life behind but my mother's over-protectiveness towards me did not change. With the addition of several dozen cows, bulls, farm machinery and the previous owner's racehorses still onsite; she was worried that I would get hurt so I was not allowed out of her sight very often. It was nice to know she didn't want me injured but at the same time, I wished I had more freedom to explore – the freedom I had looked forward to enjoying.

Towards the end of summer, I was taken into town and registered for school. I would be starting grade four at Elmdale School, one of the three elementary schools in the community. I was really excited for many reasons. A school bus would be my transportation, so that meant no more walking to school. I was also starting a new school and the prospect of making new friends was very exciting. My isolation would finally end. Little did I know how difficult it to blend into the community.

Back in 1977, Steinbach was not as welcoming to outsiders as it is today. The seemingly humble community was founded about a hundred years earlier when eighteen Mennonite families emigrated from Russia and settled in the area. Mennonites were farmers and the Steinbach area met their needs with acres of lush farmland and trees. Most of the community consists of descendants from its founding fathers, predominately German speaking Mennonites.

One of the first things I noticed when we first arrived, there seemed to be a church on every single street corner. I thought this would make my religious mother happy, but I was wrong. Once in school I learned that if you didn't attend any of these churches it was hard – if not impossible - to fit in. My naivety to my differences in religion and culture in my new home and the expectations of a great life were soon dashed. I found that being religious and Ukrainian Catholic was quite difference from being Mennonite.

Instead of flowing seamlessly into a new life, school and friendships, I was tossed into the fray like a lamb to slaughter. In a cruel twist of fate, my mother made me stand out like a sore thumb right from the beginning. When I disembarked the bus at Elmdale School on my first day of grade four, I showed up at school outfitted in a dress. And not just any dress, but a floor length, light green printed dress with pictures of *Holly Hobby* plastered across the fabric. It was identical to the dresses Laura Ingalls Wilder wore on the television show *Little House on the Prairie*. It was the typical pioneer dress complete with flowing skirt, long sleeves, and a bibbed front that tied in back. It was a style reminiscent of a hundred years ago and not at all fitting for anywhere in the seventies. It was so ironic that the television show I was so enthralled with was so out of step with reality. My mother made it for me, and while I loved it, the dress did not have the same reaction on my classmates. From day one, I was picked on and bullied. There was zero tolerance for being different, and I was as different as they came. Instead of flourishing in my new environment as I hoped, each day was a fight for acceptance by students and teachers alike.

All I wanted was to fit in but it would never happen.

CHAPTER EIGHT

When you are a child, you don't understand why adults do the things they do. You look at the way you are treated, and if things add up in your head, then that becomes your truth until someone teaches you otherwise. In my case, nothing made sense. When I found out at the age of ten that I was adopted, I believed I really must be an awful person. To be given up by one mother and then horribly rejected by the woman who "chose" me to be her daughter through adoption translated in my mind to "downright unlovable".

Unfortunately it took another three decades for me to discover the truth. I've since realized it wasn't me, I was just a victim of other people's choices. But as a little girl, I was left feeling rejected and despised. It was like my very existence ruined everyone's lives.

I found out I was adopted about a year after we settled in Manitoba. Despite my mother's eagerness to put distance between her in-laws and our family, my mom, sister and I took a trip back to Welland a year later to visit my father's family. My dad stayed home on the farm with my brother.

We took the train and for three days the rails carried us through every small community in southern Ontario. The scenery was spectacular as we travelled through tunnels and over bridges. In some ways the trip seemed to take forever. At my age, being trapped within one car of a moving vehicle for nearly three days was bordering torture but at the same time, I was on an adventure. Pretending that I was on some fantastic journey kept my mind occupied. When we finally arrived in Welland, we spent two weeks at my grandmother's house.

One evening, my father's family including my aunt and uncle (my dad's only brother), my mother, sister and grandmother were gathered around the dining room table drinking coffee and chatting. My two cousins and I were just off to the side in the sitting room playing, while I tried not to eavesdrop on the adults. At one point, I overhead them talking about adoption, but since it didn't apply to me, I hardly paid attention. I already knew both my cousins were adopted so it was not an uncommon topic to be discussed. It was easy to push it aside because it was not relevant to me. My mother, assuming I had overhead the conversation planned to address the subject when we returned home.

My understanding of my life changed forever the day I found out how relevant the conversation actually was. I remember my mother coming to me one afternoon and suggested we go for a walk. She was in the kitchen making perogies and began taking off her apron as she spoke. Taking a walk with my mom was exciting. I really missed my mother's undivided attention – I craved it. Since moving onto the farm there was always too many chores and no time set aside for leisurely activities. It was the middle of the afternoon and we were going for a walk? Life looked great from a ten-year-old's perspective. Eagerly I followed her down the driveway, until we crossed the road and heading into field across the road.

Mom was unusually quiet as we trudged down the dusty trail surrounded by budding alfalfa. I forced myself to contain my excitement but all I wanted to do was hold her hand and skip along. She was not very receptive. She finally halted in the middle of the path, and I stopped. I half expected her to wander off because she spotted something in the field. She always kept her eyes open for wild berries, birds or gophers so it was not uncommon for her to have one thing on her mind and then she'd get sidetracked.

"There is something important I need to tell you," she hesitated as she started to speak. By this point, my curiosity was peeked but I was also starting to grow apprehensive. My parents kept all major discussions to themselves and including me was a huge red flag. Even when we moved, I was told afterwards and not included in any discussions. Were we moving again? Unsure of what to do, or say, I kicked at the dust with my foot, waiting for her continue. I watched her face change. Whatever she had to say was making her visibly sad and worried. This was big and I was suddenly scared.

"First, I want you to know you are here because we both love you." she started. That was my first red flag. My mother rarely disclosed how she was feeling unless it was in anger. Since we'd moved to Manitoba the year before, she'd changed considerably. I couldn't even remember the last time she told me she loved me. I felt completely shut out of everyone's life.

"Do you know what adoption is?" We started walking again.

"Not really," I admitted. I had heard of the term often enough because my two cousins in Ontario were adopted, but I did not understand how it related to me and my life.

"Well, your father and I are not your real parents," she continued, fidgeting with her skirt. She didn't seem very comfortable with sharing this story with me.

"What do you mean?" I was puzzled. This was not something I expected to hear and it confused me. They'd raised me, provided for me, and I called them Mom and Dad, so how could they not be my parents? I didn't understand.

"Well, we wanted a baby really bad and couldn't have one – so we went to a special place where there were other babies and picked you," she explained. "Your real mother couldn't keep you, and so we took you in and gave you a home."

This conversation did not make any sense to me; yet I knew it was life changing. Unsure of what to do or say I started to cry. I was terrified the next thing she'd say was that she was going to get rid of me. They picked me, so they could give me back. As understanding (and childish worst-case scenarios) slowly filtered into my befuddled brain, I started asking questions. I wanted to know everything.

"What about my brother and sister?" I asked. I knew they loved me and yet there was a part of me that sensed that something was not right. I always felt different, like an interloper and this explained everything in my child's mind.

"They are not really your brother and sister either." she replied. She went on to explain that while they were not my brother and sister by blood, they were her children through birth. As she spoke it suddenly hit me – they had all hid this secret for years and kept it from me! What else didn't I know?

As the reality of what I just heard sunk in, I grew terribly upset and remember ending up sobbing in her arms; looking for comfort while trying to understand how my entire world had just changed. But understanding eluded me. I suddenly knew I didn't fit in nor would I ever fit in with this family. I was suddenly the stray cat that was found on the side of the road. This meant that, like a stray cat, I could also be dropped off at the local pound or wherever they take unwanted children. I'd already been threatened with being dropped off at an orphanage if I didn't behave; it all made sense. I was positive that the reason she was telling me this story, I was on borrowed time. In my head, her telling me was a warning that if I was naughty in any way I'd be dropped off somewhere and forced to watch them drive away and leave me behind. These are the things that went through my head in the days following Mom's big announcement.

My mother swears this is when our relationship changed forever.

Maybe if I had known the truth about my birth from the start, I would have reacted differently. I would have understood I was special from the beginning and life would have made sense. Instead, this new truth had me second guessing everything. I became oversensitive to the different ways she treated me from my siblings and even the way my siblings treated me. I was suddenly waiting for the other shoe to drop, constantly believing if I screwed up once, they would decide to throw me away. As I pondered things further, I tried to understand why my birth mother gave me up but these are questions my adoptive mother could not answer. I felt such loss, but most of all, abandoned. Instead of being part of a family, I felt temporary and replaceable.

It seemed that once I knew the truth, things didn't matter anymore. I guess my mother sensed my withdrawal as I tried desperately to find my place. She must have taken it as the ultimate rejection so she stopped pretending to be loving and caring (as sparse as those moments were) and returned her focus on keeping our immortal souls from eternal damnation. She stopped being a mother and became my warden and keeper.

She grasped onto her faith with a fervour that was frightening. She constantly dwelled on Bayside's doomsday prophecies. Any free time was spent reading the leaflets sent to the farm on a regular basis and praying. She continued to force us as a family to kneel for an hour each night to recite three rosaries. Of course, by the time the second set of beads was started, I was snoring with my face in her bedspread along with my father, who had been up since before dawn doing the daily chores of milking and feeding the cows.

Crying exhaustion, my father eventually stopped joining us during family prayers. This angered my mother and caused many arguments between my parents. She was convinced my father no longer believed in God and she could not allow that.

She was constantly berating him to the point he would eventually avoid her completely. I don't ever recall my dad standing up to her. She berated him for buying the farm. She berated him for not going to church. She berated him for spending so much of his time doing chores. She would have berated him for breathing wrong if the whim hit her. By the time I left home he rarely left the barn except to eat or sleep.

This was extremely difficult for me because my father and I were very close. My mother's irrational mind had polarized our family into two distinct groups. The "good family members" included my sister and herself. The "bad ones" were my father, my brother and of course, me. My mother is the only person I have ever met who could rant and rave for hours without swearing yet make one feel tiny and insignificant. I learned at a young age to tune her out, but many of her hateful words are seared into my brain. Her voice and words have faded over time but during dark days of insecurity they still rear their ugly head.

Thinking her words carried less weight, over time my mother added a new torment to her arsenal. My mother believed fasting was the best way to purge an evil soul and because I was deemed an "evil child" in her head, I had to be starved into submission. Fasting provided cleansing of our bodies and souls, she said. The Saints did it, Jesus did it and we must do it too. She began putting me on two, three and even seven day fasts where all I could have in my belly was water. I was just a kid and didn't understand the entire process other than that it made me weak and after a few days became physically painful. Fasting was always preceded by some perceived transgression on my part. It was getting to the point that everything she did translated her hatred towards me. I was hungry, hurting and living in fear.

I guess fasting was not enough to purge the alleged demons

living within me. As I grew older and headed into my teenage years my mother started to become more physical. Instead of hugging and kissing me like a mother should, I found myself cowering whenever she raised her hand. She'd tell me to look at her when she was talking and then slap me across the face for staring at her. There was no pleasing her. Unless I concentrate really hard, to this day I still have problems looking at people in the eyes when I am talking.

Part of surviving my mother's wrath was learning to hide what was going on at home very well. My mother had an ironclad rule - anything that occurred in the home stayed within the home. This, I am sure, stemmed from her childhood when all the Ukrainian immigrants were scared of authorities, having fled a country ruled by the NKVD, a predecessor to the KGB. I grew up hearing stories of how people couldn't trust even their own family members. For the right price, they would turn in their loved ones to the authorities even if they knew it would end with a death by firing squad. She was terrified that I would tell people at school what was going on at home. When I eventually did escape, I committed a cardinal sin by her standards in telling the authorities what happened at home and she never forgave me.

So many secrets were piling up, and my mother was growing more unstable.

About a year or two after we moved to Manitoba, my brother decided he no longer wanted to be partners with my father in the farm. He sold back his half of the operation to my mother for a dollar bill. Before he left home, my mother acted like she hated him and blamed him constantly for our being on the farm. Every single day she reminded him of her misery and eventually he too would stay away from home for days on end to avoid her wrath. This succeeded in angering her further because instead of respecting her authority as a parent, he was trying to find his own way in the world.

Everything came to a head one afternoon when my brother came home from work to find all his belongings in the middle of the driveway, burning. My mother was doing his laundry earlier when she'd found some records she deemed demonic and went ballistic. I vaguely remember a Black Sabbath album cover among her finds. Furious at his perceived disregard to her rules, she hauled everything out of his basement room and set it ablaze with no regard to his privacy or feelings. She sure loved the sense of finality the burning gave her, plus it assured her that no one else obtained items she deemed Satanic.

Livid, my brother packed up the remainder of his things and left. He left so quickly he didn't even say goodbye to me. I remember chasing him down the driveway and watching him disappear in a cloud of dust. I was devastated because he was my only friend even though he considered me a pain in the butt. Before he moved out, I had followed him everywhere. When he was in the shop working on cars, I was there too, watching and helping. When he was playing music, I was hiding outside his room listening. I may have been his annoying little sister, but in my eyes, he was a hero. I envied his ability to leave but I never blamed him. He made his escape. He had to and so did I – I just didn't know it yet.

Once my brother moved out, things got worse for me. Mother no longer had my brother to yell at, and in her eyes my sister was flawless so she set her eyes on me and my dad. She tormented us in many ways. Somehow I always got blamed for anything that went wrong, even when I wasn't even home. I was convinced she despised the very sight of me. There were days I would get off the school bus and sneak quietly into the house, not knowing what mood my mother was in. The slightest thing could set her off – including my very presence. It was like living in a life sized game of Russian roulette and I was always losing.

At this stage of my life, I was starting to love writing so I would scribble on whatever I could find. I found solace in sharing my thoughts on paper. I wasn't allowed to talk to anyone, so I would pour my heart out on paper and hide it. I was able to tell my mother how I felt without feeling the sting of her hand because I disagreed, or defended myself against some false accusation. Unfortunately, I never found good hiding spots. Mom would be in my room collecting laundry and find my scribbled thoughts. She would misunderstand what I'd written and overreact. At first she would scream at me irrationally while tearing apart every word I wrote; then she would demand an explanation. She'd ask me questions and if she didn't like the answer I gave, I earned a slap. These exchanges could be brief or go on for hours depending on her mood. I learned very young to sit quietly and not say a peep unless spoken to. Even then I had to make sure I was expected to answer because if I spoke out and I was not supposed to, I was slapped across the face as a vicious reminder.

I never meant to talk back, but in my child's mind I was defending my honour. I hated being accused of things I didn't do because when that happened, I would end up hurt – and I do mean hurt. Anything I did or did not do "right" made me fair game for a beating – not picking the eggs, breaking an egg, spilling chicken feed, forgetting to lock up the birds at night. I felt like a moving target. If we were outside, she'd grab a broom, a loose board, tree branches, or anything else she could use to hit me. She never used her hand because it could hurt her. Then there was the infamous strap, which was really one of my father's old leather work belts. Even the flexible rubber hoses used to herd the cows were used as weapons.

In a rage, she would grab my arm and start swinging. She always aimed for my backside but my squirming made it difficult to get anything other than the back of my legs. I was brave and scared enough to try and fight back, trying to get away but it was fruitless. Eventually I learned to outsmart her by dropping to the ground and curling up as best I could to make myself a smaller target. Undaunted, she would lash at my back, legs and arms while I screamed in agony until she tired herself out. Once she started, she would not stop until she was so exhausted she couldn't lift her arms. If she still had energy, she would grab me by the hair and drag me to the top of the stairs to my bedroom and toss me toward the door. I made a very quick exit before she could change her mind and start all over again.

Sadly my father never stepped in to save me from my mother's wrath. At first my father tried to stop her, but his feeble pleas fell on deaf ears. When she'd ask him to whip me, he refused. He never liked spanking me. There was one time she was in the middle of beating me when he wandered in from the barn. Already tiring, she yelled at him and tried to get him to take over. He refused, even though she berated him, calling him a coward.

I lay there sobbing, watching and waiting until finally he looked at her, took the belt from her hands and raised his arm. I expected a vicious lash but instead he gave me a half-hearted smack on my already tender backside. I didn't even whimper. Dropping the belt on the carpet, he turned away but not before I spotted the hurt and defeat in his eyes. I forgave him instantly. Without looking back, he walked out of the room and house. Not long later that brutal strap disappeared never to be found again. I had nothing to do with it – I wouldn't dare.

CHAPTER NINE

While my home life was so distressing, I struggled to find my place at school. It was my only escape from reality. But no matter how I tried, it was impossible to make friends due to all my horrible secrets. When I was at school, I was not allowed to get close to anyone because my mother didn't trust me to keep my mouth shut about what went at home. If my story came out by accident, either during recess or a classroom discussion, she always seemed to know about it when I got home. This almost always led to accusations and some sort of corporal punishment so I learned to be secretive and deceptive. This did not help me make friends.

To further complicate matters, if I did make a friend, I was forbidden to have or make phone calls when I was at home. Giving out our home phone number was a punishable offense. I could not go to their houses nor could they come visit me on the farm. There were other kids in our neighbourhood my age who could come and go as they pleased. If they happened to see me outside as they were pedalling past and dropped in, I would make them leave before my mother spotted us. I remember being afraid she would assault my friends the way she attacked me. I didn't understand yet that her behaviour was only directed at me.

Even school functions, like classroom Christmas concerts or plays took place without me even though I desperately wanted to participate. I loved to sing and perform; even though I was shy and insecure, I enjoyed the spotlight. In music class, I would sing the loudest and practice the hardest but I could never do anything with it, because I couldn't commit to being at performances.

When I was in grade 5, our class and the grade 6 students decided to put on a play called *Robin Hood*. I wanted to be a part of it so badly, I begged my teacher to give me a role even though I was already in the choir. I told him the only way I could attend was if I earned a part. It took a lot of courage for me to approach him; it was a delicate matter asking for a part and keeping it from my mother that I had asked. If she knew my attendance was an option not a necessity, I would never be allowed on stage. I ended up playing a butcher, it was a small role with only two lines but I treasured it. The hair, the makeup, and the costumes; I loved drama and I adored performing. Outsmarting my mother was a small triumph but unfortunately, it was short lived. This was the only time I was ever allowed to participate in any type of choir or drama performance outside of regular school hours.

It wasn't until grade 6 that the truth I was being physically beaten and starved at home finally came out at school. I stood out like a sore thumb because of my wardrobe so the girls loved to criticize me. My mother believed shorts were too provocative so I couldn't even change for gym class. She even sent a note to the school asking I get excused from class. The school's policy stated changing for gym was required for participation and because I was excused I was forced to sit on the bench during every class.

The girls disliked the perceived favouritism and took it upon themselves to provide me with shorts and a T-shirt so I would finally have no choice but join them in gym class. But I refused to defy my mother, knowing that if she found out I'd be punished severely. Somehow she always found out and it wasn't worth it. One particular morning, a couple of my classmates ganged up on me in the locker room and started to force me to change my clothes. While two girls held me, a third tried to tug my shirt over my head. I fought as hard as I could, but I was small for my age and it was easy for them to overpower me. I was mortified the girls would do this to me. They'd finally managed pull it high enough to expose my shoulders when they stopped cold and stared. They sat back, questions in their eyes. So intent on modesty, I had forgotten a beating I received from my mother a day or two earlier. She'd used a broom handle this time. My back was riddled with welts and bruises, in various degrees of healing. The entire experience was humiliating, yet such a relief. My horrible secret was finally out.

One of the older girls went to the school principal, but at that time child abuse was not viewed the way it is today. I was eventually called to the office and questioned. At first, I refused to talk. But eventually with encouragement I confessed everything. As I told them the truth I could tell they did not believe a word I said. Eventually I was sent back to class, not knowing they'd called my mother. She came in and was questioned but she managed to explain everything away and the event was forgotten. Except by me - my face still burns with embarrassment when I remember how humiliating it was to be ganged up on and stripped by my classmates.

This was not the only time my mother got called into the school. Each time my mother was always cooperative when the authorities investigated so it seemed to me they never believed a word I said. She always told teachers and principals that I was a pathological liar, with an overactive imagination so they let it go. That, combined with my seemingly unusual behaviour in school, meant I never stood a chance of getting real help from anyone. I guess it was easier for them to believe her, than the horrific truth.

Once I went into grade seven at the Steinbach Junior High, I was able to blend in better because it was a bigger school. The grade six students from all three of Steinbach's elementary school came together for the first time in grade seven, tripling my odds of making a new friend my age. But, it wasn't that easy. Most of the girls I went to school with had already spread the word that I was "odd". My classmates continued to treat like I had the plague despite my efforts to prove everyone wrong. Kids can be so cruel without even realizing it. Trying to focus on other things, I tried to study hard but I lost interest in all my classes. Nothing was ever good enough at home or at school so I stopped trying. Instead, I turned to reading and devoured book after book. Getting lost in a world of make-believe was my only escape from reality.

It seemed as I grew, so did my mother's resentment towards me. She acted like she hated me and constantly reminded me of that fact. Emotionally bruised and battered I took everything she said to heart. She would get so angry over minute details and was always quick to lash out. I was constantly walking on eggshells. Sometimes, she was downright cruel.

For as long as I could remember, special events like my birthday and Christmas were celebrated with mixed emotions. On one hand, I was eager and excited as any child would be; yet deep down I was afraid and always prepared for the worst. Each year my parents would buy gifts which I would open in excitement. Many times I'd get things I really wanted (within reason) but then if I was deemed "naughty," my mother would take everything away, hiding or burning it. I learned quickly not to get attached to anything because I never knew when it would be stripped away and destroyed. My problem was keeping up to her ever changing definition of naughty. It took raising my own children to realize most of my punishable actions were done out of pure curiosity and childhood innocence.

I loved learning about my environment. After all, I lived on a farm – what a great classroom it could have been if had been allowed to flourish instead of being held hostage by my mother.

As I got older and physically stronger, I tried my hardest to be useful and less of a "troublemaker". I especially enjoyed helping my dad in the barn doing chores. The dairy farm was a busy place. Dad got up most mornings at four o'clock and after a quick coffee and toast he would spend the next three or four hours milking, cleaning the barn and feeding the cows. Then he'd come in for a quick breakfast before heading back out again. Afternoons were usually spent getting other stuff done before it was time to milk again after an early supper. This was our routine, seven days a week. I was thrilled when I was finally strong enough to carry the five gallon steel milk buckets full of milk and be able to dump them into the step-saver. The step-saver was just that; it sat in the middle of the barn, hooked up with an airline to the bulk tank and after milking two cows the fresh milk was dumped into it and sucked into the main tank. Once I was able to do this without help I became an indispensable helper for my dad. I remember thinking that if I helped Dad with chores there would be time to spend together like in the "old days" but that never happened. There was always something else to do. Eventually doing chores with my dad became our "quality time" together.

Haying was also a fun time because even though it was hard work, it meant I was spending days with Dad, and not with my mother. It's kind of funny when I think about it; my mother used to try to teach me to knit, crochet, paint Ukrainian Easter eggs and other things she felt would benefit me later in life when I became a wife and mother. But she would get so frustrated with me that she would end up calling me useless and telling me I would never learn anything; then she'd tell me to go find something else to do. Yet when I helped my dad, I never heard that; he never criticized me.

When I wasn't working, I was exploring our property. I was strictly forbidden from crossing the fence line but within our property boundaries, I could go anywhere. I was fascinated by the peaceful pond across the road. In the summer I would pedal my bike across the field then spend hours reading while listening to the frogs. In the winter, I'd drag my toboggan through the snow, along with a snow shovel and an old pair of figure skates. After painstakingly clearing the ice, I would spend hours performing before an imaginary audience. I was always a star.

This obsession started while my brother was still living at home. He had defied Mother and successfully smuggled a little black and white television into the machine shop where he worked on his cars. After watching the movie, "Ice Castles" while my brother was restoring an old Chevelle, I dreamed about becoming a figure skater. I was so desperate for the mental freedom skating provided that if there wasn't ice in the pastures that I could use, I'd clean a patch in the manure pile – skating on cow pee. I treasured those hours where I was lost in my own little world. As long as I was home in time for homework, chores or supper, I could be gone for hours and no one would care. When I would disappear like this, it was the only time I was genuinely safe from my mother's wrath.

Even though I had siblings, for the most part I was a lonely child living off the fuel of my imagination and my many imaginary friends. Without real, tangible friends, I yearned for something to love, and if I couldn't have people then I wanted a pet. You'd think with all the animals I had access to I'd be content but they were off-limits to me. I wanted something four-legged and furry all my own. I needed the unconditional loving acceptance a pet provided. Somehow I knew if I had something alive that I could hug and love, it would provide me with the comfort my family denied me. But my mother kept saying no, I was "too irresponsible" to take care of our farm animals so obviously I couldn't take care of a pet.

While I remained without a personal pet, my mother was obsessed with birds and cats. At one point, she had fifteen cats. Every morning each cat was tied up outdoors to old milk cans or cement blocks; and every night they were brought back inside. They were never allowed to run free because she didn't want them killing the goldfinches and hummingbirds who loved her flower gardens. She also didn't want them running away or getting killed on the farm or road. She'd already had one cat who had cost hundreds of dollars in vet bills because she got hit by a car. We also had a couple of dogs over the years, but they too were always tied up. I always felt sorry for the animals because they were never allowed to be free. When no one was looking, I would let them go so I could play with them as best I could. This would lead up to one of the most horrific memories of my childhood.

Before my brother moved out, he adopted a part collie mongrel and named her Tina. She was tied up near the barn to alert us of visitors and never allowed to run free. She was a cute dog and definitely lived a lonely life attached to a chain. A prisoner myself, I felt sorry for her so I spent time with her when no one was looking. What I didn't know or understand was she was not fixed and one day I let her loose to play and she wandered off. A few weeks later I was excited to find out she was going to have puppies. Our cats were all fixed and while we did have a couple of surprise litters of kittens over the years, we'd never had pups before so this was a big deal. I begged and pleaded; finally my brother promised me the pick of the litter and I was bursting with excitement. I would finally have my own pet.

I don't remember what led up to the incident. I just remember my mother was angry that this dog had a huge litter of pups. They were adorable and every chance I got I would sneak over and play with them. When I wasn't doing my chores, I was sitting in the doghouse with puppies crawling all over me. One afternoon my mother was on one of her tirades. I remember her telling my brother that he had to get rid of all the dogs. She was relentless. I watched him put that poor dog and all her pups in the doghouse and nail the entrance shut. I could hear their cries of fear but I didn't understand what was happening, yet. The next thing I knew he'd backed up his car, and parked it against the doghouse. After attaching a hose to the house, he left the car idling. Eventually I clued in as my mother forced me to watch as he attempted to gas the dogs. I could hear Tina crying and scratching to get out then I could hear her vomiting.

I stood and bawled while my mother screamed at me the entire time that it was my fault the dogs had to die. If I had left things alone, the dog wouldn't be suffering. It was like she knew I loved those dogs and she had to destroy them because of that love. To make things worse, when all was silent, my brother would open up the doghouse to check to see if they were dead and the fresh air would revive them. It seemed to take forever to kill those poor animals. Eventually, totally inconsolable, I ran off and hid in the shed where I sobbed for hours. My dreams of ever having my own pet were dashed by her cruelty.

I started to withdraw into myself after this incident. I was determined to be a "good girl" and not do anything to earn my mother's wrath. She'd shown me what she was capable of and it terrified me. Every chance I got, I hid. I built tree houses in the bush, turned an old outhouse into a playhouse and even converted one of my brothers' abandoned project cars into a hiding place. If my mother ever needed to find me, she would have to search many places before spotting me. This was the only way I felt safe. But I could only hide for so long. When I would finally show up, she would accuse me of all sorts of things. The truth was, I was usually lost reading a book or writing as far from her screeching voice and false accusations as I could get. Anything was preferred to all the work I was forced to do, mostly as punishments.

One summer afternoon my mother was putting up a pigeon box in the grainary. I was in the garden weeding and it was hot. I was wearing a woollen turtleneck sweater and a long cotton skirt and it was pure torture being in the garden; there was no shade. I was lost in the tedious task unaware things were happening elsewhere until the sound of sirens filled the otherwise quiet summer day. Emerging from my chore, even though I knew I would be in trouble, I wandered to the yard in time to see an ambulance pulling into the driveway.

I hid out of sight and watched as the paramedics eventually took my mother away. Later when I asked my dad what happened, I found out she had fallen. Somehow the ladder fell backwards away from the wall and my mother landed on the concrete floor on her back. She fractured several vertebrae in her back and spent several days in the hospital. When she got home she spent months sleeping on the bare living room floor.

The one thing that struck me about this incident was that I was blamed for the accident. Whenever anything bad happened, it was my fault. She was convinced I was so angry with her for punishing me with the garden task I had wished her to get hurt. Convinced I was possessed by the devil, she actually started to be afraid of me. Believing demons resided in me she took me to see a priest. He performed an exorcism at her request. I was just a child, so I believed what she believed. If she thought I was possessed who would argue. Agreeing kept me from being beaten and starved. But it didn't matter; I soon learned that no matter how good I tried to be, I was still always being punished. To add insult to injury, my own sister joined the fray. I remember her breaking a plate once (something I was notorious for doing) and I got a beating for it, while she stood and laughed. My pain seemed to entertain her. Maybe she felt that if she didn't take my mother's side, the wrath would turn on her, but as far as I could see, it never did. I already envied her because my mother obviously loved her more than me but eventually, I grew to dislike her, even while trying to earn her love and acceptance.

The thing that killed me the most was for all the verbal and physical abuse I was suffering, no one ever believed a word. I tried to tell the school, my teachers and the few friends I did have. It even came out in my school work. I recently found an old school project from elementary school. Our assignment was to create a children's book complete with original artwork. Once done, the books were given to the grade 2 students who read and graded them. My book was carefully drawn and bound; it looked like a real book. Titled the "Loveliest, Loneliest Reindeer" my story was about a pretty little reindeer who was bullied and mocked. Even though she was smart, pretty and good, she had no friends. Reading it now, I realize I was writing about myself and it breaks my heart for the child I once was.

But my cries for help and attention fell on deaf ears. It was like my stories were so horrific no one could imagine it, never mind believe someone they knew was suffering such extremes. No one seemed to care and I felt isolated and alone. Except for my father; his quiet companionship was the only thing that kept me going during those days. No matter what my mother said or did, I knew I would find comfort in his company. My mother might despise me but I knew my father felt very different. In his quiet unassuming way, I knew he adored me and I took comfort in that.

CHAPTER TEN

By the time I started school at the Steinbach Junior High I felt pretty screwed up. I was living this horrific existence and school was my only reprieve from reality. But school did not offer the reprieve it should have. I stood out even more in high school because of my clothes and my family's faith. People assumed that because I wore the same couple of dresses all the time that we were poor. When kids would ask about my family life, I would lie creating a more ideal situation than actually existed. I didn't dare tell the truth because if it followed me home punishment was severe.

I started to exhibit some behaviour problems. I loved to learn and when I understood things I became a very enthusiastic student. My teachers constantly told my mother I was disruptive in class which made teaching the other students difficult. I don't believe I was intentionally disruptive; I just paid attention and liked being asked for the answers and for my opinion. I didn't have one at home and it was nice to be noticed in a positive way for a change. School was the only place I had a voice and I loved being called upon in class, but the teachers found it disruptive because no one could get a word in edgewise. With a little praise I became an over-achiever and know-it-all.

Thinking back, in elementary school this was already a problem. In Grade five, my teacher set up portable walls around my desk. Like an office rat, I had my own cubicle. I could see the chalk board, but not the rest of the students. I hated being segregated like that, but I turned it into something special. I had an office, not just a desk like the rest of the class. Meanwhile, my classmates despised me because it appeared I was getting special treatment. This made me a target for bullies.

By grade six, my survival instincts kicked in which made it even more difficult for my classmates to like me. Food was plentiful at home, but since I was always getting into trouble in my mother's opinion, I was forced to fast often. I was always hungry which made it difficult for me to concentrate in class. In desperation I began to sneak food from my schoolmate's lunches. I ended up getting my first spanking at school for stealing an apple out of one of my classmate's lunches. She always had a lot for lunch and I didn't think she would notice. I was famished and the pilfered apple was delicious. The spanking was worth it but no one likes a thief!

As I got older, I grew bolder with my thievery. While volunteering in the Steinbach Junior High library, I stumbled onto where the librarian kept the late book fines. I was soon helping myself to the cash to buy a hot dog, or pizza pop from the school canteen. In Grade nine, I discovered the home economics teacher left her purse unattended in the classroom and she always had cash on hand. After class, I would slip back to the classroom and help myself to some of her change. I was not greedy nor did I want to raise suspicion so I never took more than I needed. I'd only take enough to buy myself a pizza pop and a carton of chocolate milk. This would keep the hunger pains at bay and help me make it to the end of the day. I am not proud of this but sometimes, it was the only food I would have until the next day. It all depended on my mother's mood when I got home.

When it came to friends, I made my first real one in grade seven. After three years of living and going to school in the community, it was a big deal. She was in my homeroom and I don't remember how we became friends just that we did. Once she heard about my family and life, she started to invite me over to have lunch. Finally able to leave school grounds without permission, I enjoyed hanging out with her and her family. Her parents and little brothers always made me feel welcome. In all my twelve years this was the first time I actually spent time with someone else's family and could see the blatant differences between how other families operated compared to mine. I am not sure if she really believed me when I would talk about home but she listened and did not judge me.

Unfortunately our friendship only lasted a single school year. I was devastated to find out near the end of the year that she would be leaving. Her family took on a missionary post in Zaire, Africa and we became pen pals. I eagerly waited for the little blue airmail envelopes that came every month. At first my mother passed the letters on to me – opened and read – but eventually they stopped coming. I assumed my friend stopped writing but my mother admitted to me many years later she destroyed them. One of her biggest complaints was how each letter contained comments about praying for me and passages from the Bible for encouragement. To me, the letters were supportive but to my mother, they were a threat to my faith; she did not want anyone converting me. I lost touch with this friend until about eight years later but we were unable to ever rekindle a relationship.

When grade eight started, I was apprehensive. My only friend was gone and since making new ones proved more challenging I expected it to be a long, lonely year. But, I got lucky – I made a new friend. She had spent the first year of junior high at the Steinbach Christian High and came to our school the second year. Her father was a minister and she practised what he preached.

As our friendship grew so did my trust in her and eventually I told her about life at home. She was one of the first people to ever believe my story and she never called me a liar. I sometimes wonder if she was friends with me only because she considered me a project but I took her kindness for what it was and accepted it. She would even bring extra treats in her lunch so she could share with me.

While she knew I was living through hell, she didn't know what else to do to help. So she offered to pray with me. Despite my feelings toward religion at this point, I found myself dropping to my knees on the floor of the girls' bathroom one day and allowed her to pray. It was the first time I said a prayer in public that wasn't a rosary or a novena. It was also the first time I acknowledged there might be something else, other than what I had been brainwashed to believe. I felt different afterwards and filled with inner strength. It's kind of funny how when we returned to math class our teacher asked where we were and my friend openly shared with him what we'd just done his attitude towards me totally changed. Suddenly there was hope for me.

Unfortunately, my classmates failed to agree. By this time, I was bullied by my classmates on a regular basis. Boys would punch me when they passed me in the hall just because they could and girls would play mean tricks on me. With less supervision in the two-story school it was easy to get cornered and punched or kicked without anyone knowing. The school bus was another great place where kids would antagonize me without repercussions. The constant mistreatment made school difficult but I took it all in stride. It was just something else I had to accept. I guess I got to the point that since I was battered at home and school all the cruelty just flowed into one in my head. The kids were just reiterating what I was already told, so I couldn't hold it against them. Besides the kids couldn't really hurt me, but my mother, on the other hand could kill me if she really wanted to.

I had actually forgotten or blocked out how bad the kids really were in junior high until very recently. A short time ago I received a surprising email from one of my former classmates. He was one of the more popular boys in my class and we spent many grades together. Now he was grown up, married and a father. He is also a youth minister at a local church. In recent months there have been numerous young people committing suicide because they're bullied at home, school or on the internet. This has led to an international anti-bullying campaign. He confessed he'd never forgotten me or what he witnessed when I was in junior high.

"I apologize for my behavior back in school. I am sorry for teasing you and treating you badly, and for not sticking up for you when my friends teased you. I realize that I must have made your life unbearable and I am sorry," stated his heartfelt apology letter. *"Bullying is a horrible social disease. If it is any consolation, my wife and I have tried to teach our daughters to look out for those who are bullied. Your memory has affected my life to the point that I teach loving all of God's children, with your face as my memory. This may sound weird, but thank you for changing my life."*

I was stunned. Thirty years after the fact one of my bullies is telling me I changed his life? At the time, I was hell bent on survival. I never expected to affect anyone's life in such a significant way. He went on to recall a particular incident at the end of grade eight where our class spent the afternoon swimming at the Steinbach pool. I'd never gone swimming before so a friend loaned me a bathing suit. My mother was clueless to the entire event. I was excited. However, when we got to the pool I was too scared to go in. I wasn't sure how deep the pool was and I knew everyone was watching to see what I would do. I knew they were focused on me because everyone stopped talking the moment I walked out of the locker room in less clothing than anyone had ever seen me in since I was a child.

I guess the kids knew this was a big deal for me but they weren't sure why. At some point, the popular boys started bugging me about being too scared to get in. Determined to prove I was fearless (and not the loser they said I was) I thought I would show them. I climbed the ladder of the diving board, walked out to the edge and jumped in. Like a boulder I sank to the bottom and felt myself float to the top. I remember opening my eyes and seeing the sun shining through the water as I fought desperately to break the surface. When I finally did, I floundered a few times but kept going under. Then it hit me - I was going to drown right there, surrounded by my classmates and they were going to let me. All I remember next was a lifeguard in a skin tight purple Speedo pulling me onto the deck.

I've told this story to my children over the years; using it as an example of why it is important to know how to swim. I've told my children how ignorant I was to think I'd instinctively know how to swim; I just needed to jump right in. But I'd forgotten how my classmates fit into the picture. All these years I've just thought about what my bullies taught me. While raising my own children, I encouraged them to befriend the underdogs in their class. If someone new started school or someone got picked on or had no friends, I would tell my kids to talk to them, don't judge. It changed me and what I believe but most of all, it's changed how I treat people. But I have never thought it had an effect on anyone else – I didn't even think anyone noticed.

I didn't respond to his note right away. I had to digest its contents first. But when I did, I thought I would share with him what was going on in my life at the time. His response was to voice regret that he judged so quickly and just jumped on the bandwagon without getting to know the real me.

"It is horrible that kids have to survive when they should thrive. I did not know that about you (the abuse at home), *that's the saddest part. We should have attempted to get to know you. It is all making more sense now."* his letter concluded. Incidentally, of all the kids who beat me up and picked on me at school, I've only had two render heartfelt apologies. I am

grateful for both. They were more than apologies – they were affirmation that this was not in my head; it was all real and others could see something was wrong; they just didn't know or understand the truth behind my behaviour; nor did they know how to change it.

It wasn't until the end of junior high that I finally began to do something about my situation. I had no choice in the matter at this point. I was a late bloomer and it wasn't until grade nine that I started reaching puberty in a noticeable way. I knew nothing about sex or what happened to boys and girls when they matured. I'd listen to the girls in school talking about boyfriends and getting their periods while secretly wishing that I had both. It became a big deal at home too. My sister teased me about being flat as a board. I also knew that my mother and sister were keeping their eyes open for when I started my period. In my mind it meant something special; I equated it to acceptance. I'd finally be like my mother and sister, no longer a little girl.

The moment my mother noticed my breasts start to develop her viciousness gathered steam and hit new lows. She became focused on keeping me away from the opposite sex. I was forbidden to be around when the milkman came or any male visited the farm. I would look at my reflection in the mirror and failed to see anything special, so I couldn't understand her attitude. She started telling me that I shouldn't bother looking at boys - I was ugly and no one would want me. If I was lucky enough to attract the interest of a boy, he would only want one thing and when he was done he'd toss me aside, she would add. While other kids were told they could be anything they wanted to be when they grew up, I was told I would be nothing but a whore: used up, washed up and worthless. This was always punctuated with the painful footnote that my real mother knew this, which is why she gave me up – to save herself from raising such an abomination.

I believed every single word as it sliced into my heart like a knife. It was easy to believe because I would watch the boys and dream that one of them would notice me but the way they picked on me, I knew it was impossible. Meanwhile my mother cut off all my hair and dressed me in ways no one would ever consider attractive. When I finally started my period, things came to a head in a big way. First, she was convinced that it wasn't my time of the month; she assumed

I'd had sex and lost my virginity. That earned me a beating despite my protests to the contrary. Then she was convinced that since I was becoming a woman, I would end up pregnant like my birth mother and she was adamant she was not going to deal with an unwanted child.

Convinced I would be nothing but a tramp anyway (her exact words), my mother decided I would not be attending the Steinbach Regional Secondary School. Girls like me did not need an education, she said. She felt strongly if I went to high school she would not be able to control me. For once, I stood up for myself but despite my protests the decision was made that I would be home schooled. Well, you can understand this was the last thing I wanted or needed. It was bad enough I had to come home to that farm after school and during the summer. Just thinking about being there day in and day out (except for church on Sundays and feast days) was more than I could take. This was a total one hundred and eighty degree turn from the utopia I had dreamed of five years earlier.

That summer I began to plot my escape and to steal money in preparation. My sister had a great job and rarely kept track of her cash. Because she seemed to despise me as much as my mother did, I felt no qualms about helping myself to her wealth in the event I would need the extra cash. It became a game to see how much money I could pocket as I helped myself to the bills in her wallet. By the end of July I had two of everything including a pair of twos, fives, tens, twenties, fifties and even a pair of one hundred dollar bills. If I hadn't gotten caught she never would've missed a dime.

I might not have gotten caught if I hadn't asked my neighbour for help. She was the same age as me and lived just down the road. We'd gone to school together and we even had some of the same classes. We tried to be friends since the day I moved onto the farm but it never really happened. Her family never understood why she was never welcome at my place or why I was forbidden to go to hers. They were also strong Christians and here too, my mother worried about them trying to convert me. What my mother didn't know was when she left me alone to go to town, I would sneak over and play for awhile but the visits were short and too far between to foster a real friendship.

Regardless of our relationship, I was desperate and needed help.

Somehow I was going to school and there was no way my mother was going to stop me. To make this happen, I gave the neighbour some of my pilfered cash and asked her to pick me up a few things I would need for school. My list included some clothes, a backpack and basic supplies like pens, paper and binders. I begged her to keep it a secret from my mom.

I never expected this to be a problem but I guess her mother was concerned about the amount of cash I seemed to have, so she approached my mom and filled her in. Unaware, I heard my mother calling me and I emerged from my playhouse behind the grainary in time to see the neighbours leaving our driveway and walking home. The neighbours had barely left the yard and my mother already had me by the hair. She dragged me bawling toward the barn where she grabbed a rubber hose and proceeded to thrash the truth out of me. I admitted to the theft but I never confessed how much money I actually took. I was forced to return what I admitted to taking back to my sister, but I managed to keep half of it, just in case. Later my neighbour admitted she could hear my screams while they walked home and if she had known what I was doing and what would happen, she would have never told a soul.

I spent the rest of the summer locked out of the house, living in the old van that brought us from Ontario, now broken and abandoned in the implement shed. I slept on a bed of fresh straw, covered with old sleeping bags left over from our camping days. For food, I would sneak into the garden and pick ripened vegetables. I didn't dare help myself to milk from the bulk tank because Mom swore she measured it every day and could tell if a single drop was missing (yet I was accused of it constantly).

The only time I dared steal food was when my mother and sister went into town shopping. If I knew they were leaving, I'd watch and wait until Mom would lock the front door, then I'd sneak behind her and unlock it. Then I would wait until I could no longer see the dust rising from the retreating car. When the coast was finally clear, I would sneak into the house and steal a package of soda crackers and a quarter pound block of butter to take care of the hunger pains. I knew if I got caught it would cost me dearly but after two or three days of no food, it was worth the risk.

Thankfully, when I was on a "fast", I was not expected to do chores. I could spend my days curled up in the van reading or wandering the bush around the farm. I was living like an animal, sneaking around to avoid my mother's unpredictable wrath. It was at this juncture in my life I became obsessed with running away. It was no longer a matter of IF I would run, but when. I started to hatch a plan.

Towards the end of summer I was finally able to reclaim my basement bedroom in the house, but my mother was still not allowing me to go to school. It took some effort before I could finally execute my escape. I took a backpack, along with a pup tent and I climbed out the basement window and made a bid for freedom. I made it to a mile from the house before braving my fears and knocking on the door of a neighbouring farmhouse. It was owned by a little old widow who had no idea who I was or where I came from. It struck me as odd that we had lived within a mile of this family for four years and they did not even know I existed.

I was terrified that someone would call my mom but I desperately needed help. It was three miles to town and I was petrified of getting caught. The lady who answered my timid knocks was nice enough to let me use her phone and from there I called a boy I knew from school. He was someone who barely knew me but was kind whenever he crossed my path and he had a drivers licence. Soon afterwards I was riding between him and his best friend toward Steinbach, and my first taste of freedom.

For three days I camped out in the corner of Barkman Park along Main Street in Steinbach sleeping in that little blue pup tent. On the first day, I tried applying for some jobs around town, but I had no address and I was only fifteen. I admit that I was not mature enough to understand the gravity of my situation. But I did not care. I was not going home – I really believed that my mother would kill me if I did. I had defied her and she hated defiance.

On the third night I awoke to the flashing of a light in the tent and muted voices. Startled and frightened I sat up bolt straight and listened until I heard voices say they were police officers. They coaxed me to come out. Terrified I crawled out of my tent and I was asked to come to the station with the officers. I didn't know the town well enough to know that I had pitched my tent right next door to the police station, which is now the community's fire station.

After hours of questioning and my adamant refusal to go home the police had no choice but to take me to a foster home in Ste. Anne, a neighbouring community until it was decided what should be done with me. Finally someone was listening to me and checking into my story. I felt hope for the first time in a long time. Unfortunately it was short lived.

After a week, I was returned to the farm and as expected my mother's horns had grown even larger. Her hatred toward me grew worse because I had humiliated her by bringing in the authorities. However, thanks to Child and Family Services (CFS), I had won a small battle; my mother was told since I was not sixteen yet, I had to go to school whether she liked it or not.

CHAPTER ELEVEN

At the time the Steinbach Regional High School (SRSS) was a melting pot of students from throughout southern Manitoba. Students were bused in from communities over an hour away such as Falcon Lake and Sprague because it was the region's largest high school. The biggest draw was the vast selection of vocational classes which made it almost like a college and high school combined.

No longer stuck in a predominantly Christian environment like in grade school, my classmates were more tolerant of differences in each other. Soon I had several friends my age and older. For the most part I actually blended right in. I hung out in Banger Hall, which was located on the southeast end of the school where all the "rejects" and smokers gathered. For some reason I always gravitated towards other misfits. I loved how they accepted me, despite my haggard appearance and what I considered blatant flaws.

Some of my newfound female friends felt sorry for me and they would bring hand-me-downs. I would come to school looking drab and dowdy only to quickly change into my new wardrobe so I wouldn't have to wear the concealing ugly dresses my mother favoured to school. The girls would also bring me makeup and hair clips. I even had friends in cosmetology class who would do my hair at no cost. This was a blessing at the time; in a rage my mother had hacked my hair just before school pictures. She assumed I'd killed one of her geese and in disbelief at my denial she grabbed my nearly waist length locks and started chopping. The truth never changed, but my appearance had. My grade ten school picture is my worst photo ever.

You can imagine my astonishment when the boys started to take notice despite my mother's attempts to keep me unattractive. About a month after school started, I had my first in-school boyfriend. He was in grade 11 and in power mechanics class. Through him I made tons of new friends and as my self-confidence grew I become more popular. I could finally relax and be myself.

He seemed really sweet and thought I was cute which surprised and appealed to me. During spares we hung out at the local pool hall and yes, Steinbach had a pool hall and arcade in those days. One afternoon, after a day of skipping and playing pool, we were standing at the back of the school waiting for the bus. We were talking when I was suddenly pushed back against the brick wall. Before I could protest he gave me my first real kiss, and boy did I like it. I floated home. The next day he asked to be my boyfriend even though he knew our relationship would never flourish outside of school hours.

A week later he was declaring his love for me - I hadn't heard those words in recent memory so I believed him. I glowed under his attention. It was easy because kindness and tenderness was something I rarely received. He told me I was beautiful, wonderful and smart, completely contradicting what I'd heard at home. Too naïve to know boys often say things they don't mean, I thought I'd died and gone to heaven. I would have done anything to be with him.

This new relationship was all I needed to start taking risks I normally wouldn't have. We started skipping classes together and many stolen afternoons were spent at one of his friends hanging out and playing cards. It was in the basement of his friend's house I would eventually allow him to take things past the making out stage. It was not the most pleasant experience. To be frank, it was my first sexual experience but to this day I don't believe he actually completed what he started. I was terrified and no matter how he approached the situation, it hurt like hell. Afterwards I was left wondering what actually happened. On one hand, I was horrified about what we'd done, but at the same time I felt powerful and wanted; emotions I'd never felt before. I had finally experienced the innocence of first love or what I thought was love.

I was happy – genuinely happy and my mother had no idea why but she was determined to find out. My mother accepted what Child and Family Services ordered to her to do but she didn't do it willingly. She would show up at school and conduct spot checks to ensure I was in class or doing anything else she wouldn't approve of. I came out of English class one afternoon to find her tearing apart my locker. I stood dumbfounded and mortified as she cut up my precious stash of borrowed clothing. The more incriminating evidence she found, the angrier she got. Soon my textbooks and schoolwork also lay in shreds on the hallway floor. Yet, no one stepped in to stop her. I watched in horror from down the hall until she finally spotted me. Her rage escalated as she surveyed the jeans and makeup I was wearing. I had left home that morning wearing a skirt and shapeless sweater. I knew it was going to get ugly when I got home. Even worse, she'd humiliated me in front of all my classmates. Her behaviour succeeded in making me stand out even more.

But I was okay because I drew strength from my budding relationship. Until an innocent incident turned ugly and my fragile world came crashing down.

During exam week at the end of the first term I was goofing around with some friends on the landing between the first and second floor of the SRSS. We were talking, laughing and play wrestling when one of the boys picked me up, and threw me over his shoulder. He carried me up the stairs into the boy's bathroom on the second floor. He'd playfully threatened to carry me away but I didn't believe he would or could. He was one of my boyfriend's buddies and I assumed he wouldn't disrespect him.

My girlfriends remained perched on the window ledge laughing, thinking it was all a joke. I was too naive to completely realize what he was capable of until it was too late. My dress made it easy and my panties were soon on the floor. He sexually assaulted me right there, in the school on the bathroom floor. In those horrible moments he managed to finish what my boyfriend had started. I still remember the cold marble against my skin, and his slimy fingers tearing at my skirt as he violated me.

Accustomed to being powerless, I didn't fight back - I didn't believe I had the right. I was sobbing and bleeding when a special education student found me a little while later. He walked in, got scared and ran to the main office to tell a teacher what he'd seen, but by the time they returned I'd made a hasty shameful escape. I remember going home in a state of confused shock. I didn't really understand what happened, yet I felt like I'd done something wrong.

I may have lived on a farm but what happened in the bedroom between men and women was kept from me. Since my mother's back injury, my parents slept in separate bedrooms and they were never a passionate couple. They didn't even hug each other. Without a television or movies to watch, I didn't get an education there either. Even when the cows were being bred I would get locked in my room. I really was clueless about anything sexual, so I kept the rape to myself.

Meanwhile, the teachers were on the lookout for the girl who allegedly had sex in the school bathroom. While I attempted to carry on as usual, it took awhile for the school to figure out my identity. At barely five feet tall and less than a hundred pounds, I was smaller than the majority of students in the school so initially the assumption was whoever was in the bathroom was not a student. I was standing outside the cafeteria one afternoon when a teacher who spotted me leaving the bathroom that awful day, caught up with me and questioned my identity. Later I was called into the office and questioned again, this time by the vice principal. Subsequently my mother was called to the school and given a complete run down on events. Despite hearing my side of the story, I was suspended from classes for three days. My mother was livid over the entire situation. I know she never believed that I was raped.

After my suspension I returned to classes and things went downhill from there. During my absence the entire school heard about my shame and my story was fodder for the local gossip mill. My "boyfriend" was waiting for me when I got off the bus. We had not spoken since before my suspension. He was furious at my perceived betrayal and deemed me a slut. He dumped me on the spot despite my attempts to explain and defend myself. My heart was broken and humiliated; I wished I could vanish. Adding insult to injury my classmates were equally unforgiving. Alone and unpopular, students ridiculed me everywhere I went. They even nicknamed me "Corn Hole Mary." No one ever wanted to hear the truth. Once again I was just a disgusting outcast.

There was a brief ray of hope during those horrible days. A random act of kindness helped me believe that despite everything, someone cared about me. I was called to the office one day and a large package was waiting for me when I arrived. There was no card or note attached but I eagerly tore it open. Inside was an adorable yellow teddy bear; he was the cutest thing ever. Tickled pink by the surprise I carried the bear all day, showing it to everyone I knew. I didn't care that I was in grade ten and wandering through a high school with an oversized teddy bear; I loved it. Later I took it home and showed it to my mother. Instead of being happy with someone's kindness she came unglued. Convinced someone was using the bear to poke fun, she pointed out the bear's fat belly saying it looked pregnant. She grabbed a pair of scissors and I sobbed my eyes out while she proceeded to shred it to pieces. Once again something I enjoyed was stolen from me.

So far everything my mother predicted was coming true. I had become a whore; I had no friends and my family was disgusted with me. I was worthless. My insecurities escalated and so did my risky behaviour. I believed anyone who said they cared about me without questioning the validity of their words. I was desperate for love and attention – and it didn't matter what kind.

There were a few people who stood by me; most of them were boys. As an adult now, it is obvious to me why (they were teenage boys after all) but at the time, because I related to my brother and father so well, it seemed safe and natural. Shunned by the majority of the school and my own family, I would do anything to be accepted and liked. Desperate for attention and approval, I even posed nude for a grade eleven student who claimed he needed practice for photography class. I thought if I did it, he would like me but like many men to follow, he used me for his own personal pleasure. It was all a ruse. It's difficult to admit to being so gullible and ignorant. One thing led to another and by the end of the second term, I was expelled from school for inappropriate behaviour. The vice-principal caught a grade twelve boy touching my thigh while we were studying together in the school library. This time, I was kicked out of school immediately and the culprit was allowed to graduate.

Once expelled, I was thrust into the constant company of my mother. Her hatred toward me for humiliating the family was evident constantly. Instead of going to school, I lived life walking on eggshells, waiting for the other shoe to drop. She tried not to hit me as much because of CFS's earlier involvement but that did not stop her vicious tongue. I was forced to sit and listen to her rage on for hours. I had no choice. I was forbidden to leave the room until she was done and I didn't dare just walk out like my dad did. My mother could be vicious without cursing yet every word she used was a stab to the heart. When angry she would scream "You're ugly", "No one loves you or will love you", "You're a tramp" or "You're worthless". For the longest time I even believed I had native blood in my veins because she called me a "useless black-eyed Indian"; my eyes are a gorgeous golden brown. One day she actually grabbed my crotch and told me sex was all anyone would want from me, ever.

Her personal attacks did not stop there.

Any remaining freedoms or privacy I had, which was already limited beyond reason, was taken away. My mother maintained complete control over my actions. This way, she believed, I would return and remain on the straight and narrow. I would be woken up in the middle of the night, because she would suddenly get the urge to go through my things. I'd be out helping my dad with the chores, only to come back and find my room trashed with nothing left but a mattress on the plywood floor of my basement bedroom. Her rages were spiralling out of control. At this point, I was alive but not living. As far as the outside world now knew, I didn't even exist. I knew I had to get as far away as possible and soon. With all my heart I believed if I stayed she would eventually kill me.

I dreamed constantly of escaping and freedom and in March 1984, two months short of my 16th birthday, I was finally successful.

CHAPTER TWELVE

For the life of me, I cannot remember how the fight started but I will always remember how it ended.

I was in the kitchen leaning against the stove while my mother shrieked at me about something. I don't recall what it was about but I must have said something which she considered talking back. It was rare for me to speak out while my mother raged unless I was positively innocent; then I'd adamantly defend myself in vain. Before I knew it, she grabbed a fist full of my hair and started smashing my head against the kitchen cabinets. Over and over she slammed me into the doors. Crying, I begged her to stop but she was relentless as she screamed, spitting in my face.

Absolutely terrified and in agony I was convinced this time, she would go too far; she was going to kill me. Blinded by tears, snot and hair I swung at her in desperation. My little fist made contact with her soft stomach. That single act of defiance on my part left my mother blubbering in shock and fury. Instantly she let go and stepped back blinking in astonishment. Shaken, I remained frozen in place as she shook handfuls of my hair onto the floor.

How dare I touch her? What gives me the right? She screamed at me. She charged across the room to the phone and started to call our priest, thinking that he could help. As soon as she was distracted I refused to stick around. I made a mad dash to my basement bedroom. Within five minutes I had a few things tossed into a pillowcase, and I climbed out the window. I ran and ran until I couldn't run anymore. As desperate as I was to get away, I was not stupid; I hid behind buildings, I cowered in the fields, I ducked behind trees. My terror of what could happen if found kept me moving when I couldn't take another step. I have never run so hard in my life.

Cowering amid a grove of poplar trees behind the family farm, I waited for what seemed like an eternity for the moment I could dash across the field, across the road and to freedom. I had only one moment of doubt. From my hiding spot I could see my mother's white Oldsmobile driving back and forth along the dirt road. Pressing myself out of sight in the tall prairie grass I could hear my dad calling my name. Hearing his voice I felt a twinge of remorse. I couldn't help but cry. I was shocked he was the one looking for me. I knew it was milking time and yet, he'd dropped chores to search for me. But, instead of revealing my presence, I blocked out his voice.

It seemed like an eternity before the car finally returned to the yard. When it seemed safe, I bolted out of my hiding spot, across the road, and away I went. It took me forever to practically crawl along the bottom of the ditch, the entire three miles to Steinbach. Every time I heard a car I didn't wait to see who it was; I would duck into the tall grass and not move a muscle. My heart pounded in fear. There was no way I could be caught and sent back home. Not after striking my mother. I had done the unthinkable - I had finally fought back.

It was nearly dark by the time I eventually made it to the outskirts of Steinbach and I had no place to go. With no option other than taking a chance and relying on strangers, I ended up on the doorstep of a family on the east side of town. I chose them because their daughter and I were in the same grade for years. I didn't know her parents but she was one of few classmates always kind to me, no matter what was going on. I also knew that they were Christians who seemed to be one of few who actually practiced what they preached. Somehow I knew they wouldn't turn me away. It was nearly ten o'clock at night when I finally I knocked on their door.

Spotting the bag over my shoulder they knew immediately I had run away. Yet without question they welcomed me in anyway. I was hungry, so they offered me a late night snack. As I filled my empty belly, they listened to my horrific tale and when I was finished they swore I was safe. They agreed to help me and not tell my family where I was. A few days later they admitted to calling my family after I went to bed just to let them know I was safe. However, true to their word, they did not tell my family where I was staying. I ended up staying in their home for about a week while CFS found a place for me. I refused to go home and thankfully my social worker agreed.

During that first week I took full advantage of the situation. After years of living like a hostage on the farm I was finally within city limits. I enjoyed freedom unlike anything I'd experienced before. Until I ran away the ability to come and go, even within reason, was foreign to me. This meant I could see friends I'd missed since getting expelled and have some fun. I could also finally check out the town I'd loved for so many years yet hadn't explored. Since it was March break and school was out, I also could hang out with classmates I'd gone to school with but had never seen outside of classes before. The possibilities seemed endless compared to my previous reality.

At the top of my list of friends I had to see was one of the boys who'd helped me run away the first time. He and his twin brother were always kind to me and they lived down the block from where I was staying, so I started spending time with them. Their mother loved me and I basked in the attention I received. Instead of being ostracized for my experiences, I was welcomed warmly. I wasn't used to positive attention but I definitely enjoyed it. We spent so much time together I eventually started seeing one of them. We became inseparable and I really enjoyed his company. He took me for ice-cream; we watched movies and played video games (something I'd never done before). I felt like I'd won the lottery. For the first time in my life I was enjoying life, freedom and real attention. The added bonus was the boyfriend.

At the end of the week, I was officially taken into temporary custody by CFS and assigned a new full-time social worker because I still refused to go home. Even though my mother denied everything I told the social worker, the authorities listened to me, and I was placed in a foster home in Landmark. It would be a several months before I saw my mother again.

After publishing the first edition of this book, I found out more to this story when the twins attended my first official book launch. I had not seen either of them in decades. My heart stopped when I noticed them slip into the room; I was not expecting them. The brother who helped me run away the first time explained how my mother had showed up on his doorstep the second time I ran away. She knew he'd helped me the first time, and automatically assumed he knew where I was hiding. When he refused to give her the answers she sought (even though she threatened him) she went to the Steinbach police and told them about this lead. Meanwhile my friend who was buddies with one of the investigating officers, had already spoken to the police.

"The police knew exactly where you were staying and were ready to go, pick you up and take you back home," he told me after my launch. "I told him (the officer) there was more to the story and that they needed to listen to you; no matter how much your mother threatened me, I stood up for you."

Until recently I had no idea that I owed my freedom to his bravery. I have referred to him as a hero many times, and now I know he really was my hero!

Once I was free of my mother's iron fist and placed into foster care, my life changed drastically. Where I was once a prisoner in my own home, I now had freedom to explore life and learn how to be a normal teenager, if there is such a thing. The first few months I lived with my foster family was challenging for everyone. For me, the hardest part was learning how to coexist with a family other than my own. I was so used to being shut out I initially hid in my bedroom, out of the way. The last thing I wanted was to do something that could land me on the streets. But my situation was not like that all.

My foster parents were a young married couple without any children of their own. My foster father worked in Winnipeg, while my foster mother owned and operated a successful equestrian centre east of Landmark. Before my arrival there was already two other foster girls my age living on the farm. I actually went to school with one in Steinbach and we had tried to be friends but she ended up not liking me because she'd caught me in a few fibs. I had told her about the horses on the farm and how I loved riding and grooming them; unfortunately the truth was that the horses belonged to someone else and I was never allowed near them. To me, it wasn't a big deception but to her, it was a reason to dislike me. Once we lived together she heard the complete truth and was able to understand better where I was coming from when I was in school. Over time we became sisters and friends.

I loved that my new home was an equestrian centre. After all these years, I was finally able to be around horses. No stranger to chores, I threw myself into helping around the farm. In exchange, my foster mother taught me to ride and I did every chance I got. There was an indescribable freedom to galloping along the diversion banks, east of Landmark. I felt alive and hopeful during those moments.

My foster family was determined I discover all life had to offer as long as I didn't endanger myself or anyone else. I was not naturally careless but like a convict released from prison an overabundance of freedom could have spelled disaster. But my mother's influence ran deeper than anyone had anticipated.

Emotionally I was timid, withdrawn, and insecure; physically, I was strong but very thin. I was barely ninety pounds when I arrived and soon I began to put on weight. This was easy because at home, I worked hard and anything I ate was quickly burned up by my body. But it was soon evident that I had food issues. I had to learn I could eat whenever and whatever I wanted and not have to steal food. My foster mother once told me that I ate like I never expected to see a meal again. My foster mother encouraged me to cook and eat; soon I learned to love making meals for the entire family. I learned quickly how to gain praise for working hard, so I was always doing something to make people smile. I was like an eager puppy learning new tricks and the more I was complimented and praised, the more I did.

The hardest part was learning I no longer had to sneak around like a wraith. My life of walking on eggshells was over. I was not beaten for simple mistakes and I was no longer belittled. My foster mother encouraged me to speak my mind, something I'd never been allowed to do. I had an opinion and it actually mattered. Most of all, for the first time, I felt like I was part of a real family.

It was my foster mother who taught me how wonderful a hug could feel. She was a big "hugger." At first, I was terrified. I was not used to the kinder side of human touch. It was tough at first, but once I finally believed the rug wouldn't get pulled out from under me, I began to thrive. Knowing where I had come from, I commend them for trying to introduce normalcy into this budding teenager's life, especially since I'd been led to believe I was a hopeless mess.

My foster parents also liked my boyfriend and allowed us to spend time together both on and off the property. We went out for two months and things were going great until we decided to take our relationship to the next level. It was my sixteenth birthday and we decided to finally sleep together. It was the first (and only) time. Unfortunately, I was not ready for that crucial step. Afterward I was overcome with remorse and fear. After the fact it hit me like a ton of bricks; I was living up to my mother's expectations and I couldn't handle it. I broke up with him within days.

Sadly he never understood my reasoning; nor did his family. His mother contacted my foster home a few weeks after the breakup and asked what happened between us. She admitted a genuine liking for me and confided I'd broken her son's heart. I felt like a heel and I hated hurting him but somehow I knew healing needed to be done before I could become involved with anyone. I was not emotionally prepared to handle the situation. I would find out later she really cared about what happened with me; she was the one who sent me the teddy bear to school which my mother had so callously destroyed. Her intent was to make me smile and give me hope; not what my mother had viciously assumed.

No longer distracted by a boy, it was time to focus on healing and deprogramming. I call it deprogramming, because what I had learned (and believed) before was far from normal. Most of all, I had to learn what normal really was. That was the hardest part, because I still expected my mother to come down on me, even though I had absolutely no contact with her. Her voice rang constantly in my head and I could not stifle it. As warped as it sounds, eventually I would have to go home again and I didn't want to be someone my mother would not accept. I was no longer directly under her thumb but she still maintained control in my head.

This was obviously a real problem. My social worker and foster family decided I would benefit from the help of skilled professionals. By mutual agreement, it was decided to admit me into the McEwen Centre in Winnipeg at the beginning of June. Located in a separate building but operated by the St. Boniface Hospital, the facility had an in-patient treatment program designed to help teenagers overcome difficult issues, similar to mine.

Before admission, I had two months to explore my new community and try to make new friends. When I ran away, it was spring break and the start of the new school term so I wouldn't be able to start classes until the fall. This gave me a chance to get my act together but at the same time, it made it difficult for me to socialize with other people my age. But my foster family encouraged me to get out and find friends. Both my foster sisters helped by introducing me to people they knew and it was wonderful to be welcomed and accepted for a change.

Not many people in Landmark knew my past or where I came from, so many of the teenagers I met seemed more open and welcoming. One of the first friendships I made was with a girl who lived a few doors down from us. Her father was the minister of the local church and she was very involved in bible study groups and youth activities. She convinced me to come with her to "Young Peoples", one of the youth groups at Prairie Rose EMC in Landmark. The meetings were held once a week and something I looked forward to attending on a regular basis.

It was after one of these meetings I met the man who a few years later became my first husband and the father of all my children. My foster mother's little brother moved in with us not long after I did. He was a fun guy who played drums with a local band. On weekends, the band would gather in the house or garage for jam sessions and anyone who wanted to listen, dance or drink (or all of the above) could just show up. I came home from church one evening and the living room was full of guys, mostly in their early twenties. One of them caught my eye; I thought he was cute, but he was obviously shy because he didn't say much to me that night. He was six years older and I had just turned sixteen so I never really expected him to notice me but being a typical teenage girl, I hung around just in case.

Under the circumstances, my foster family discouraged any budding relationship. But over time he would become my first true friend and confidante. I had other friends but there was something about him that encouraged me to trust him in a different way.

I realized he was special and not playing me when he eventually called me for a first date. It was hard to explain to him I couldn't go out with him because of the foster care situation. Knowing it would lead to questions I may not know how to answer, I told him everything. Part of turning over a new leaf and making a new start in life was to be honest with myself and everyone else. Besides, I had no reason to lie, and now that the truth about my past was coming out, I had nothing to hide.

Despite hearing about my traumatic life, he still wanted to spend time getting to know me. Unfortunately, his timing sucked. The weekend he suggested we meet up was also the same weekend I would be admitted into McEwen. He didn't seem to care. Not wanting to waste a moment getting to know me, he offered to be my first visitor at the in-patient facility. I didn't expect to really see him but true to his word, he showed up at the start of visiting hours and spent the entire day with me.

It was my first weekend as a patient so we could not leave the premises. Instead we spent the day playing cards, telling stories, laughing and watching television, which was still a novelty to me. He was so kind and didn't seem to look at me like I was a freak, even though he was visiting me in a mental institution.

His actions left a lasting impression on me because it was such a sweet gesture and completely foreign to me. Unfortunately for us, life would get in the way and I wouldn't hear from him again for several months.

CHAPTER THIRTEEN

When the movie "Girl Interrupted" starring Angelina Jolie and Winona Ryder came out, it was like watching my life in McEwen. I was suddenly thrown into the midst of people who were, in many ways, more damaged than I was. For me, it was a scary place.

The building itself was located on the St. Boniface Hospital complex in Winnipeg, just off the Norwood Bridge. On the main and second floors, adults were institutionalized and I was no longer sheltered from the more sordid side of life. I learned that while my life was horrible, it could have been a lot worse. I drew strength from that knowledge and it helped me heal. I was no longer alone yet I had so much to learn.

I was one of eight troubled teenagers living in a ward located in the basement of the building. The ward was co-ed and we were split into rooms of two or three. We lived locked up, under the constant care of psychiatric nurses, psychologists and therapists. My fellow in-patients consisted of drug addicts, were abusive or had been abused, sexually molested or were suicidal. I was labelled "promiscuous".

Dealing with my mom was one thing, dealing with a ward full of messed up teenagers was a whole new ballgame. I ended up sharing a room with another girl. She seemed nice but was always under lockdown. If she went outside, she'd make a break for the Red River, intent on killing herself. She would sooner kill herself than face her father in court after he'd molested her for years. Thankfully she was never successful or at least not while I was there. One of the boys was always in the "rubber room" because he would have violent outbursts, which terrified me. I would wake up in the middle of the night to hear him screaming as the staff tried to get him into the foam protected room before he could hurt himself. Anyone uncontrollable would get locked in and I was glad I never had to spend a moment in solitary confinement. I had learned a long time ago that it was safer not to break the rules. This lesson served me well during that time.

I spent the next six months living in McEwen during the week and spent weekends in Landmark at my foster home. At this point sending me back to my family was not on the agenda. While in care my days consisted of group or individual therapy sessions. This is where the hard work began.

During countless hours of group therapy and private sessions, I was encouraged to speak openly about my life. No matter how intense my story became I was never called a liar. In individual therapy, one of my toughest tasks was to look into a mirror and verbally deny everything my mother ever told me about myself. My counsellor would make me meet my own gaze and tell myself things like "you are not worthless"; "You are beautiful"; "You are smart", and "You are lovable". At first, I couldn't do it. I would start crying as soon as I focused on my eyes. Over time, as I began to believe the words I spoke, it became easier but I don't think I ever completely believed in what I was telling myself.

In many ways, living in McEwen was good for me. I had access to people and activities normally foreign to me. Twice a week, we went to a public pool where I taught myself how to swim; I didn't want a repeat of the diving incident. My near drowning in grade eight made me afraid of complete submersion under water but I was determined it could be overcome. When I was finally confident I wouldn't drown myself, I attempted to jump off a diving board again. I recall standing at the edge of the board for nearly the entire half hour we had the pool. Instead of jumping in, I'd move aside so others could go first. I was not going to be rushed despite the encouragement from my group. Just before the buzzer rang signalling swimming was over, I took the plunge. This time, instead of sinking to the bottom and needing help to get out, I surprised myself and swam to the surface and got out of the pool on my own. It was not nearly as bad as I thought it would be and I was eager to do it again.

Unfortunately our time was up and I'd have to wait until next time.

Once I was out of my mother's clutches, I started to blossom and be myself. During my stay at McEwen I learned how to bowl, roller skate and even went to the movies in a real theatre. All of these activities were forbidden by my mother. I had fun discovering my interests, likes and dislikes. I learned to laugh and that I was good at making other people laugh. I was making a lot of new friends but most of them were male. Females had always been so cruel to me so I did not trust them.

When we weren't going places or participating in these activities I tried to study. My determination to finish school was always in the forefront. Because I was a ward of CFS (and not in regular classes) I was able to do some of my high school classes through correspondence. The course materials and textbooks were mailed to me and I did my school work on my own time. I signed up for grade 11 biology and English; when I was done, I worked on my grade 10 Math. I was determined that despite everything, I was going to graduate from school and make something of myself. I was determined I would prove to my mother that I was not as worthless as she assumed. Maybe if I became everything she didn't think I could be, she would finally love and accept me.

Being a teenager is challenging enough for anyone. In my case, all the years of belittlement, starvation and rejection really messed up my thought process. I genuinely believed I must have been a terrible person to be rejected by my adoptive mother. Combined with the knowledge I was given up at birth, seemed to be the nail in my coffin. I was absolutely convinced I was the most unlovable, horrible girl in the world because of this incorrectly perceived reality.

As a result my foster family was charged with daunting task of teaching me this was not the truth. Completely naïve, I had to learn what was real and what was not when it came to people and relationships. To this day, I am grateful for the many people who played a part in helping me overcome my mother's brainwashing. Finding self-worth was my greatest challenge. Her constant belittlement left me terribly insecure and afraid of myself. I believed I was nothing and would remain nobody for the rest of my life. She always told me no one would ever love me, except for what I had between my legs; and I believed it.

Along with freedom, came the ability to make unwise choices. My insecurity and desperate search for love and acceptance sometimes placed me in situations I would like to think I'd otherwise have avoided. For example, invitations for coffee with local boys would sometimes end up in situations where I would be used sexually. It was easy to take advantage of me because I felt I had no right to protest. I didn't think I had the right to say "no." Looking back, I am lucky to be alive.

One such incident occurred on one of the first weekends I was in McEwen. It was a Sunday, and for the first time since leaving home I was close enough to a Catholic Church. My foster family did not attend regular church services and I'd spent the first sixteen years of my life without missing a mass, so it was strange to not be going. In my opinion, I had no excuse not to go. Knowing my mother would be pleased that I went to church on my own, I was determined to attend. I obtained permission from the staff to take a city bus down to a church on Mountain Avenue. It was my first trip on a city bus yet somehow I managed to find my way downtown where I waited for my connection. But I got lost; I didn't know what bus to take next and there was no one to ask.

As I stood along Portage Avenue outside the Eaton's Building trying to decide what to do next, a young man on a motorcycle stopped near me. He asked where I was heading, so I told him. By that time church was almost over, so he offered me a ride back to St. Boniface. Without thinking twice I got on the back of his bike and we drove back to the hospital. I should have sent him on his way but instead of saying goodbye, I made him wait outside while I checked into the ward. Then I headed back out because he'd asked me for coffee.

We ended up in his apartment, where I smoked my first joint at his urging. The next thing I knew we were naked and I let him have sex with me. I had a disgustingly submissive quality in me at the time. He was nice to me, so I was nice to him. Several hours later when he was done with me, we returned to the facility. I never even knew his name.

Looking back on this incident, I realize how ignorant and naïve I was. I could have disappeared and no one would have been the wiser.

It was a real eye opener. The incident also managed to prove to me I was the whore my mother always predicted I would become. After that, I kept myself away from the opposite sex unless I happened to run into someone on the street. If that happened I would offer a few pleasantries before moving on. I wouldn't allow myself to be alone with anyone.

That first summer flew by and in the fall school started for everyone but me. I would have gone into grade eleven, but being in McEwen, school was not yet a priority, healing was. Yet over the summer, I met some of the neighbour kids and for the first time, I was actually allowed to foster relationships.

The preacher's daughter next door became a favourite person to hang out with when I was not with my foster sisters. Having grown up in Landmark she knew everyone our age and she encouraged me to attend events with her, especially Young Peoples. My foster parents also encouraged me to attend because it was a great opportunity to make friends my age. It was after one of these meetings that I learned how precious life was.

In foster care I was allowed to dress how I wanted, encouraged to take care of how I looked and was even allowed to wear makeup. The ugly duckling I'd grown to see myself as started to turn into a swan. This was evident by the attention I received when I finally stepped out into the real world and I loved it.

Looking good attracted attention and this particular night, I caught the eye of several local boys. Everyone wanted to know the new girl. Standing outside the church having a smoke we chatted and got to know each other. After awhile, one of the boys invited me along for a ride on his dirt bike. Seeing no harm, I told my girlfriend I'd return shortly and I jumped onto the bike behind him. We tore out of the parking lot and it was really dark out on the highway, but my companion did not seem worried. Even after we went off the road and ended up in the middle of a farmer's field he wasn't concerned. I was more than ready to turn back, but he was determined to show me where he lived. We headed back onto the highway toward Linden, a hamlet about three miles west of Landmark.

The last thing I spotted before we were sliding across the asphalt was what appeared to be headlights. I'd peeked over my shoulder, spotted the lights and tried to warn my companion. I never had a chance. I felt our bike get hit then start skidding sideways. Time slowed as I felt myself fly through the air, hit the asphalt road and slide along the highway face down. When I finally came to a stop, I recall looking up to see if the culprit who'd hit us had stopped but all I saw was the black of night. Whoever had hit us was long gone.

Shaking, I stood and immediately realized I was unable to bear weight on one of my ankles. My newfound friend ordered me to stay put while he grabbed the bike and found our shoes which had come off in the crash. Despite my fear and insistence we walk, at his urging I got back on the dirt bike and we drove back to the church. He parked the bike behind the church while I was carried to the pastor's car so they could take me home. As we left the church, a little Honda Civic hurried past us with horn honking and lights flashing. Barely slowing at the stop sign, it turned southward towards Steinbach. We wondered why the car was in such a hurry, but it was soon forgotten in light of what just happened to me.

Within the hour, my foster family was taking me to the Ste. Anne Hospital, where I was admitted overnight for observation. Other than a twisted ankle and severe road rash, I was okay. The next morning, my foster family picked me up from the hospital. On the way home my foster mom told me the police would be coming to question me about the accident. I was confused but it also made sense because from my perspective the incident was a hit and run. The officers took my statement and when we were done they explained someone else had been involved but it wasn't a hit and run.

While I was searching the night for taillights from a disappearing vehicle, there was actually another teenage boy dying in the ditch mere feet from where we'd stopped. The police explained he was driving his dirt bike behind us, but by the time he spotted us it was too late. Trying to swerve to avoid hitting us, his front wheel caught our back tire catapulting him in another direction. It turned out the car which flew past us the night before actually carried his broken body to Steinbach. His neck had broken on impact and the move killed him. He was only fourteen years old.

For months afterwards I was terrified to drive anywhere at night. I would be sitting in the front seat of my foster father's little Honda Civic and the sight of oncoming headlights would cause me to hit the floor. I could not stop thinking about the flash of lights before we collided. I am grateful for the patience my foster dad showed because I am sure it was not easy for him to deal with me and my fear.

Any progress achieved at McEwen up to this point was undone with this single incident. I became more convinced than ever I was a bad person and a curse like my mother predicted. After all these years I had concrete proof; someone died because of me. If I hadn't been trying to make friends and meet boys, the accident would not have happened. I became more determined to not affect people. I closed myself down and kept people from getting to know me. I had enough confirmation that I was bad luck and I was not going to drag anyone else with me.

Then something happened which started to draw me out of my shell again.

About a month after the accident I received an unexpected phone call. The young man who'd shown an interest in me earlier in the spring and spent the first day in McEwen with me wanted to know how things were going in my life. What started out as a simple phone call lasted about three hours. I filled him in about my summer, my friends and finally, the accident. This news surprised him. As it turned out, he knew the boy who died very well because his family farmed down the road. He also played hockey with the victim's older brother. He knew all about the accident but like many people, he did not know I was involved.

What amazed me was that despite everything I told him, he still wanted to get to know me. It was not an easy process but eventually I let him in.

CHAPTER FOURTEEN

Over the years I have learned I can do a lot on my own, but I need encouragement and love to be able to maintain this newfound independence and strength. With a simple phone call I learned that this man (he was six years older than me) was willing to give me the attention I craved, on my own terms.

The first thing I did was establish ground rules. The most important being: we would be friends but I would not sleep with him. I needed to know I mattered to someone without strings attached. My history had already proven otherwise. But the therapy I was receiving taught me I was worth more. What I needed was someone to prove to me that what I was hearing was true. Amazingly, he accepted that.

While an amazing friendship grew, it was not the ideal courtship. My foster parents had already decided that since he was a grown man we could not be alone together. It was for my own protection. They made sure he knew that if we were intimate he would be charged to the full extent of the law. They actually sat him down and explained this to him. But he was not scared off. And believe me, he should have been.

A few months later at Christmas, this was reinforced strongly by my foster family. We hadn't spent a lot of time together so he didn't know what I really wanted as a gift. Instead of a present he presented me with a Christmas card containing a crisp new one hundred dollar bill. I was grateful, because I rarely received cash of my own. On the other hand, my foster family freaked. Instead of believing it was a gift, they were convinced the cash was payment for sexual services. We were brutally questioned; subjected to threats of him being charged with statutory rape but our story never changed; we were both innocent. Eventually they were convinced. His innocent gift was sullied but our relationship persevered. I was terrified he would think ill of me, turn tail and run, but he didn't. He took it all in stride and stuck with me.

Over the next year and a half we became inseparable. He would come over after work or on weekends and we would sit for hours in the living room watching television. After having no television or radios most of my life, I was addicted to sitcoms and recorded music. He had fun watching reruns he'd already seen over and over while I giggled and gasped as I watched them for the first time.

A farm girl at heart, I loved being outside and sometimes he would help me take care of the horses. We would just spend hours walking and talking. Never good at keeping secrets eventually my entire life story was laid out at his feet. He never judged me or treated me differently.

He was respectful of me and my foster family's rules; it was six months before he kissed me for the first time and another two months before the second kiss. Both of these I initiated. After that we couldn't keep our hands off each other but we still behaved. His patience drew me to him and I slowly learned to count on him. Eventually my foster family learned to trust us, and we were allowed to leave the farm on our own. We would go to movies or for supper – all things I'd never done before. He always treated me with respect and kindness which was exactly what I needed.

After I'd been in foster care for about a year I was finally able to say goodbye to living in care at McEwen. Meanwhile, my foster mother's parents had returned from Nova Scotia to the farm which, it turned out, they owned and my foster family was just renting. My foster mother began looking for a new farm where they could move with the horses. Eventually, my foster mother found the perfect place in a farm outside of Oakbank. She wanted acreage with an indoor riding arena so she could continue to teach riding lessons and host riding camps.

At first this was where I thought we would part ways. Not understanding the foster care system I assumed I wouldn't be moving with the family. I was terrified to go back home. During the year and a half I was in McEwen I only saw my mother once, during a family meeting with my therapist. I knew then I would never be able to return home. She denied everything she ever did to me and attempted to convince my counsellor I was the one in the wrong. Thankfully, he saw through her words and recommended to CFS that it would not be in my best interest to return to my adoptive family - ever. My mother signed over custody to the province not long after that meeting.

Subsequently I was thrilled to learn that I was not going home. Soon our things were packed and we moved into our new home. Even though it now took thirty minutes to drive to our new place, my boyfriend (I loved calling him that) made the trip almost daily.

While he was the perfect boyfriend and friend, I still did some self-destructive things. I did not doubt the love we had for each other but I still tested him to see if he would hurt me like everyone else in my life had. I had come so far but I couldn't squash my deep-seated fear of being unlovable and he would eventually prove me right. He would go home with bruises on his legs, where I would pinch him to gain attention. I never noticed I did it, and he never complained. Seeing the evidence while swimming one day, it scared me that he allowed me to do this without complaint, yet it was reassuring that he never raised a hand to me.

When that didn't chase him away, I did other things. The worst was to pose naked for pictures for a stranger. A friend from McEwen and I were walking in downtown Winnipeg when a man approached us and offered us cash to pose for a magazine. Thinking it was legitimate, we both met him in a room at the Holiday Inn. I realized afterwards that while sex was not involved it was not the smartest thing to do. My guilt ate me up because I had betrayed his trust. I wanted him to believe in me and I had just proved that I couldn't be trusted when left alone to my own devices. I had to tell him.

As I confessed my betrayal and watched his face, I knew his love was real and not a ploy. He was devastated - I had never seen a man cry before. He tried to leave but I ran sobbing after his retreating car. I had gone too far and in my heart, I knew if he left, I would never see him again. Thankfully he stopped and turned around. We ended up talking for hours and managed to deal with the situation. I swore I would never hurt him like that again.

With the move came several big changes in my life. The biggest being, I would finally be able to return to school. It was the first time in two years I would attend regular classes since getting kicked out of Steinbach. I spent the first semester attending Transcona Collegiate in Winnipeg during the mornings. This allowed me to continue attending afternoon group sessions at McEwen as I transitioned back into a normal life. After first semester exams I "graduated" from McEwen and I transferred full time to Springfield Collegiate in Oakbank, one of the reasons being so I could take Driver's Ed. I enjoyed both these schools because the students were very different from my previous classmates in Steinbach. The students were more open and welcoming, not cliquish and judgmental.

For the first time in my life I was encouraged to become active in activities outside of the classroom. I loved to sew and participated in the high school fashion show. At the end of the year, I proudly accepted a few awards after beating out the boys by getting the highest marks in Carpentry. While I had struggled in Steinbach over the years, I was now thriving. I got great grades, studied hard and was thrilled when I finished grade eleven near the top of my class. I was well on my way to proving my mother wrong. I was going to make something of myself come hell or high water.

Near the end of the school year, I was turning eighteen and faced some tough decisions. As an adult I would no longer be under the care of Child and Family Services. Because I was under psychiatric care previously, I was offered the opportunity to get an apartment while I collected social assistance for the rest of my life. At the time, this was the solution to adulthood CFS offered to wards of the province. I did not know much but I did know that was not the future I wanted.

Without social assistance I couldn't remain with my foster family anymore because there was no money for my support. My foster parents graciously allowed me to stay until I finished school at the end of June even though my birthday fell at the beginning of May. But on the last day of school, I would be homeless.

My boyfriend made my next decision easy. On my eighteenth birthday he surprised me with a diamond ring. He'd carefully picked it out on his own and it was a perfect little cluster of diamonds. Parked in his car outside my high school he asked me to marry him. I loved him dearly, so I readily agreed. Engaged meant he would eventually marry me, so we decided at the end of the school year I would move back to Landmark with him and his two roommates.

My biggest regret at this point was how I left my foster home. I don't feel I ever gave them a proper good-bye or thanked them for saving my life. For the previous three years they'd been my only family; my foster dad had sacrificed so much driving me to McEwen, dealing with my accident, and everything else I did. While my foster mom wasn't perfect, she was the only woman who ever tried to be a real mother to me. But in the end, I turned out to be a monthly stipend and not a real daughter to them. I withdrew from them completely during the last month before I moved. I kept to myself and was gone with my boyfriend nearly constantly. On my very last day, I said goodbye and walked away without looking back. I dropped in for a visit about two years later to say hello but I have never seen them again.

Moving in with my fiancé and his two roommates was fun for me. For the next four months, the four of us shared a mobile home, and I enjoyed taking care of our home just like a wife would. I didn't have a job yet so in exchange for living with the guys, it was my responsibility to keep the place clean and cook. Not only did my labours help with paying the rent, but it also helped me realize I had learned many positives from my mother. Not only did I have fun playing the good housewife but I learned I could manage a home. It was great practice as I learned to cook, clean and take care of the man who would eventually become my husband.

Now an adult, I could make the decision on my own, if I wanted to extend the olive branch to my adoptive family. While I did not think I was ready, my fiancé eventually helped me reconnect with my mother. He came from a large family and had eight brothers and sisters. His mother ran a small country store outside of Landmark, while his father farmed and drove a truck. Family was important to him and, while he understood my hesitancy with reconnecting with my mom, I knew he'd be there if things did not turn out according to my fantasies.

Initially when I was in foster care, I expected that once I healed, eventually I'd be able to move back home with my family. But any contact I had would set me back in my treatment. It never failed, as soon as I was around my mother I returned whipped and insecure. The emotional trauma ran too deep. Eventually my family was forced to sign away their rights and I became a ward of CFS. Yet in the back of my mind I still believed if I became the daughter my mother wanted in the first place I would eventually be welcomed home with open arms. That never happened.

I remember how proud I was to finally see her again, this time with someone special in my life. I believed I'd found someone who loved me even though I was considered damaged goods. How could she not be happy for me?

Little did I know she disapproved of our relationship from the beginning. First, my fiancé was German and a Mennonite, which made her dislike him on sight. How dare I think of not marrying a Catholic? He was blond with blue eyes which she associated with the supreme race Hitler once tried to create. There was never any logic to my mother's thinking, but she kept her opinion to herself for once. I would hear about it later from my siblings.

Now that I was living on my own, my mother and I tried to rekindle a more adult relationship. Things were very strained. For one thing, I was lying to her about my living arrangements. I hating deceiving her but I knew she would disapprove of my living with my fiancé along with two other men. She would never understand or accept it so I didn't bother trying to explain. I hid the truth knowing it would disrupt our budding relationship. It was easier to spend a few hours hiding the evidence of male occupants before she would arrive for a visit.

While I was thrilled to have my mother in my home, the visits were awkward at first. My foster mother had taught me to love and accept physical attention and affection such as hugs and I hoped to pass that on to my mother. She stood in tense shock as I fell into her arms and welcomed her into my new home. Eventually she put her arms around me but there was a stiffness emanating from her; an invisible wall that I was never able to destroy.

Despite my proved independence, she was still not happy with my choices. What I don't think she ever realized was that I had no choice. For the past three years I had been forced to take control of a situation that could have completely destroyed me. I believed I was making great progress – I was in love and happy; I was managing a home, what else did I need? I definitely did not need her condemnation and constant criticism. So I attempted to keep her in my life but at arm's length. Even without her constant presence, I lived my life in a manner I knew she'd approve of (without her knowledge) in hopes that eventually she would open her eyes and see who I really was. Unfortunately, that never happened – ever.

Meanwhile, my fiancé and I were playing house. While we knew we were getting married we had not set a date, I was in no rush. Before I moved in, I made him promise we wouldn't get married until after I graduated high school. This was my goal and I would not be deterred. However, going back to school and everything else would be put on hold when an unthinkable tragedy struck his family and changed my thinking.

It was a hot Friday in August, and we'd been living together for just over a month. I made supper and was waiting eagerly for him to come home. He always came home right directly after work. We didn't have a phone in the trailer but our neighbour accepted phone calls on our behalf. Late in the afternoon she interrupted me while I watched soap operas to tell me my fiancé would be late. She did not know why, but he was at home with his family and he was upset. Knowing I didn't have a valid driver's license, she let me take her car and I drove the five miles to the family's homestead. The house was chaotic; there were family, friends, and neighbours crowding the tiny house and everyone was visibly devastated. When I arrived I soon learned that my future father-in-law had passed away.

He had been missing for a few days but no one was suspicious at first. It wasn't unusual for him to go hunting or drinking with his buddies and disappear for days on end. Earlier that fateful day, a neighbour had spotted his red truck parked on the property across the road just a few miles from Niverville. Curious, they went to investigate and found his body lying in the grass beside the truck. He died from a self-inflicted gunshot wound. The police were called in to investigate and his desperate plot was exposed. He had set up the gun on the back of the truck hooked with a line attached to the steering wheel. All he had to do was close the truck door and the deed was done. He did not leave a note.

I will never forget the horrific sobs of my fiancé's mother when she found out her husband of forty years had shot himself. That morning they were supposed to sign papers to sell their family home.

They'd lived there since 1942 and raised their entire family there. Just over sixty, he was a big man and his knees were causing him problems so they'd decided to move to Steinbach. His family had believed he agreed. His actions spoke otherwise. Instead, for the weeks prior to his passing, he did many unusual things. He made a point of spending time with all his children. My fiancé's mother was shown where the accounts were, titles to the land and his will. This should have been a red-flag. Despite running the store for three decades, she did not even know how to write a cheque. No one made the connection until afterwards.

Those days were very difficult for me. I had never lost anyone I loved nor did I know anyone that had been affected by such tragedy. I felt very inadequate. But I loved my fiancé and I stood by him. His father's sudden death was hard enough to cope with. Add the cause of death and it was almost too much to comprehend. He tried to withdraw but I didn't allow it. Knowing better, I didn't press him to talk, but I let him know I would not leave his side.

As my fiancé's enormous family descended on the old homestead, I found myself drawn to them. This was the life I wanted. They were a close-knit group, and I had proved my worth by sticking by my man during his most difficult time. It also made me decide that I couldn't wait for our life together to begin. In the midst of our grief I suggested we set a date and he agreed. We would get married two months later on October 25. The wedding invitations were sent out within weeks of my late soon-to-be father-in-law's funeral notices.

When I decided to get married, I thought that my mother would be happy and approve. Despite her predictions, I had found love and devotion. He didn't use me; he respected me and cared. In a way, she approved but I later found out it was all an act.

My sister got married that August and I was shocked when she asked me to be her maid-of-honour. It was fun to be finally welcomed and included in something by my sister even though it was a token position. Her friends (the other bridesmaids) did all the work; I was never really included in any of her wedding plans. It didn't matter. She had a beautiful wedding and I was so happy for her. She was marrying a man she worked with and had a crush on since we moved to Manitoba. I remembered Mom sewing her gorgeous outfits for work so she would attract his attention. I guess it worked eventually and they started to date. I was thrilled to see her so happy and in love.

She was not the only one that was in love and happy. During the heat of the summer of 1986, wedding fever took over as I excitedly planned my own nuptials. I knew my family wouldn't pay for anything, so we tried to keep it as affordable as possible. We hosted a social at the beginning of October which helped us raise money to pay for the wedding. While my sister had hundreds of guests, our list was around a hundred, mostly my soon-to-be husband's family. I proudly sewed my own dress – my mother helped me pick the material and paid for it. It was a completely hands-on wedding. I even returned the favour and asked my sister to be my matron-of-honour.

For once, life seemed normal and exciting until I asked my father to walk me down the aisle. It was something I really wanted – to have him give me away. Initially he agreed, but later he called me to retract his acceptance. I was heartbroken. I did not expect rejection from my father. I found out my mother was livid he accepted without consulting her first and forbid him from doing it. I think she was also angry because we got married two months after my sister's wedding. I had not considered any of that. I was just eagerly looking forward to my own future – a future I never dreamed possible.

Despite the drama, we got married on a glorious fall day in the St. Michael's Ukrainian Catholic Church, in Sarto, a tiny hamlet south of Steinbach. It was the closest Catholic Church to my parents, and my family had been members there since we'd moved to Manitoba. I handled most of the arrangements myself – other than a few bridal showers my fiancé's family threw for me. There was very little involvement from my own family.

Looking back at my wedding album which I have kept all these years, I cannot find a single picture of my mother with a smile on her face. Yet, I distinctly remember making my wedding plans with her in mind. I even sewed my own wedding dress – not only to save money, but to prove to my mother that I had left home with something she'd taught me. But it didn't matter. She was constantly disapproving.

Despite that, I was happy. For once I didn't care. I was marrying an amazing man who loved me despite my flaws. I couldn't ask for anything more.

Before taking our vows, I returned to the family farm for the first time since I ran away from home. My mother allowed me to stay with her during the two days prior to the ceremony. As far as I knew, she was still oblivious to our living together so I was trying to make it right by staying apart for a couple days before the ceremony. It was also closer to Steinbach and the church. This was our first separation since moving in together in June.

It was in the bathroom of my mother's house, the day before my wedding, I discovered a shocking but pleasant surprise.

I was pregnant.

CHAPTER FIFTEEN

For the first time in memory I was truly happy. My once damaged heart was bursting with joy. I was in love, newly married to a wonderful man, expecting my first baby and making our house into a home. Things were perfect and it didn't matter what my mother thought. I had my new husband to please, not her. My future was full of hope and promise.

I really wanted my new husband to see where I had been raised so we took a road trip down to Niagara Falls. It may seem a cliché to visit the honeymoon capital of the world on our honeymoon but there was more to the story for me. It was a trip home, to visit my dad's family and return to my roots. We used the money collected during presentation at our wedding to pay for the trip. It was nice to go home and show him some of the places I'd talked about so fondly. I showed him my old house, the school I'd gone to, and we checked out the magnificent Niagara Falls. Even in late October, it was still breathtakingly beautiful.

A trip home would not be complete without visiting the family we had left behind so many years ago. My grandmother was thrilled when we stopped in Welland and spent a few days with her. She had not seen anyone from our side of the family in over a decade. She was invited to the weddings, but could not travel alone. She missed my father so much and she couldn't believe he had stayed away for so long. Once my father moved to Manitoba he never returned home to see his mother or brother; he didn't even go home when his father passed away. It broke my grandmother's heart, but she knew how my mother was. She didn't understand it, but she knew — they all knew. When I told her I was expecting, she hauled me into the basement. From a dark corner in the back, she pulled out an old white crib. It was my crib from when I was a baby. I couldn't believe she still had it after all these years. We loaded it up and took it home, vowing we would refinish it and use it for our children.

On the way home, morning sickness kicked in. It was the smell of the nickel mines in Sudbury that made me ill. For the next three months I suffered. I couldn't keep anything down. Thank goodness for the commode in the basement, although it got quite nasty, so I would spend mornings dry heaving into the kitchen sink.

Our new home was my husband's family homestead. When my husband's father passed away, his mother closed the store, sold the old homestead house and moved to Steinbach. His many brothers and sisters wanted the house to stay in the family, so we decided we would buy it. His parents bought the house in 1942 and raised all nine children there. It made sense that we would continue the tradition, plus the price was good.

I was thrilled to have our own home and threw myself into becoming the perfect housewife and soon-to-be mother. I may have been born and raised to be a traditional homemaker; but it was not as easy as I thought it would be. There was so much I had to learn. Our first winter together was the hardest for me. My husband worked construction out of town at the time, so I spent a lot of time alone.

While we had a house, it was not modernized. There was an old monstrosity of a wood furnace in the basement we used to heat the one and half story house. I had to learn how to keep the place warm and chop wood. We didn't even have a modern bathroom the first year. There was an outhouse in the back and a homemade commode in the basement for days when going outside was too cold. It was a fairly big house, but we limited the living space for the winter. One third of the house which once housed the store was closed up and forgotten about. Despite the hardships, it was cozy, warm and ours.

When my husband worked out of town, I lived for the weekends when he came home. I missed him terribly when he was gone. He was my only true friend and confidant and I was lonely. I felt inadequate trying to maintain the home and when he returned, he'd help me restore things to order. Learning to be a real housewife was harder than I expected. Looking back, it must have been difficult for him to come home on weekends. While I spent my weekdays missing him like crazy, he'd work his fingers to the bone making an honest living for our budding family. Instead of appreciating it, I resented his perceived freedom. He had friends and guys he worked with while my loneliness grew. I didn't have my license yet, so I was housebound three miles from town. With the exception of going to the neighbours for tea I was pretty much left alone.

I felt guilty I was at home growing fat with child and laziness while he would come home to cook, clean, do laundry and return the house back to order. I admit that it was not fair but he never complained. To make things worse, when I'd call my mother and shared my feelings instead of reassuring me, she'd point out that if I didn't learn soon, I'd lose my husband.

As my pregnancy progressed and some problems started, I grew more passive and lazy. I was a horrible homemaker. I did what came naturally and turned to my mother for help. Surprising everyone, most of all me, she was very helpful. She even came to the hospital with me several times when I started spotting so I wouldn't be alone if I happened to miscarry. My pregnancy seemed to have drawn us closer. We talked daily on the phone and when the weather finally started to warm up, I spent days with her on the farm. For the first time in my life, my mother was being a mother.

We would draw up chaise loungers under a massive tree in the yard sipping homemade ice tea and talk. I soaked it up. This was what I had always wanted: not to be criticized or condemned. This was when she started to share her story. I had learned it was also okay to start ask questions. More importantly, as an adult I was not afraid to ask them. During these afternoon chats, she confided how her father had molested her as a teenager. As her story unfolded, I started to understand. She explained this was the reason behind separating me from my father and her over-protectiveness when men were around. She admitted that she'd recognized my budding beauty and feared for my safety. It was nice to have so many gaps filled up but, at the same time, it was heartbreaking to hear her story.

This was also when she finally dug out the paperwork for my adoption and started to encourage me to find my real family. I was actually surprised she did this. It was the first time I'd seen the documents – I didn't even know they existed.

Despite all the progress we seemed to make that summer, my

mother still took my past behaviour as hatred and rejection over her adopting me and would not acknowledge her role in anything. No matter how I tried to explain all I ever wanted was her love and acceptance, she never heard me. In her mind, she was convinced I was a problem child because I wanted my real family and was punishing her for it. She never apologized for the abuse she inflicted on me; she didn't believe she had done anything out of the ordinary.

During our talks I grew less afraid to tell her how I felt. She couldn't hurt me physically now, and there seemed to be a newfound respect. Once I was able to tell her how she had made me feel, I was able to start letting things go. Most of all, it felt good to stand up to her for once. I was no longer afraid of her. It hurt immensely that she never took responsibility, but I decided that I needed to let things go and look at this as a new start.

Being pregnant made me feel wonderful, nurtured and loved because I was doing something special. I was pregnant with my parents' first grandchild or so I thought. Around this time, my sister-in-law announced she was also having a baby. My brother was finally expecting his firstborn. This excited me even more because my brother, who was always my favourite, was sharing a mutual experience with me. My baby would have an instant cousin.

Sadly, my mother found no peace or joy in having two grandchildren. My sister and her husband were also trying to have a baby but with no success. For her, my sister's not getting pregnant was more important than her impending grand-motherhood courtesy of her two least favourite children. But she wore a smile whenever she was around me and afterwards I would hear all about what she had to say from whomever she spoke to. Yet, I still sought her approval! Why is it that children who grow up in situations like this are forever in search of what they have lost? That love, acceptance, faithfulness. A mother! After I gave birth to my oldest, I never understood how my mother could treat me the way she had. I had this most beautiful daughter, but I still had a hole in my heart; one that I felt could only be filled by a mother's love.

While things were getting better between my mother and me, not all was as it seemed. My mother's insecurities and fear of men started to show again, but this time I recognized it better. She didn't like that I was alone so much and was convinced my husband was cheating on me when he was out of town. Not a great thing to be feeding an already insecure and very pregnant woman. When he came home I was accusing him of things he wasn't doing – because the bee had been put in my ear. He'd come home on weekends and have to spend time assuring me he loved me and would never hurt me.

Despite this emotional rollercoaster, my husband and I drew closer as my pregnancy progressed. He changed jobs and was no longer working out of town. He also participated in the pregnancy by attending doctor's appointments, ultrasounds and even prenatal classes. I was due at the end of June and he worked hard on improving the house, too. We got rid of the commode in the basement and renovated the old master bedroom into a full size bathroom. The store part of the house was renovated into a living room and we moved our bed and the nursery to the second floor.

I was growing excited with the prospect of becoming a mother, and very impatient. My due date came and went without the appearance of our bundle of joy. On the advice of my mother-in-law, I dug out the castor oil without breathing a word to anyone. Apparently drinking it would cause a woman to go into labour. In my case, all I succeeded in doing is cause problems. After two days of leaking amniotic fluid, I was finally admitted to Bethesda Hospital. A quick exam proved that baby was at risk and I was quickly transferred to St. Boniface Hospital.

All my fantasies of the perfect birth and delivery were shattered over the next few hours. In an overcrowded delivery room in St. Boniface Hospital I was subjected to poking and probing from nurses, doctors, interns and medical students. So many people came and went. The janitor could have checked if I was dilated and I wouldn't have known or cared. It was terrifying. Everything I learned in Lamaze class was tossed out the window. Finally, after three hours of induction it was decided I needed an emergency c-section. We welcomed our tiny daughter into the world at 3:00 a.m. Despite the complications, my husband never left my side. I remember holding my baby for the first time and feeling so complete. As the most perfect love poured out of me, it really hit me what I had missed with my own mother.

The next couple months were spent learning how to raise a baby. My husband adored being a father and enjoyed his little daughter. She was a tiny little thing with a shock of brown hair and big blue eyes – she was perfectly beautiful and I was proud of her. I'd watch him curl up with her and my heart would swell with love and pride. Our little family was happy but I also couldn't help being a little sad.

I felt cheated and disappointed in myself because if I hadn't messed with the castor oil she would have been born naturally. One of my husband's cousins had the nerve to tell me I was not a real woman or mother because I didn't give birth naturally. His words hurt deeply. It didn't take much for the feelings of insecurity and shame I had lived with the majority of life to resurface. Minus the many therapists I'd had in recent years, I felt myself regressing.

Needing to find something to keep my mind occupied and focused I decided to go back to school. Even though I had a little baby, I knew I could do both. Unfortunately, I was forced to put my plans for graduation back on hold again. When our little bundle of pink was only three months old, we were in for a shocking surprise.

I was pregnant again.

CHAPTER SIXTEEN

Finding out I was expecting again came as a shock to both of us; but I took it the hardest. I was not ready for number two. When the second pregnancy occurred, I was breast feeding. My mother-in-law and others had assured me if I was nursing, I wouldn't get pregnant and I believed them - they were the experts after all. My body proved them very wrong.

Our first baby was sort of planned. Birth control was against the rules within the Catholic faith. While in foster care, CFS put me on the pill and I stayed on it until we set a date for our wedding. Even though my mother had no knowledge of my actions, I still tried to abide by her rules and what she had raised me to believe.

Needless to say, baby number two was unexpected. I was just getting comfortable with my new situation and planning for the future. I had already developed a plan. When my baby was old enough to be weaned and stay with a babysitter, I was going to hold my husband to his promise that I could go back to school and graduate. With a second child this was not going to happen and I became resentful.

It shames me to admit that, for the first time, I actually hoped the problems I had with my first pregnancy would manifest themselves and I'd eventually lose the baby. Where I wouldn't lift a finger during the first pregnancy, I was now shovelling snow, tobogganing, snowmobiling, skating and any other physical activity I could do. I knew what I was subconsciously trying to do and, thankfully, nothing ever happened. Obviously, God had other plans, because our second daughter was born in August the next summer. I was determined and tried to give birth naturally and again, there were complications. After thirty hours of labour and no progress, I was finally rolled into the operating room for another C-section. From the moment she was laid in my arms, I knew she was special and I fell in love with her instantly and deeply. Overwhelmed with emotion, I was deeply ashamed for ever wishing this tiny infant any harm. She was a little angel.

We christened her an old-fashioned name my mother once mentioned she loved; it was Ukrainian. In a drug-induced fog, it was the only name I could think of when the nurse asked if we had a name picked out. I vaguely remembered mom mentioning the name and I chose it as a small tribute to her. After all this time, her opinion still mattered.

It was like this new baby knew that at one point, she was not wanted – she clung to me from day one. While my oldest daughter would spend hours curled up with Daddy, the little newborn clung to mommy. This suited me just fine. It felt wonderful to be needed and wanted by someone so tiny and helpless. My recovery from my second C-section was less dramatic than the first, but I still took it easy – or at least as easy as I could with two babies in diapers. My husband was always a huge help. I couldn't have done it without him.

While I was pretty useless as a wife during the first year, I now embraced my new family situation. Some of the healthy ideals – if somewhat old fashioned - my mother instilled on me surfaced. I made sure my husband had hot meals at the end of the day and the children were always well taken care of. My mother stepped in and helped when she could but over time, she seemed to resent the fact that I needed her. I was actually shocked when, after I gave birth, she would come and take care of the babies so I could rest and recover. It was wonderful to share raising my little daughters with her – things were as they should have been all along. I guess in my own way, I knew it was too late for us, so I offered her a chance to redeem herself through my children.

But it was difficult raising two little ones and the reality is - I was terrified to get pregnant again. I was only twenty and, once again, my husband was working out of town. The baby was only six months old when he started going north to work in Thompson. Despite my religious beliefs (which I followed even though I didn't go to church) the first thing I did when he left was go on back on the pill. Unfortunately, this affected nursing so I was forced to wean my baby quickly. Already overly attached to me, she did not like that at all – she went on a hunger strike. I put her on solid food because she refused to take a bottle no matter how hard I tried. I was just as stubborn even though it pained me and finally, after a couple of days, I found a formula she would take.

Meanwhile, someone in my husband's family grew concerned I was alone all the time with the two little ones, many times without a vehicle. They contacted Child and Family Services, raising concern the baby was not thriving. She was a tiny girl compared to her older sister in the first place so it was understandable that someone would be concerned. The battle for the bottle caused her to lose valuable weight, but she was otherwise healthy. A social worker came to my home and conducted an investigation. This was the first time I understood how my mother truly felt when I was little.

I was petrified that no matter what I said the authorities would take the kids away. I even assumed that, since I was a former ward of the province, they would automatically take the babies. Maybe it was because in my heart I didn't feel like a fit parent. I was scared, alone and clueless on what I was doing. It was the days before the World Wide Web offered help just a click away. I was learning on the spot and, in my opinion, I was really uninformed. Look at the castor oil incident and the not getting pregnant while breast feeding thing. I was making mistakes left right and centre just because I didn't know any better.

Instead of removing the kids (there was no reason to) the social worker offered me a homemaker. This helper came into the house twice a week and watched the kids while I got things like daily chores done. Through Child and Family Services I was also introduced to a "Young Mom" program offered in Steinbach. Once a week, the kids and I packed into her car and we attended the afternoon mothers support group. I finally had a social network of my own and made some friends with other young moms. We learned about parenting, discussed our relationships and even did craft projects. These groups made the weeks I was alone not so terrifying.

Once both girls were a little older, I once again looked at going back to school. I was determined and I was not going to give up. The only way I knew I could graduate was to go back to the Steinbach

Regional High School. It was hard walking through those doors again. I hadn't been there since I was kicked out years ago. It felt strange walking those same halls I'd wandered fearfully through years ago. I expected them to deny my request to attend classes but they took me back despite my school record. I was twenty-one, married with two children, and the oldest grade twelve student in the school.

A lot of my classmates looked up to me; I was popular for once and I soaked it in. I even allowed myself to get talked into running for school president. The rebel in me came out and on the day I had to give my campaign speech, I rode into the gym on the back of a motorcycle. Yes, you read right – I rode on the back of a motorcycle through the halls into the school gym. It was the first time I'd gotten onto a bike since that horrific accident when I was sixteen. I didn't win but I got more votes than I ever expected. And people recognized me! Instead of a horrible school experience, I had turned it around and it felt great.

Unfortunately, I messed that up for myself by investing more time with making friends instead of going to class. Soon I was skipping classes, drinking and starting to smoke pot. While my classmates' parents received phone calls from the school about ditching classes, my husband was the unwelcome recipient of notices when I skipped. I was reliving my teen years instead of doing what I set out to do. It got so bad that teachers would watch the activity around my car and eventually the police began checking things out.

On the day I finally dropped out my car was searched by the police three times. Trying to be nice, I let my friends smoke in my car while I was in class, never thinking they'd take advantage of the situation. Smoking wasn't allowed on the school grounds, so I parked my car on the street, unlocked for that purpose. There were rumours of a theft and that my vehicle was involved. I was in class but my car was unlocked, and I really did not know what was going on until someone told me the police were searching my car. I realized that I didn't need that. I had to think of my kids. In an effort to relive the youth I'd missed, I was putting their lives in jeopardy, so I walked out of school that day and never went back. My timing was actually perfect – within a few weeks of dropping out of school, I found out I was expecting baby number three.

While I was excited to be expecting again, my mother returned to her bitter self. You see, since they'd married my sister and her husband was trying to conceive with no success. I was so caught up in my bliss over my growing family I failed to notice the sadness in my sister's face when she saw my gorgeous babies. She bravely stood up as godmother for each of their baptisms but meanwhile her heart was breaking. She yearned to have a baby of her own.

I was thrilled when, within a few days of telling my mother I was pregnant, she confided my sister was also expecting. She was due in June and I was due in August. I was ecstatic - my sister and I were both pregnant together. Once again, just like when we got married, my sister and I had the foundation for a real relationship. As we grew plumper, my sister and I spent countless hours together, talking about our babies and pregnancies. I was younger, but an old pro in the baby producing department and I loved my older sister seeking advice. She may have been a decade my senior, but I was a wealth of information both about pregnancy and raising babies – it should have been a wonderful bonding time. But she had a hard pregnancy. While mine progressed without any complications, she suffered from prenatal diabetes and a tumour which grew at the same rate as her baby. I prayed for her constantly and offered my unconditional support.

Over the summer our relationship had come so far but the fragile bond of sisterhood was severed in August when my niece was born. She was tiny, ill, and the doctors did not think she would survive at first. On one hand, I was thrilled for my sister's new motherhood but on the other hand it broke my heart that things were not as we all expected. Understandably my mother focussed her undivided attention on my sister, helping her during this heartbreaking time. I was once again abandoned.

My third daughter was born a month later without even a phone call from my family. When I finally heard from my mother, she refused to listen to me talk about the new baby, the other two children or our family. All she talked about was how hard things were for my sister. She had been elevated to sainthood in my mother's eyes because their daughter was diagnosed as severely autistic. The worst part was, as bizarre as it sounds; I was blamed for my tiny niece's health problems. My mother accused me of somehow cursing my sister. I was asked by my own mother if I hated my sister so much that I could have wished something this horrible should happen to her.

"You don't deserve to have perfect children," my mother told me over the phone one afternoon. Those simple words cut like a knife. I realized my mother had never changed her attitude towards me at all. Her real self was hiding deep inside this entire time. I tried arguing back. We had just found out our third baby was born with a heart defect which could affect her all her life – she might even need open-heart surgery. Foolishly, I thought this would make a difference. Then I realized nothing ever would. She was an angry, hateful woman and ultimately I did not deserve to be treated this way.

When we finally hung up, I sobbed for all that I thought was, but in reality turned out to be only an illusion. It was sickening to realize I believed my beautiful daughter's heart defect would please my mother and make her love me and my family more. What kind of mother did that make me? My concern should be for my children; not what my mother thought.

It was at that point that I realized that I would never be the daughter my mother seemed to want. I also realized no one could be that hateful unless something else was eating him or her up inside. But when you have been subjected to the same emotional roller coaster ride, over and over, year after year, you eventually get to the point where you have to walk away. Or at least shut yourself down from all the pain and heartache such a relationship can give you. I had to cut the strings she had on my heart and move on. Admittedly, it was the hardest thing I had ever done. It tore me apart but I had to walk away. At this point I was determined to accept my husband's friends as my friends, his family as my family, and I, by choice, did not have a family. I had to do it. My mother's suspicions, accusations and manipulations could cost my marriage and my sanity.

I was extremely lucky when it came to my husband's family. My mother-in-law was an amazing woman. She was the type of woman who even though she had nine children of her own, she accepted, loved and treated all the extended family and grandchildren like they were her only child. I have never met such a giving woman like her before or since. Having her unconditional love and acceptance in our lives made it easier to close the door on my condemning family.

Over the next four years, I kept in touch with my family but there was no real relationship. My doors were always open but my parents and siblings never came to visit, even before the riff. I would return to the farm when my mother would invite us over but later I would hear she told my brother or sister I only came to visit because she had something for me.

I hated being manipulated and there was so much emotional pain attached to her yo-yo type love. But as the matriarch of my own household, I had learned my strengths and I refused to be drawn in. I kept my distance and at the time it was the best thing I could do for us. Finally, without my mother feeding my insecurities I could thrive; both as a mother and a wife.

CHAPTER SEVENTEEN

I knew I would be condemned for it, but at the time putting distance between my mother and myself was the best decision for me and my family. I remember my husband telling me that he could tell as soon as he got home if I had talked to my mom during the day. He said it was like a different person was waiting for him. In one phone call, my confidence and security would crumble at the sound of her voice. It made perfect sense that each time I would walk away from my mother and her influences, I would become more settled and calm.

Determined to be a good mom and not like my mother, I would focus my efforts on raising my children and pleasing my husband during those hiatuses. I prided myself with bringing some of the good things that my mother taught me into my home. I don't compliment myself often, but I was a good wife and partner. In many ways I am very old fashioned. My goal was to make sure that as long as we were taken care of; my husband was taken care of in return. Unlike the first few years, he would now work his construction job and come home and relax. I made sure the house was clean, the kids were taken care of and the yard was even mowed. I believed that the less he had to do when he was finally home, the more time he could spend with me and the kids.

I learned that I loved to cook and each day I planned a dinner meal for when my husband came home. Like my family when I was growing up, we would sit around the table and eat together. As the kids got older, we moved into the living room and would picnic on the coffee table. Mealtimes were always a time to share stories and be silly. If he worked late then I would feed the children and wait until he got home to eat dinner with him. When he was out of town, we would do our own things and keep things simpler.

It was the hardest for me when my husband was working out of town. Keeping up with the care of our home and the children was a lot of responsibility. Sometimes I was really scared to be alone with the kids. When he was home, I knew if I got upset or frustrated he could talk me out of it. Maybe it would have been different if I had family backing me up or friends I could call when I needed a stress reliever, but for the most part it was just me and the kids. It was during those days that I was genuinely worried about becoming my mother.

The girls were little and full of mischief. It never failed, but the two oldest were always off doing something. They would scare me by wandering off. One afternoon, if it hadn't been for their hot pink rubber boots, I might have lost them in the neighbour's sewage lagoon. The oldest was always the one who got into trouble. Not that she was the leader, but because daughter number two was super sensitive. My middle daughter was so timid that if you looked at her the wrong way she'd burst into tears. So when I'd get angry, I'd focus on the oldest. I used to believe in spankings until I took it too far one afternoon. The two girls were fighting in the living room, something they seemed to enjoy doing a lot. It's amazing how even at a young age siblings seem to know exactly what sets the other off. After telling them to settle down several times without success, I decided to step in. Without thinking I grabbed the oldest and 'fired' her into the corner chair. I didn't pick her up and drop her or place her gently; I grabbed her by the arms and threw her. She landed in the chair, bounced onto the floor and landed on her back at my feet. I remember looking down at her and stomping on her fragile little chest in exasperation.

As she lay there gasping for air, I was overcome with remorse. I fell to the floor and started bawling. I had done the unthinkable. I had tried to hurt my child. I was inconsolable. In horror, I called my husband and demanded him to come home immediately. I told him I was going to call the police and report myself for child abuse. I couldn't believe what I had done! Meanwhile the girls were shocked and couldn't believe it either. Their tear-stained faces as they watched me freak out were unforgettable.

When my husband finally got home, he talked me out of calling the police. So I tried packing my bags, intent on walking out on all of them but he wouldn't allow me to go. Eventually he calmed me down and we talked it out. Once I was consoled, I went to see my daughter. As I held her and cried in shame I apologized; swearing that I would never lay a hand on my kids again in anger. I was not going to subject them to the same pain I felt. Even worse, I now knew I was capable of the same violence I had been subjected to. I was horrified. Determined that I would not let my upbringing affect my children, I threw myself into being a good parent. I wanted my babies to have what I hadn't had – loving parents, and a relationship with each other. I also wanted them to have many fond childhood memories. Most of all, I wanted them to love me, not fear me. I knew that pain and they deserved better. They deserved a childhood.

Determined that my children would have a good life and many pleasant memories I did my best with what we had. There was never enough money to do anything fancy so we would get creative. During the summer, we would go to the Blumenort pits for the day instead of sitting at home watching television. I was now hanging out regularly with mothers my age and we loved getting together and letting the kids play. We would stake out a piece of the local gravel pit and stay there until dinner time. This made the days go fast and was a great time for me because we all parented together. Once I had my son, it was harder for me to hang out with the group. It was exhausting to haul four children around and expensive, so we had to look at alternative sources of entertainment.

One year I wanted a swimming pool and a friend of the family had one for sale. He wanted $500 which was more than I dared ask my husband to spend. Instead, I held my first garage sale and invited the neighbours to join. Our huge shop was packed with tables and items spilled out into the yard. It was a great success and a few weeks later we were enjoying our pool. It was one of best investments I have made because we got many years of use out it.

Some of my fondest childhood memories consisted of camping as a family and we followed that tradition. In exchange for shingling the neighbour's roof we earned a hardtop tent trailer. My husband was a seasonal worker so we could never take holidays during the summer so we improved. I decided it would be fun to take the camper to St.

Malo during the week and instead of his coming home to the house, he joined us at the campsite. It was not quite the same as having a week off, but he enjoyed that I made the effort and he had a mini-vacation.

This became a yearly tradition – a week in July and a week in August until the camper canvas started rotting to pieces. This also gave me a wonderful chance to spend time with the kids without interruptions like television and chores. We would have wonderful adventures that became grander as the girls learned to ride bikes. Sadly, when my marriage fell apart these outings were gone forever. I could never afford to replace the camper or to find an inexpensive replacement.

When my husband and I were dating, it was a weekend tradition for his buddies to play baseball on Sunday afternoons, a tradition that continued for a few years after we got married. We even built a baseball diamond in our back yard one year. Once the pool was built we'd play ball and swim. Those were great summers.

Each summer we would plant a big garden. Here too, my mother's influence reared its ugly head. It was amazing that our garden grew well considering I never took care of it. Each spring we would plant it together as a family but I refused to weed. I loathed weeding. It always brought me back to when I was a little girl and I would be forced spend summers on my hands and knees in the searing heat dressed practically like a nun. I'd always get yelled at because I was a terrible weed picker. I was more intent on finishing and finding shade than caring if I did a good job or not. Many times I was sent back two or three times to do it properly because roots would still be left in the earth. Thankfully my husband understood and he actually enjoyed weeding in the evenings or on weekends until the mosquitoes threatened to carry him away.

My contribution would be the big job of getting ready for winter by harvesting everything and canning. I loved canning and even had some of my mother's recipes. I'd make pickles, salsa, tomato sauce, pickled carrots, cabbage, and fruit. I also filled my freezer with everything I could so we would have plenty during the winter. The girls' contribution was to sneak into the garden to eat peas and tomatoes straight from the vine. I never minded.

We didn't have extra money to do things or go places but we found other ways to have fun. My. My husband built a little trailer to pull behind the lawn tractor. The girls would eagerly beg for him to take them around the neighbourhood for rides. They loved how he spent time with them. As a little girl, I loved skating and being outdoors, but as I got older this wasn't as much fun. I spent my winters indoors while the kids and their dad would always be outside. He would make them amazing forts in the yard. The way the house and shop sat, the middle yard would fill up with snow. He'd make the pile higher as he pushed snow throughout the winter until the mountain was as tall as the house. Then the shovels would come out. I loved watching the four of them digging in the snow, making snow forts. Safety first, he always put a piece of plywood across the top so that it could never collapse on the kids. They'd spend hours making snowmen.

Then there was the winter of the snowmobiles. One of our friends offered us a good deal on a couple of TNT snowmobiles. The snow-machines were ancient and rarely went faster than the dog could run but that didn't matter to the kids. A huge sled was built and soon the kids had free rides around the neighbourhood. Even I spent hours outside playing in the snow that year along with the kids.

It was important to me that each of the girls had a slight education before they started school. I would spend afternoons teaching them the alphabet, counting and how to write their names. The older two girls would often compete with each other to see who knew more. My oldest was often annoyed that her little sister could count to twelve while she could only count to six. Most of all, I remember teaching them to love music. We would dance down the road to get the mail, each of us holding hands singing: *"There she was just-a-walking down the street."* Those are precious memories.

Once the girls were older, they discovered their own love for music and we were subjected to many well-choreographed performances. They would spend hours in the basement practising dance routines. The *Spice Girls* were huge at the time and a favourite for their acts. When they were done practicing (and fighting), they would set up the living room and put on a show. The girls were very creative with their acts and, with the exception of the youngest daughter interrupting all the time, they did very well.

When the girls were little, I admit it was very difficult to parent them. There is only so much that you can do to entertain a toddler at least they were easy to take care of. It used to scare me at how close my children were in age – heck, I had three in diapers at one point. But once they got older, taking care of them got easier. The hardest part of those years was that we did not have a lot of money. With only a single income, many of the things that we would have liked to do were never done. I was also terrible with finances.

My husband's biggest mistake was to rely on me to deal with the money. We lived from disconnection notice to disconnection notice because I would forget to pay the bills. He'd work during the summer and get laid off in winter. It always took forever for the first unemployment check to come. We even had to crawl to the municipality a few times for food vouchers or to keep the power on when times were really tough.

But it didn't matter – for the most part we were happy. The kids were happy too. I was living my life the way I wanted to and raising my family the way I believed they should be raised.

CHAPTER EIGHTEEN

Things were not perfect in our growing household but they were less complicated. I had settled in to happily being a wife and mother. Even though my heart yearned to include my mother, father and siblings, I had done what I had to do - carry on and live.

In 1994, we decided to try to have another baby. Despite my doctor's discouraging advice - I'd already had three C-sections, we decided that we would just see what would happen. I was determined to try one more time to have a son. My husband needed a boy, a namesake, someone to carry on the family name. This baby was planned and it was a great pregnancy. There was a lot of pressure on me – everyone pointed out that with three daughters we HAD to have a boy. I'd already decided it would be my last baby, so a boy would be nice, but I knew I'd be happy with a healthy baby.

When our little boy was born, I was thrilled. Finally, after three daughters, I had fulfilled what I had felt was my duty as a wife and mother. I had finally given my husband the son he wanted and deserved. Our son was an adorable little boy, and loved by everyone – especially his oldest sister. She enjoyed spending time with him and many times I'd find them sleeping together on the couch, where she'd fall asleep while reading him a story. He was spoiled from the moment he entered the world. With his big blue eyes; hair so white he looked bald and deep dimples when he smiled, he was very easy to look at and love.

As I raised the girls, I knew that I would be the one to influence them, encourage them and teach them to be the women they were meant to be. A son, however, needed a man's influence so I encouraged my husband to take the lead in raising him. It wasn't difficult as it was obvious from day one he was pleased with his little boy.

His birth also gave me another opening to reacquaint myself with my parents. I especially wanted a relationship with my father. For me, it became important to give this man, whom I had cleaved to when I was hurting, a chance to know his grandson.

My mother once told me that when I ran away, I broke my daddy's heart. Sadly, I believe that. Whenever the battles started in our home, my mom would come down on everyone. My dad, he would hide in the barn doing chores or meaningless tasks, just to stay out of her way. As for me, well, I hung around wherever my father was. I would tell him about my day at school or a book I was reading. I would sing while milking, which he loved, and I baked for him. He loved sweets and my mother never made them. His favourite was cream puffs. I still have the recipe, but I have never made them since I left the farm.

Our relationship was as good as it could be under the circumstances until I reached puberty. Mom turned our innocent father-daughter relationship into a nasty little affair. Later, when I found out her own father had molested her; I understood she couldn't understand that a father and daughter could have a normal relationship. Needless to say, there was no incest. We just shared a quiet and safe companionship. We spent a lot of time together but we did not even dare talk to each other about Mom. It seemed wrong, like a betrayal. We just hung around together in comfortable silence. But the damage was done. Until the day he died, my father was afraid to be alone with me because of the allegations so many years ago. Despite this, I wanted my son to have the relationship with my dad that I was cheated out of.

In my opinion, my father lost so much when we moved to Manitoba. He was too stubborn to give up on a lifestyle that proved to be a hard adjustment. He gave up his dream of being a truck driver to become a city boy with a factory job and paid holidays. He loved his hobbies of camping, fishing, travelling and photography. But the farm ultimately robbed him of his life. He never indulged himself again.

On the dairy farm, the day started early with feeding and milking and ended late after dark for the same reason. In the twenty years he operated the farm he never took a holiday. Not even a day trip. His favourite canoe rotted and fell apart, and all his camping gear was torn to shreds over the years by mice in the grainary. After what happened with the previous owner, he never trusted anyone enough to leave someone in charge.

My husband, bless his heart, tried numerous times, to get Dad off the farm, even for just a day. He missed his own father and he genuinely liked my dad and his gentle spirit. We thought if we could get him off the farm, even for a day, that he would have some happiness in an otherwise hard life. We suggested day fishing and canoe trips. Dad would excitedly accept the invitation and the pair would plan the trip. Unfortunately, these excursions never happened. As soon as we would be ready to leave, my mom would step in and before we knew it, Dad was calling to cancel for one reason or another. It broke my heart but I was not going to give up.

When my son was born, I took it as an opportunity to bring some happiness to my father's life. He'd finally retired and sold the herd, so there was less responsibility. He hoped he could start doing the things he loved again. But I guess he was tired and it was not as easy as he thought it would be. He hung around the farm and raised a few beef cattle to keep busy. Visiting with him was now easier because he was no longer running off to do chores nor was he as exhausted as he used to be.

He would beam when he'd see any of his grandchildren. I took it as silent praise and acceptance. What he didn't say in words I could read in his eyes and it made me feel happy knowing he loved and accepted me and my family. I wanted my son to get to know his only living grandfather – they both deserved and needed that loving influence. My brother had a son, but they rarely came by the farm, and I know that hurt Dad. But I also understood why my brother kept away – I was in the same boat.

My dad had so much he could teach my boy, and I wasn't going to deprive him of the opportunity. I picked up the phone and started making regular visits to the farm to help them cement a relationship. Whenever I would go visit, my dad would leave the barn so he could see his grandchildren. While he adored the girls, I could tell that he was hesitant and standoffish. They didn't understand – but I did. If my mother accused him and me of things, there was nothing keeping her from making the same accusations about the granddaughters.

But it was different with my son. From the day he learned how to walk and talk, my son was fascinated by the animals and all the farm equipment. I'd spent a lot of time mowing grass when I was pregnant and he seemed to have an inbred love for tractors and farm machinery. Every chance he got, he would beg to go check out the tractors and my dad would take him for rides. We even got him collecting cards, similar to hockey cards, except with tractors and farm equipment. He loved them and would proudly tote his binder to show his grandpa. My dad would beam with pride as my little boy would name the different brands and types. He could tell the difference between a swath and a combine; Kabota or International Harvester. His favourite brand was John Deere. My son adored his "grandpa with the tractors."

One of my fondest memories of their relationship took place about a month before my father passed away. My son managed to charm a trip to the barn to check out a newborn calf with my dad. After I got him dressed, the pair ventured outside. I don't know what drew me to the kitchen window, but I found myself looking out into the yard. Tears welled as I watched my father walking across the yard holding my son by his tiny hand. I couldn't hear what they were saying but I saw the love and admiration pass between grandfather and grandson. My son adored my dad. That picture is something I will treasure for as long as I have a memory.

Unfortunately the relationship would never have a chance to bloom.

CHAPTER NINETEEN

The reality of my life kicked in after the birth of my son. No longer required to breed I looked forward to raising my family with the plan that eventually I would look for something to make myself feel more complete. It is not that I wasn't happy being a wife and mother. I just hungered for something of my own.

I was twenty-six years old with four kids and a husband who was working out of town again. I had never had a job, even though I tried. My husband was determined I remain a stay-at-home mom. It was the way I was raised and the way he was raised. He would sooner work hard and never see his family than have his wife get a job and leave his children in the care of others. He did not understand that I really needed to get out of the house. I felt like I was suffocating. Because money was always tight was always tight (and it was usually my fault) I needed to contribute in a greater way.

I knew once the kids were all in school that I would need something to keep my mind and body occupied or I would go crazy. All I needed was a chance to fulfill my dreams. But what were my dreams? I didn't even know. Sometimes I still don't know. When I was growing up, I was so focussed on survival that I did not believe life could be any different. To be honest – I did not even know where to begin.

For the most part, we had a good marriage, but I can see now I was extremely immature; the fact was, I got married way to young. Maybe if I had lived on my own, had a job and a life before we married I would have not been searching for something more. If we'd had some time to be husband and wife before the kids came, maybe things would have been different in our relationship. While the majority of people I knew were having fun and enjoying their teenage years, I was busy healing and fighting my inner demons. I never had a chance to really grow up. I spent years trying to be content with my life and for the most part I was. But I also always felt extremely lost and in over my head. I yearned to go back to school and graduate. When I tried going back to school and failed, I took each failure hard and personally. My husband encouraged me to find myself yet, when I tried to, he would act resentful and angry. It was like he wanted me to achieve my goals but felt threatened I would leave the family to do it. So I often tried something then quit out of guilt.

It didn't help that it seemed I was trying to relive my teens and make up for lost time and memories. I would make friends with other girls, but they were always younger than me. Our family home became the local hangout. My friends and I would drive my husband nuts by staying up all night watching movies or going bar hopping. He was indulgent and understanding but at the same time, it was upsetting to him. I was not acting like a devoted mother and wife. He didn't like me gone during the evenings. Many times I left the kids, leaving him no choice but to spend quality time with them. I believed it was only fair because if I had to take care of them alone for days on end, he could handle the evening shift. I guess I was starting to feel more like a live-in babysitter than a wife and mother.

I don't think my husband really realized how important it was for me to be able to leave for awhile or to have a social life. Without these breaks, it was difficult for me to be a calm and rational parent. Getting out gave me a chance to relax and recharge. While most people used how they were brought up as a blueprint to life, I didn't have such a plan. I felt constantly on edge and inadequate. I kept myself on a short leash and it was exhausting. Without these breaks, I felt that it would be too easy to lose control of my emotions and I was genuinely afraid I would hurt my children. Not because I wanted to, but because I was easily frustrated and did not have a constructive outlet. I remember times of going shopping and having all the girls fighting in the back seat. I would fantasize about driving off the road into a hydro pole, just to shut them up. My thoughts scared me, and thankfully I never acted on them. Although there was one time I dropped them off at the side of the road a mile from the house and made them walk home.

The common belief that victims of abuse became abusers was never far from my mind. I lived my life determined not to follow that horrible stereotype. I'd felt that pain so I didn't want to inflict that agony onto my innocent babies. Admittedly, there are times that I was stricter than I should be, but at the same time, I wanted my children to have the life I never did. Yes, I got angry at them, but in the same token they always knew we loved them and would never hurt them.

For the most part things were going well in our household until 1997. That March, my brother-in-law called me with devastating news. My father was dead – he was only sixty-six!

I had just seen Dad two days earlier and at the time he had seemed fine. His ankles were a little swollen, but other than that, he appeared in good health. I remember the ankles because my son was crawling all over his grandpa and I saw my dad flinch in pain. I asked what was wrong and he told me his legs hurt. It was then I noticed his feet – they were swollen like tree stumps.

Two nights later, he went to bed and while getting undressed for sleep, he keeled over backwards and never woke up again. My parents stopped sharing a room and bed years ago so my mother did not notice anything unusual until the next morning when he didn't come down for breakfast. When Dad didn't respond to her many calls, she went upstairs and found him sprawled across the bed half-dressed. Hysterical, she called my sister, my brother and the police. A few hours later, my brother-in-law called me to tell me that my father was gone. Not surprising, I was the last one to know.

It was after my dad's passing I really "saw" my mother for the way she was. In my grief, my eyes were finally opened. I was very angry at first. My heart ached with despair for my father because in my mind, he had wasted twenty years of his life on a farm he hated. It was like he worked his life away as penance for whatever he felt he had done wrong in his life. And he never admitted that he was wrong in buying the farm. For once, I really hated my mother for making his life a living hell; for forcing him to spend the remainder of his life hiding in the barn from her and her insane accusations. Most of all, I was consumed with anger for all the time my father and I lost. I never knew my dad and I blamed my mother for robbing me of that experience.

However, despite my heartache, I reached out to my mother the best I could. I put aside my own grief and became the strong one in the face of despair. Maybe the experience with my husband's mom when his father committed suicide helped, but I instantly knew what needed to be done. My sister was wrapped up on her own grief so I tried to take the pressure off her. It is ironic; the adopted outcast was the one who held my mother's hand throughout the whole bereavement process. From picking a casket, to holding her while my dad was buried. The one who my mother treated so callously and coldly was the one who gave the most during her time of need. Not because I wanted something, but because I knew that she needed me - because I loved her.

Not surprisingly, this caused problems with my sister and her husband. My sister was crushed by Dad's passing and her husband immediately stepped forward and took charge of everything at my mother's request. It was obvious from the start my brother-in-law was angry that my mother was suddenly turning to me. They had done so much for her while I was absent, so my stepping in was unwanted or needed in their opinion. But I only did what Mom asked of me. I remember my sister's husband glaring at me in the funeral home after my mother had agreed to use a poem I'd chosen for the back of the funeral program. Everyone offered a suggestion, but it was the one I picked that went on the handout.

"Why are you here? You don't belong," he later asked me. The contempt he felt towards me dripped off his tongue. He might as well have slapped me across the face. Who in the hell was he to tell me that I don't belong? I tried to talk to him, because I knew where his condemnation was coming from. Ignorantly I believed that telling him what I'd gone through would make a difference. Futilely I tried to explain why I kept my distance but he refused to listen and called me a liar. There was no point in arguing; he'd already made up his mind. I could never get him to understand that my sister's perspective and my perspective would differ because she was ten years my senior. The way a child sees things is very different than an adult. I soon realized that talking to him wouldn't get me anywhere so I left it alone. Besides, it didn't matter. I started adamantly disliking him that day.

Over the next few months, the cold behaviour I received from part of my family did not make it easy for me, but despite everything, I tried to be there for my mom. She didn't like being alone on the farm so I went there nearly every day. She did a lot of talking when we were together. It was during this time we shared meaningful mother-daughter conversations. This was when I found out how my parents met, about her father and many other details about her life I never knew. It felt good to have my mother lean on me – I was her rock. Why? Because despite all that I have written and suffered at her hands, I still loved her with all my heart. I can still say that to this very day.

While my mother and I may have tentatively reunited, my relationship with my husband began to slowly fall apart. I remember lying in bed the day after my dad died and sobbing myself to sleep. My head and my heart were in turmoil. I was mourning his death and how he wasted his life on the farm. Most of all, I mourned the loss of any relationship I could have had with him.

When my husband should have offered comfort to my broken heart, he lay there beside me and ignored my obvious distress. Not once did he reach for me and even attempt to ease my anguish. I could not help but feel rejected by him. While I was trying to grieve for my dad, he acted like he wanted it to go away. Yet when his father killed himself prior to our wedding, I held his hand each step of the way. I guess a part of me has my mother's unforgiving side, because that's when I started to pull away from the man I swore that I would cling to for the rest of my days. In my heart, he had let me down when I needed him the most. I didn't know if I could forgive him and I guess in some ways, I never did.

The months following my dad's death were hectic so it was easy to put my growing marriage problems on hold. First there was the great flood of 1997. The entire Red River Valley was devastated by what would be called "The Flood of the Century". It has always been easy for me to avoid my emotions by throwing myself into physical labour and that is exactly what I did. I physically threw myself into service and spent weeks mourning my father by sandbagging and helping others save their homes. I worked myself to physical exhaustion. When I was at finally home, I locked myself in a little room in the basement and painted bird houses. My dad loved birds and I loved to paint, so many of those houses I made in his honour.

Being busy helped me grieve and avoid the budding problems at home. I didn't want to deal with anything. I was mentally and emotionally incapable of it. While sequestered I would dwell on my own life and how things had been messed up all along. I realized I did not want a wasted life. I wanted to embrace life and enjoy everything it had to offer. But I felt so trapped. I loved my husband and I loved my children, but did I really want to spend my life locked in the house with no friends and no future? I know I should have been content – in many ways I had a wonderful life. Yet after years of hearing that I would never accomplish anything, I yearned to prove the world wrong - mostly to prove myself and my mother wrong.

But I was not ready to do anything about it yet. I had to concentrate on my mother and her needs. After the spring flood waters receded, we as a family began looking at how realistic it was to allow Mom to stay on the farm. I remember my mother-in-law wishing she hadn't moved out so fast, but the reality was, winter was coming and there was no way that my Mom could stay alone. There was no way she could stay on the farm by herself. We all came together as a family for once and immersed ourselves in the preparations to move my mom off the farm, selling all the farm equipment and helping her build a new house.

Selling the farm would be the hardest decision for my mother to make. It had been her home for twenty years. So much blood, sweat and tears were shed over that place – yet in the end, she did not want to leave. She begged to stay on the farm. One afternoon when I was helping her pack, she asked me if I would consider moving into the house. She was willing to give one of us the entire farm in exchange for letting her stay there until she couldn't anymore. She'd obviously given it some thought because she had already considered moving a mobile home onto the yard. It was ironic how she seemed to hate the place for so many years and suddenly she did not want to leave. But it was the only home that she had for the past two decades, so I can understand how difficult it was for her. She'd already asked my brother and sister if they would consider it, but they both refused. I didn't even consider it because my husband and I had already taken over his family homestead. If I had known what I know now, I would have taken her up on that offer in a heartbeat.

My husband and I spent most of the summer helping clean up the farm, liquidating things and packing. My sister and her husband took over the planning for my mom's new home. They offered to let Mom build a new house on a lot right next to their place. The next thing I knew, the farm was listed for sale and in a matter of days it was sold. I found out about the listing and subsequent sale after the fact. My mother called me one day sounding sad and despondent. She had just signed the offer to purchase. I was happy she had made the decision on her own. However, that attitude changed when I asked who bought the place. She informed me it was a neighbouring farmer who lived just down the road. I was stunned when I heard who it was. This same farmer used to mock my dad as often as he could. My father farmed his eighty acres with a 1942 International and an Oliver 77 front end loader. While the neighbouring dairy farms had modern milking parlours, he still milked his cows with a step-saver and bulk tank system. Most of the money he made went back into the farm, so he never splurged on new equipment. Meanwhile, the neighbours always had new tractors and would drive them back and forth. Sometimes in their arrogance, they would drop in and show off their latest purchase. My dad was never an envious man but it hurt his feelings that his neighbours made fun of him.

Needless to say, I was stunned when my mother admitted this was the man who bought the farm. In her defence, she explained that my brother-in-law had come to her with the offer and convinced her it was the best she would do. The house, buildings and farm were old and deemed worthless in his opinion. It was rare for me to speak up against my mother's decisions (I still didn't believe I was allowed to have an opinion) but I distinctly remember telling her my father was rolling in his grave over the sale. But there was nothing she could do about it – the papers were already signed.

Knowing how my father felt about this neighbour, gave me just one more reason why I ended up angry with my brother-in-law. He should have known and respected my father's wishes. But in the end, it was all about the money and getting my mother into a place we hoped she'd enjoy the rest of her life.

CHAPTER TWENTY

With the farm sold I gracefully bowed out of the picture. I believed the reason my mother chose to live adjacent to my sister's place was her way of telling me she'd made her choice – my sister was the one she wanted to be close to. I felt like an interloper. Despite my numerous attempts to be helpful, my sister and her spouse made it very clear they did not want my involvement. I vowed I would help when I could, but I had already put my own family aside long enough. I had spent most of the summer at my mother's side and my husband was growing impatient with having me gone. I discovered something about myself that summer. I could handle my home, and anything else I set my heart to. I had proved to my mother and myself that I was not useless. I just needed to stop being paralyzed with fear and find my own way in the world. It was time for me to grab onto a little bit of life for myself.

At the time, my son was three and in two years he would be in school. Money was always tight so I thought a part-time job would be right up my alley. But I was not sure what I could do. I was already volunteering at the school, coached my daughter's ball teams, and actively involved with the local skating club. While I was eager to help with almost anything and had lots of great ideas, I was emotionally bound by a constant feeling of inadequacy. I was terrified to put myself out there without any education, so finding my niche was not an easy task. Yet, I just knew I had to do something.

It was through the mother of a friend of my oldest daughter that I landing a job working for the *Dawson Trail Dispatch*, a monthly newspaper that covered news from throughout southern Manitoba. The head-writer was looking for a little help. I was surprised at the faith she had in me, but at the same time I was pretty excited. When I was in junior high, I proudly launched and edited the schools' little newspaper. I still have all four editions from that year. I also loved to write and had for years so it was very appealing. My husband agreed because I could stay at home and bring in some extra cash writing freelance. If I could make it work, it would be a great fit for me and my family.

I was so excited when I picked up the October 1997 issue of the paper and spotted my first four by-lines. I visited Mom one afternoon with a brand new issue in hand. For once, she was very supportive and told me how proud she was of me. Those words were like manna to my ears – you could have knocked me over with a feather! When she heard I was borrowing a computer, she asked if I needed help. I told her it would be nice to have my own computer but we didn't have the extra money. I was surprised when she suggested I look for a used system that would meet my needs and offered to pay for it. After all, I had helped her all summer and did not ask for anything in the process, so she wanted to thank me.

This was significant because I made a point of no matter how bad things were for our family – we even had to visit food banks sometimes – I never asked my mother for money. She would give me food, eggs and chickens but I drew the line at cash. It was something we never did. The fact she offered to spend money on something I really needed at the time and my acceptance was a major milestone in our relationship.

Once I had my computer system set up, I threw myself into writing. I was paid by the story so the more I wrote, the more money I made. I no longer felt like a burden on my husband. Instead of spending his money on things I wanted or needed, I had my own money coming in. I was elated at my newfound independence. My husband, on the other hand, was less than enthusiastic as I began to spend more time going to meetings, grand openings and other things. In theory, having a working wife was nice – the money helped. On the other hand, I was no longer as available to him and the children like I used to be. Tensions started to rise and soon we were constantly bickering about why I had to leave, where I was going and what I was doing so I stayed home as much as I could. The more we argued, the more I tried to avoid him. I have always run away from confrontations of any kind.

Unfortunately, that computer opened up a few doors that should have remained closed. Instead of staying at home alone, taking care of my son and doing the household duties I normally did, I discovered the joys of wasting time on the Internet. Instead of cleaning house and doing laundry, I was spending hours chatting in Internet chat rooms to strangers far and wide. I fell under the spell; hook, line and sinker. Within a month, between working for the paper and discovering the Internet, my marriage quickly fell apart. I was at home alone so much it was easy to fall victim to the allure of chat rooms and instant messaging. The recluse I had become to please my husband was suddenly the life of every chatroom I entered. While my husband immersed himself in work, I flourished in a world of make believe. I discovered I had a sense of humour and I was encouraged to use it. I basked in the attention.

Things were pretty tense at home due to my new obsession and even though I believed things were pretty innocent at that point, my guilt ate me alive. I was speaking to other men, who were telling me things my husband had long stopped saying, so it was a major ego boost. Some of the men I talked to encouraged me that if I was so unhappy I should leave my husband and start my own life. Eventually I got involved in a few emotional flings. When I look back to it now, I see how vulnerable I really was. The relationships were not real, but I was hearing what I needed to hear.

In reality, I was still fairly young with four children and married to a man who seemed to be done with me once I had our son. I was lonely and discouraged. That, combined with the fact I had gained significant weight and despised how I looked and felt. I was an easy target. I soaked up every compliment and encouragement like a dry sponge. In my heart I knew none of these relationships were real or ever would become real, yet I felt like I was cheating on my husband. My irrational guilt consumed me and I started to fear the worst. I was convinced that he would eventually find out and blow his top. His increasingly cold and quiet attitude added to a fear totally irrational – yet, very real.

While he'd never raised a hand to me, in my head I was convinced all it would take was pushing the wrong button. I'd heard many stories from his friends on how he was the enforcer when he played hockey or would get into violent bar-room brawls – he even butted a cigarette in someone's face. He would lose his temper with the girls so I knew he was capable of anger even though it was never directed at me. But after years of being hit for stuff I didn't do, I expected that if he ever found out what I was doing it would bring out his wrath at its worst. The more involved I got with people on the Internet, the more I feared my husband – rational or not.

At the end of October, this irrational state of mind, fed by my guilt led to the end of my marriage in the form of a "zero tolerance" arrest. I was on the phone talking to a man I had met in a chat room. He was a trauma surgeon at a hospital in Washington. A background check confirmed his identity. We started chatting and soon he was promising me the world. He told me everything I wanted and needed to hear. I knew it was wrong but I believed him. He knew I was married, but when I told him about my life, he encouraged me to move on. He said my inner restlessness was justified and my life could be much more. I felt guilty about these conversations because, even though we were not physical, I was sharing intimate details of my life, which should have been my husband's alone. This guilty conscience led to the catalyst that would end my marriage.

As our online affair escalated my heart and head were consumed with unfounded fear and guilt. I feared my husband leaving me, I feared him hurting me, and I feared everything. Maybe it was because I had hurt my husband so badly in the past, I was convinced this would be the last straw. In my head, I had blown up this crazy scenario to the point that my husband would find out and in his anger beat me to an inch of my life. After all, I felt that was what I deserved. Because this fear was very real to me, I shared it with a few close people who also became afraid for my safety.

One afternoon, I was lying on my bed chatting on the phone with my doctor buddy. My husband came home from work unexpectedly. Not finding me downstairs, he snuck upstairs, intent in surprising me with his early arrival. When he couldn't find me downstairs, he came to our bedroom, where he found me laying face down on the bed engrossed in my conversation. I never heard him come into the room until he was at the foot of the bed. He smacked my bottom and I screamed in surprise. In my haste I accidentally hung up the phone. My friend tried calling back several times, but I was too afraid to answer the phone. I was already feeling guilty for getting caught.

When I didn't answer the phone, he called a mutual friend right away. She tried calling me too, but I still would not answer. I was too busy trying to act like I had not been doing anything wrong.

I didn't know the police were called until they showed up on my doorstep a few hours later. The officers wanted a statement regardless how much I argued. I told them it was a misunderstanding but they still wanted to check everything out. I did not want my husband arrested because he didn't do anything wrong. But due to the zero tolerance laws, there was nothing I could say or do. A few hours later my husband was arrested in Steinbach and charged with spousal abuse. He was picked up at his mother's house with my two youngest children in tow. I can't even imagine the horror my children felt watching their father be escorted to a police car in cuffs. He was released a few hours later after being questioned but was told he had to stay away from me and the children, at least until his court date.

Later that night my husband's brother and sister showed up on my doorstep, demanding answers. They were both convinced, based on what my husband told them, I would pack my bags and leave with the kids in the middle of the night. I guess he had been checking to see what I had been doing on the Internet and suspected I was planning on running off with another man. While the thought may have crossed my mind, the reality was I had no money, no destination, and four children to take care of. I wasn't going anywhere. The hardest part of that night was being told by his sister that if my husband ended up killing himself over this, it would be completely my fault. It was that night I discovered his siblings had already assumed that since he was so much like his father, my husband would end up taking his own life instead of living with the humiliation I had just inflicted.

The next few months were horrible. It was difficult learning to manage things on my own. I no longer had the support of my husband and my actions had cost me nearly every friend I had. Despite a restraining order preventing my husband from coming near me, I allowed him to spend as much time with the children as possible. I was not going to deny him the right to see his children. I also recognized I was a complete mess. While things were confusing the kids deserved stability while we attempted to put our lives back together. Eventually ignoring the order seemed easier. It was a lot of work to ensure the children did not suffer because of my mistake.

They were all victims of circumstance and I genuinely believed I was minimizing their suffering.

The wheels of justice slowly turned and court was scheduled for May. Meanwhile, my husband was still determined to fix things and maintain our marriage. But I couldn't let it go. While he was willing to forgive me for the arrest, for cyber-cheating on him – for everything, I could not forgive myself. I firmly believed I had ruined his life just like my mother had ruined my father's, just in a different way. Because of my shame, I couldn't accept that he loved me enough to forgive my betrayal. I still remember the tears streaming down his face when, in a last ditch effort, he told me he forgave me and would always love me. I knew it took the entire fibre of his being to bare his soul and heart to me. Instead of accepting his forgiveness, I coldly handed him my wedding band and engagement ring. This was the second time I made him cry and it tore me apart. But what I lack in brains, I make up for with stubbornness. With a torn heart, I started divorce proceedings.

This life change was the beginning of a slow downward spiral for me. On the outside, everything appeared wonderful. I tried to remain strong for the children but my head and my heart was a disaster. Soon I was out to hurt the one person to blame – myself. I became a bitter shell. The divorce cost me my family, his family, and most of our friends. For the first time in my life, I was on my own, and all alone. Not completely alone because I had my four babies – but in my opinion, I had nothing else. It was time to make it or break it.

The hardest part was sitting my mother down and telling her my marriage was over. I didn't want her to hear it from someone on the streets. I knew eventually someone would run into her and offer her their thoughts on my separation. I will give her credit. To my face, Mom acted supportive and all, but I knew what I was doing was gravely against what she believed. She felt strongly a marriage was until death do us part – no matter what. I avoided speaking about my filing for divorce but she knew it was coming. The thing about living in a small town is that everyone knows what is going on in your life, sometimes before you do. She actually kept her opinions to herself for a change – for the time being.

What I failed to notice was while I was trying to deal with the mess I had created; my mother was in an increasingly fragile state. I can see why now. She was already in her new house and she hated it. The woman who was once excited to be living right next door to her favourite daughter and two grandchildren refused to leave the sanctity of her home. She eventually stopped driving too. It seemed like her guilt over her life with Dad was eating her up alive. I seemed to be the only one that could tell that she was willing herself to die.

I went to see her as often as possible but it was increasingly difficult. With no one to watch the kids, I had to take them with me. This always caused issues. Most of the time, my kids would sit on the couch quietly listening to her talk about things they didn't understand because they were afraid to move. Yet, she would accuse them of going through her stuff and hurting her cats. One of my daughters recently reminded me of an incident when one of my mother's cats got sick and died. After a visit my mother called the house and accused my children of killing it. It turned out she lost all her cats one-by-one to feline leukemia. But the damage was done - my kids never wanted to set foot in her house. Instead of spending time and appreciating her grandchildren, she made us all uncomfortable and stiff. Unfortunately, these are the only memories my children have of their grandmother.

As for me, instead of finding the peace and acceptance of a mother's heart that I desperately needed, I would go home heartbroken and hurt. All she spoke about was my father and the end of the world. I would tell her about things going on at home, but she never really heard me. Her religious obsessions had grown to the point it was all she talked about. I could tell she was depressed but she would refuse any help I offered her. I never pushed it because I knew my place when it came to her so I left the responsibility in the hands of my capable sister and brother-in-law.

My mother's renewed rejection forced me to suck it up and carry on. I was bound and determined to prove to everyone including myself that I was not a loser, I could be someone; I was lovable and most of all there was a purpose for my life. I just wasn't sure what it was yet.

CHAPTER TWENTY-ONE

The two years after I walked away from my marriage were the hardest years of my life. I made some horrible decisions during that time frame and I hurt a lot of people including people I considered good friends. In my desperation to survive I painted myself into a corner and I didn't know how to get out of it. I lived in a fog of fear and regret. Instead of dealing with it, growing up and apologizing to those I needed to, I withdrew into my house in shame. Eventually, I only came out when I needed to work and even then, I would try to avoid this as much as possible. I hated the life I'd created for myself and my children but I had no idea how to change it. There was so much we needed – physically, spiritually, emotionally, mentally, and financially but I was so afraid to ask for help – even from God.

My life had become a dirty little secret.

It was at this point I really started to mess things up on my own. I turned my back on an eleven year marriage and was now a single parent of four children. The girls were nine, eight, and six and my son was three. I still didn't trust my ability to parent without incident but at the same time I had to fill the role of both mother and father. It was not an easy task.

After my husband moved out, the first thing I had to do was find a way to support my family. From the start, we qualified for social assistance and while I hated living off the system, I had no choice. My baby was three and I had no education. While I worked freelance for the paper, I did not have a full-time job that provided financial security. Yes, I worked for the paper, but I was still learning the job, so I could only submit a few articles per issue. I was paid freelance so it was not a steady or reliable income at that point.

As I muddled through life the first year, I did more hiding from life than anything else. When I was not attending council meetings and press conferences for the paper, I was on the internet still hiding in chat rooms. I would put the kids to sleep and stay up all night chatting. Some mornings I was still online when they were getting ready for school. There were many things I stopped doing. There was no more volunteering at school, the girls couldn't skate anymore due to the lack of money. The ladies in town made it easy to drop out of the community. Once word got around town about the status of my relationship and life, people avoided me and the kids. It was easier to hide at home than to face a judgemental world.

My biggest regret was relying on my oldest daughter to help raise her siblings while I tried to stand on my own two feet. She would get them ready for school, make lunches and herd them all onto the bus while I slept my pathetic life away. It became very easy for me to escape the reality of life. And it forced her to grow up way too fast. I was grateful for her help but I didn't recognize it was not her responsibility.

Thankfully, my ex was able to put aside his feelings toward me and maintain a relationship with the children. When we first split up, he was convinced I was going to either take the kids away or keep him from seeing them. The thought never crossed my mind. The last thing I wanted was to cut the only reliable parent out of their lives. To prove him wrong I did the exact opposite. He could come and go as he pleased and take the children whenever and wherever he wanted. I began to live for the weekends he would take the kids and I was not responsible for them. I didn't believe that I was capable of taking care of myself; never mind them, so I was grateful for the reprieve.

Eventually I allowed myself to enjoy the new freedom and spent my weekends covering fun stories like rodeos, car shows and community events. Without the kids in tow, I was living life. Sadly, it was all a delusion. We were always broke, and even with the monthly welfare cheque, we were barely making it. My ex stubbornly refused to pay child support at first.

While we struggled in many ways, I was thankful that we were not homeless. Amidst the divorce proceedings, it was decided that instead of selling the house, my ex would forgo his share of the equity in exchange for not paying child support for the first year or so of our separation. I didn't want the house – it was his birthright and as far as I was concerned, I had no right to expect it. But he admitted to the judge he did not want to live there anymore so the title was put in my name. I was able to stay in the family home but it had a mortgage. I also had a car and everything had to be maintained.

The first few months I supplemented my meagre income by selling furniture and the many antiques I'd collected during my marriage. When that fell short, I would have to visit the local food bank. It was humiliating. I remember going in one day and the lady who took my application recognized my name from the newspaper. She asked why I was there – by then, my name graced many bylines and people were starting to know who I was. It was assumed that since I was working as a reporter, I'd be able to take care of myself. No one knew our desperate situation.

Eventually, my heart cried defeat. I realized I had created quite a mess and I needed to walk away for a while. I was convinced that taking a break from my life for even a short time, I would be able to get things sorted out in my head and pick up the pieces. Thankfully my ex agreed and offered to help even though he thought I had lost my mind. He agreed to move back in with the kids for a month and I packed my bags and took off. I took my entire welfare cheque and booked a flight to Corpus Christi, Texas. While it was a stupid thing to do, it was a significant step. I had never flown before, nor had I ever been to Texas. We'd travelled a lot when I was a child but I didn't remember any of those trips. Running away was the ultimate defiance but so important. For once, I was doing what I wanted to do – not what I was being told or expected of me.

While the purpose of my trip was to sort out my head and my heart, the real reason I was going down was to meet someone I had chatted with on the internet. He was younger than me and a paramedic. He invited me to stay with his family while I was there. He believed a change of scenery and a chance to take a few deep breaths and experience life would bring me back to life and help me recharge. It was a dangerous thing to do in retrospect, but at the same time, it was the best thing I had ever done. I was so lost and I had to find myself.

While there, I started a journal.

Thinking back to those first few days – from the simplicity of walking along the sea wall in Corpus Christi to standing on the beach on Padre Island, I can't help but smile. For the first time in my life, I followed my heart and threw caution in the wind and I let my soul run free. Oh - the freedom I have experienced. The freedom to love, be loved; and the freedom from pain and worries. For the first time in my life, I am responsible for no one but myself and my happiness is forefront in my mind.

While sitting on a tree log washed up from who knows where on the beach in Padre Island, I made a startling discovery about myself. I have never felt so alive. Closing my eyes, I concentrated on smelling the salty sea air of the Gulf of Mexico, and listened to the sea gulls crying in the wind. Bathed in the sound of the rolling waves caressing the sand the essence of my being was soothed and healed. I let the breezes calm and relax me.

In the twenty-nine years of my life I have never had the luxury of being selfish. I refer to it as a luxury because it is an emotion that is uncommon to me. I had the opportunity to fly on wings that have never been tested and I felt my soul soar.

I can feel my heart and soul open like the sweetness of a single rose. Slowly, but surely, the beauty is revealed to the eye of any observer that cares to stop and smell the pure ecstasy of a new bloom. Out here no one knew my past. Other than the scars that mar my skin it is non-existent. I was no one's daughter, sister, wife, or mother.

I felt my burdens wash away in the sweet air of Texas, under the rustle of palm trees amid with the cries of sea gulls and crashing waves. I am finally free.

That glorious February spent in Texas affected me deeply. It was freeing to blindly put myself into someone else's hands and just enjoy the experience. From running away in the first place, to visiting towns and people I never knew existed. My friend and I visited San Antonio and I explored the Alamo. We ventured below the surface to explore caves north of Austin and visited the state capital building. It wasn't just the places we went. It was the freedom to explore without condemnation that I grasped. I was experiencing something beyond my imagination. I soaked it all up like a child on her first field trip.

Maybe if I'd had a normal childhood and teen years the hunger to experience the unknown wouldn't have been so strong. When I finally I returned home, I had a renewed sense of hope and strength. Instead of feeling tired and old, I believed I'd figured out what would make me happy. I was determined to stand on my own two feet – one way or another. I had already burned a major bridge when I filed for divorce; now I had to focus on making a better life for my children.

While in Texas, I fell in love with emergency medical services. I spent some time that month riding along in the ambulance that was owned by my friend's family in Premont, Texas. While there, I went on a few calls from heart attacks to car accidents. I enjoyed it so much, that when I returned I was going to become a paramedic locally. After some research and hard work, I registered to take the emergency medical responders course in St. Pierre. It was a ten month program that would eventually lead me to a job. I really enjoyed it because I knew I was making a difference to people during the most critical moments of their life. It gave me a sense of accomplishment and personal fulfillment to be in those situations.

Before starting classes, I made one more trip to Texas to see my paramedic friend. When I had returned to Canada, he initially promised we would stay in touch. But within weeks our daily conversations dwindled to once a week. Misguided, I believed we were trying to build a relationship, so I was hurt by his avoidance. After all, hadn't I dropped everything to be with him? Upset, I ended up selling the only thing I had worth any money – my father's Oliver tractor which my mother gave to me before she moved off the farm. I used the money to buy my first car – a 1988 Mustang LX. Then I did something even crazier than jumping onto a plane. I packed my bags and drove all the way back down to Texas to confront my assumingly wayward lover.

I stayed in Corpus Christi with a friend of his for a few days, giving him the opportunity to come the final miles to me, instead of me chasing him down like a stalker. For the first few days, he avoided me until I finally drove to his town and confronted him. All he said was he was sorry but it was over. Later I figured out he'd started dating a local girl. I was happy for him but also very angry. Not because he moved on, but he could have saved me a trip. The least he could have done was to tell me over the phone – it would have kept me from driving three thousand miles to see him. I bid him good luck and decided to head for home.

Once again, the chat room came into play and when I told everyone what happened, I was soon convinced to drive up to Houston. Things were already arranged at home, so I quickly agreed. I ended up spending three weeks hanging out in Houston with other chat friends, meeting people and having fun.

When I finally returned home, I refocused on my new career choice. I spent the winter taking my first responder classes and working for the paper. After I passed the provincial licensing exam, I began taking shifts in St. Pierre. I enjoyed the job but it came with some sacrifice. The job consisted of twelve-hour shifts and I had to stay at the hospital, because I lived beyond the two minute response time. I was now away from home way too much and my oldest daughter ended up having to raise the family. Somehow we managed to make it work and I might have continued doing it, until our station received an emergency call which required us to untangle a toddler from a hay-baler. My own son was around that age and I realized my determination to better our lives was preventing me from seeing the big picture. I couldn't leave my babies alone any longer. They needed a mother and, while I needed a secure job, I was taking too many chances that I could not afford to take. The decision made, I quietly left my job and started looking at other part-time employment options.

By the time my son was in kindergarten, I needed a permanent source of income. The rules for collecting social assistance recently changed and anyone on the system had to get a job by the time their youngest was six years old or they would be cut off. I loved working at the hospital so I decided to become a health care aide. I didn't have the money to go to school but I could get training through the province. I successfully negotiated a deal with Social Assistance. I promised them that if they would pay for my schooling to become a health care aide, when I graduated, I would leave the system and never apply for welfare again. They agreed and I was soon enrolled in the Health Care Assistant Program at Red River College in Steinbach.

For the next year, I juggled working as the head writer for the paper while studying to be a health care aide. I loved going back to school and I flourished personally, but my kids were abandoned at home. My money was going for gas, bills and groceries so there was never anything left to do family things. There was never enough money to do the things we used to and the fun times we once had were few and far between. Without each other, they would have had nothing.

It must have been difficult for my children – they'd lost so much. When I was with their dad, we went camping and did family things. As a stay-at-home mom, there was always time to play, dance, read or just hang out. But after the split, my focus changed and I forgot how to be a mother. Where I once had time to play with the kids, my focus changed to making money, making ends meet and trying to figure out where I was going in life. Half the time I didn't even know what they were studying at school. In my attempts to do everything, I shut down my maternal side to become this shell of what I once was.

The parent who used to volunteer once a week in school no longer made it to parent-teacher interviews. My second daughter played saxophone in the school band for two years and I never saw a concert. I was constantly working or studying. It was hard for me to be everything I was expected to be and I found myself overwhelmed often. Soon I was constantly apologizing to my kids for breaking promises. It destroyed me that they couldn't rely on me anymore. And I was thankful they still had their father. We were able to maintain a good relationship despite everything I'd done, and even though we were not married, he was never far away.

It didn't help matters that my editor had high expectations. The paper was still trying to build a reputation, so I rarely missed a council meeting. With a coverage encompassing the entire southeast; a region consisting of nine municipalities, several towns, a city, a health board and two school divisions I was busy. I attended most of the public meetings but I missed my many kids' school things because of it.

In my opinion, my focus was completely off. I realized I desperately needed to settle some things before I could make a life for me and my kids. Unfortunately, I would keep making mistakes until I got to that point.

CHAPTER TWENTY-TWO

In the midst of going to school, working and raising my family, I still managed to make time for myself. When I was at home, I was still hanging out on the internet and meeting people. It was like I was searching for something, I just didn't know what yet. My ex was constantly at my house and I knew if given the chance he wanted reconciliation. But I was not ready to give in yet. To show him I had moved on, I went on a few dates but nothing serious. I lost about sixty pounds and was coming out of my shell. I attracted a lot of attention in both real life and online. I quickly learned that most men I knew only wanted one thing from me and I had already decided I deserved more than to be someone's plaything.

What I lacked was confidence in my ability to be able to raise my children, take care of myself and have a good life. So I started to look for "Mr Right". Searching for a romantic partner online seemed easier then dating in real life. There were too many expectations in person. As a writer, it was easy for me to lose myself in hours of online conversation and really get to know a person. I could share my life without being judged to my face and it was a convenient outlet. Because I loved Texas so much, I hung out in a Texas chat room. I should explain that in those days a chat room was a cyber space where up to fifty people could visit at any given time. We would talk, play games, and share stories. It was a great way to meeting people, without having to leave your own home. If life interfered, one could walk away from the computer and you were never considered rude. It was a perfect little world for the housebound.

After my two separate trips to Texas, I loved and missed the place. Maybe it was the allure of the relaxation, or the memories but I yearned to go back. Whenever life became too hectic and frustrating, my first instinct was to run away to the place I finally found myself. Finally during the winter of 1998, I had another opportunity to make a trip to Texas. A truck driver friend of mine was heading that way for a few weeks on a trip and asked if I wanted to tag along. I was itching to see my friends again, and enjoy the warm weather for a few days. I jumped at the chance for a free trip.

It was on this trip I met the man who became my second husband. We'd started chatting a few months earlier about cars and a friendship evolved. During our many conversations I found out he was thirty-six and had never been with a woman. Maybe I chalked up his inexperience to his inability to hurt me but for some reason he fascinated me. I don't know anymore. Once our trip plans were finalized, I contacted him and asked if he wanted to meet somewhere along the way. He drove up from Austin to Plano, Texas and we connected at a little truck stop outside of the city. I remember hiding behind the semi-truck and watching for him. At first I didn't spot him but eventually I noticed a guy walking through the parking lot carrying a dozen yellow roses. He was not at all what I expected. He was tall, lanky and not very attractive. But I had promised to meet him, so I stood my ground instead of running which was my first instinct.

After a few cups of coffee, he informed me a hotel room was booked for a few days just down the road. He wanted me to stay with him for the weekend. I jumped at the chance to ditch my ride for a few days as he was starting to make me feel uncomfortable. By the time we hit the Texas border he was infatuated. I eagerly ditched my ride, promising to catch up with him on the return trip from Houston and took off with my new friend. I had already decided I would not see him again, but I figured I would at least give him a weekend to remember before I walked away. I felt I owed him that. The mistake I made, besides meeting him in the first place – was to whisper "I love you" into his ear as we parted instead of just driving away. I realized it was a lie as I said it, but I couldn't take it back. I told myself it didn't matter because I did not expect to see him ever again.

I was wrong. Three weeks later he called and told me he had

bought an airline ticket and he was coming to Canada to meet my family. I reluctantly agreed, since he had already made the purchase. I should have stopped him right there - I didn't even like him. I don't know why, but I caved. Maybe I felt I owed him something, or I just didn't think I could do any better. Either way, he spent three weeks with us over Christmas before flying home after the New Year. A few months later he decided he wanted to be with me forever. He wanted to immigrate to Canada and build a relationship with me. While my heart protested, my mouth refused to work.

In February, we travelled back down to Texas together where he packed his apartment, rented a storage locker and made the move to Canada. All the while I had my reservations, but the reality was I needed the help. It would be nice to have a man around again full time. In my fantasy, he would be a stepfather to my children, help me around the house and was perfectly capable of picking up the pieces I was leaving due to my hectic schedule. I convinced myself that he would be the perfect house husband. I just had to suck it up and accept it.

In some warped part of my brain, I also believed if I got remarried my ex would also do so. We'd already been apart for a couple of years and he was still not dating. So I did the unthinkable – I remarried despite all my reservations. Maybe this is why I rarely speak of this marriage. It was a mistake from the start because I know I married him for the wrong reasons. I was scared of being alone with my children and determined to convince my first husband I was never going to get back together with him. He loathed this relationship and would not even step on the property when my new husband was there. It also really burned him that I was living in the home we once shared, with another man.

On my wedding day, I sat in the van and refused to go into the hall were all my friends were waiting. It took my two best friends to convince me to go in, although one tried to assured me it was okay to just drive away. Everyone I knew was against this marriage from the start, and I should have listened to them. Most of all, I should have listened to my heart.

Undeniably our relationship was messed up from the beginning. I couldn't believe this guy moved all his belongings from Texas to Canada to be with me when I didn't even know what I wanted. When I agreed to marry him, I hoped I would eventually fall for him. That never happened.

He was messed up in his own right. He was thirty-five when we met, and had been abandoned by his mother as a child. He feared women to the point I was his first relationship. It was like our mutual desperation for love and acceptance drew us together and it was unhealthy.   He was clingy and did not understand or respect that my children were my priority. As an immigrant he couldn't work nor study so he was constantly bored. He resented I was in school and working yet relied on me to keep him entertained, But I had my family and school to focus on. I did not have the time or inclination to deal with such a needy man.

His misery became more evident over time. He would spend hours locked up in a little room in the basement, hiding on his own computer. I was fine with that. I thought that if I ignored him, he would get the hint and leave. Instead he got more clingy and upset. I'd even wake up to find him squatting beside the bed crying, while I slept oblivious. His behaviour was starting to hinge on creepy.

What eventually led to the end of this relationship was the affect it had on my children. Not only were we always fighting, but I was always broke. Once again, their father stopped paying child support because I remarried without his approval. My cheques from the paper were not enough to support everyone's needs. Eventually I felt driven to sneak into my ex's house and steal change to buy milk. To make things worse, I found out that while I was begging or borrowing from others, my new husband had $65,000 in American funds sitting in a bank account in Austin. When I found this out, I was very hurt. I could not understand how he could sit and watch us struggle, go to the food bank, go to school, work and support him, while he was sitting on a small fortune. It pissed me off to no end.

The real turning point in our relationship was when my health started failing. A few months after we got married I started feeling ill. Unable to deny how I was feeling physically, I started to drag myself to the doctor all the time. It was beginning to interrupt my life. After numerous examinations the doctors eventually discovered several large fibroid tumours in my uterus. I suffered for months while the doctors worked to make me feel better using various medications.

I ended up in the hospital on Mother's Day, needing emergency surgery after a cyst ruptured. I was septic by the time I was admitted and very ill. During that three-day hospital stay, options were discussed on how to deal with the other unrelated issue. To ensure the tumours would not spread, I faced a hysterectomy. This terrified me because I was only thirty-four and even though my family was complete, I was not ready to face menopause and the other issues that could result. Not trusting my own decision making, I held off as long as I could.

I could have taken a Gonadotropin-releasing hormone which would have helped with the pain and decreased the tumours, but it would cost over a thousand dollars a month. These medications treat fibroids by decreasing natural estrogen and progesterone levels, putting you into a temporary postmenopausal state. For them to work properly, I'd have to be on them for approximately six months. There was no way I could come up with that kind of money, without my husband's help. All I knew was that I needed to find a solution because between the pain, weight loss and constant bleeding, things were progressing to the danger point.

I realized then my life had no value to my husband regardless of the state of our relationship. I was well aware of his nest egg, but he refused to cough up some cash saying it was his money. I flipped because he could have saved me months of agony and the eventual surgery. It was wrong to have expected him to help, based on our relationship, but at the same time, the light-bulb went on. My marriage was a farce. To continue where I was, would eventually kill me.

My children sensed my growing animosity toward my husband and acted out. They were afraid I was going to die and leave them with this man, who they were growing to hate. And they had every reason to despise him. They knew their mom was ill and expected my new husband to step in and be a father and provider, but it never happened. Knowing I was broke all the time, he would buy his own food and hide it in his office. The kids noticed and would find ways to break in and help themselves. They could not understand why they were treated this way and they shouldn't have had to. I realized I was doing to my kids what was done to me.

Any respect they had for him and our relationship was gone and they let him know he was strongly disliked by all four of them. Things came to a head one night when the two youngest started to antagonize him. He was trying to watch television and they were being playful, trying to do all sorts of things to get his attention. The more he ignored them, the crazier they got. Finally in frustration, he grabbed my third daughter, tossed her over his shoulder and carried her out the front door. All I heard was screaming and as I got to the door, I witnessed him throw her into the flooded ditch at the front of the house. That was the last straw. He could do whatever he wanted to me, but he had no right to touch my children.

Swallowing my pride and admitting I made a mistake, I told him to pack his things and leave. Within a week he packed a U-Haul and headed for greener pastures. At first he stayed with one of my ex-husband's friends in Winnipeg and he stalked me for a few months, trying to get back together with me.

It wasn't until I finally had my surgery months after we split that he really got the hint things were over between us. He showed up at the hospital before my surgery and my best friend chased him out. Security eventually escorted him from the building, but that did not stop him. Three days later he was on my doorstep and she sent him packing with a baseball bat. Eventually, he got the point and moved on. The last I heard he was living in Ontario with a new wife and her two little girls.

At this point, I was so ashamed of my life and the choices I was making I became a recluse. Not only was I unforgiving of myself but the community shut us out. I was now a twice divorced single mom. No one ever saw me outside of the house unless it was work or school related. I was alone and miserable.

I already knew I couldn't count on my mother. Shortly after I married my second husband, my mother heard about it through the grapevine and she called me. Over the phone she asked if it was true I had remarried. Having nothing to hide at that point, I did not deny it.

Her next words are forever glued to my brain: "If remaining in a relationship with you is considered condoning what you have done, thus condemning my soul to hell, then I never want to see you again."

I said fine. Just that! "Fine!" and I hung up.

I was deeply disappointed, but at the same time relieved. I could never lie to her and keeping secrets always exhausted me. Without her in my life, no one condemned me and made me feel worse than I already did. Her rejection finally gave me the out I so desperately wanted. I was guilt free because she cut the ties – not me. For once I agreed with her – I had made my bed and I was going to lie in it.

Within two months of his moving out, my phone rang again. My mother had already heard I was divorced and she wanted to rekindle a relationship. She was glad that I came to my senses and reminded me I shouldn't have gone against my initial wedding vows anyways. In her mind, I would always be married to my children's father no matter what the situation was. At the end of the conversation she invited me over for a visit. She was cleaning out the house and had some things for me, she offered. And like a cow being led to slaughter, I went crawling back.

At first things seemed okay. I went to see my mother in her new house and she seemed happy. She'd transplanted most of the plants she'd brought over from the farm, and she maintained her small but manageable house. She had built right next door to my sister's place, so she got to see her grandchildren every day. By that time, my sister had a son who loved spending time with his grandma. Yet she was sad. She'd always loved her cats and lost a couple after the move to feline leukemia. This really hurt her after losing my dad. Too many losses in such a short of time. No wonder she was so depressed.

While my heart ached for her and her obvious loneliness, I never spoke of it with my siblings. Instead, I tried to go see her every week or so but never with my children. Visits with them were never fun or full of joy as they should be. They would sit like little soldiers on the couch only leaving to go to the bathroom or outside to break the constant tension. She would offer them treats but never offer them her heart. She didn't seem to care about anything. I told her about my health, being in the hospital and needing surgery. She never reacted. She was lost in her own world of misery and despair.

I could tell my mother was not herself. She spoke of her inability to sleep and how much she missed my dad. She was gravely depressed. She'd lost an alarming amount of weight and seemed very absent-minded. It broke my heart to see my mother so sad. All she talked about were her regrets about the farm and the way she was with Dad. It was like she could finally see that he was miserable, mostly because of her attitude. She finally realized how much she loved him but it was killing her. It was too late for her to fix things and she knew it. She took solace in fasting and spending hours praying for his soul – something that gave her comfort. In my opinion, she was well on her way to trying to will herself to die.

Even though it was emotionally difficult and exhausting, I tried to visit often but once again I started to hear things along the way. I ran into my brother at one point, and he told me mom told everyone I only came over because I wanted something. She took my visits as my being a mooch, not that I really cared for her. Sure, she'd send me home with boxes of stuff. But I only took them because it seemed to make her happy if I did. When I refused, she acted so rejected. I was damned if I did, and damned if I didn't. So, I visited her less often. It hurt so much to constantly be rejected even though my intentions were pure. I didn't want her stuff. I wanted her heart. When I started to question things between us again, I knew I was on the verge of a downward spiral because of her effect on me.

As my health worsened before my impending surgery my visits began to decrease. I didn't have the physical strength. It was also becoming a nasty habit that if I pushed myself too far, I would faint so I was very careful about leaving the house. I didn't need the added stress, so I maintained some distance for my own self.

CHAPTER TWENTY-THREE

It was at this point I really started to believe with all my head and my heart my mother was right – I was unlovable and useless. Everything I had done until this point had cemented this "truth" into my head and heart. I did not trust my ability to make good choices.

I obviously had things twisted in my head. In my mind, marriage should be forever, yet I had struck out twice. There was obviously something wrong with me or people would not treat me this way, nor would I be selling myself so short. I was making the worst choices possible in an attempt to find happiness. I had yet to learn to stand on my own two feet without a man at my side. The end of my second marriage made me decide something important – I was not going to date or get married ever again.

Once husband number two left the province, I was once again footloose and fancy free. I always seemed to flourish when I could do my own thing, raise the kids the way I wanted and not have to answer to another adult. But as they say, when you stop looking for love is when it usually finds you.

While I was dealing with my most recent failure, the world changed in a single act of terrorism on September 11, 2001. Strangers reached out to each other in mutual horror as we watched the World Trade Centre buildings collapse on national television. Life changed forever for many, including me. I didn't want to be alone, but I also wanted to find someone extra special who would love me without judgement.

Husband number three sauntered into my life after I kicked out number two. We met through a co-worker who had recently moved next to my house. The pair worked together at the Mint Esso, on the outskirts of Winnipeg. She showed up on my doorstep one afternoon. She and her son had just been evicted from their home in Emerson and were looking for a place to keep her dogs. She had five pets and I had an empty barn. My heart went out to their situation so I offered to help temporarily. A few months later, she rented the little house down the road and became my neighbour and eventually a friend.

I was lonely and had lots of time on my hands. I had finally separated myself from the Internet which had become a millstone around my neck, so I was living again and helping people out when I could. She didn't have a vehicle, and since we became friends, I offered to drive her to work and back every day. Soon I was driving in and staying at the coffee shop all day while she waited tables instead of wasting the gas driving back and forth. No longer shackled to the internet, I was open to real people, real friends and real relationships. I soon learned I was not only funny behind a computer screen - people genuinely liked having me around. I was such a fixture in the corner booth that I became friends with the staff and many of the customers.

The commitment to help my friend was not easy to maintain, but somehow I managed. However, my body continued to betray me and I was getting sicker. I was not comfortable confiding my growing health concerns with anyone but eventually it became impossible to hide. No one noticed I was ill until I started to literally pass out while having lunch at the restaurant. I had to quit my job at the nursing home because some days I didn't have the strength to finish my shift.

I spent so much time at the truck stop the staff began to notice the physical changes I was experiencing. I could hardly eat, so the staff went out of their way finding things I could stomach. The cook had fun concocting things he felt I could eat without my stomach revolting. By Christmas I had developed a major crush on him. He knew I did not want a relationship and he was fine with that. Yet, we spent a lot of time together. He lived in a little rooming house in Osborne Village and soon I was driving him home from work too. We would watch movies or I would watch him play video games until

I had to go home. Even though he lived in a dump and had little, it was nicer than staying at home alone.

But I was honest with myself – this was a relationship that would never go anywhere. We were totally different people and would otherwise have never connected. It was nice to have a friendship with no strings attached – or at least no strings that I could see.

Health wise, things came to a head over the Christmas holidays. The tumours were making me bleed constantly. At one point I even ended up in the emergency ward. My doctor decided that enough was enough – nothing she was doing was working so surgery was my only option. After meeting with a specialist, I was scheduled for a hysterectomy in the middle of February. As much as I needed it, another major problem presented itself. I had no one to watch the kids for me while I was hospitalized for up to a week and the needed six weeks for recovery. My kids' father could not commit to helping because he was working in Ontario. Asking my family was out of the question. So, I almost cancelled the procedure because I had no one to help.

Now my close friends, the Mint Esso staff came up with an alternative solution. Wanting to help, my new friend offered to come into my house and take care of the children while I was in the hospital. He offered to stay for a month while I recovered. After consideration and not having other options, I decided I would allow him to help. What I didn't know was he was already telling everyone at work he was not planning to leave. While I was recovering his sweetness and sensitivity drew me to him and I found myself falling in love again. The final decision that he would move in came in after he sat the kids down and asked them if it was okay for him to stay – they said it was.

They say love is blind and in this case, it was. Because of how grateful I felt about this man, I was able to ignore many red flags. He had spent time in jail for statutory rape, he had molested his little sister, and he had past riddled with drug abuse, arson, prostitution and sexual violence. I was not there to judge him – just love him and accept him. My thinking was skewed because I expected people to look past my flaws, as I am prone to do the same. I believed that with the right person in his life, he could turn his life around and make something better of himself – and I believed I was the right person. It didn't matter that he came from an abusive background; it helped us understand each other perfectly. It was easy to open up to him because of this shared past. All that mattered at the time was I loved him and he brought out a side of me I didn't know existed.

The restaurant closed down at the end of May, and he was now unemployed. Even while I was ill, I continued writing for the paper while trying to parent my four children, who would soon be teenagers. I didn't mind, as long as he took care of things at home. I was working and he wasn't, so in my opinion, he should have been shouldering the household responsibilities such as cooking, cleaning and taking care of the yard. Instead he spent his days and nights playing video games and ignoring things that needed to be done. But he assured me when he was ready he would look for work so I waited.

Three months later, I was still recovering from surgery when the house flooded – ironically on the same day my entire family got into a head-on collision. It was July long weekend and we were going to Winnipeg to celebrate my oldest daughter's birthday. Four of us were injured and ended up in the hospital with various injuries. It took all day before we were treated and finally sent home. Meanwhile, it started to rain. It rained all day and night. There was so much rain the municipality declared a state of emergency. Despite the rising water, no one was in any condition to make sure the sump pump was keeping up. By morning, there was over a foot of water in the basement. All three of the girls' bedrooms and contents were destroyed.

It would take us another three months to clean the basement up. No matter how I begged and pleaded, that basement did not get cleaned up until September long weekend. Due to the way I knew people felt about me and my family, there was no one to ask for help. So we waited until we could physically handle the work. By then my oldest daughter had mushrooms growing out of her bed. My son started developing breathing problems and was diagnosed with severe asthma brought on by the levels of black mold taking over the house. We were already struggling financially, and suddenly my son went from totally healthy to needing expensive puffers I couldn't afford. Yet, this was all bearable, because I was in love and convinced that eventually, things would be okay – I just had to stick it out.

Much to my surprise, in October 2002 my new beau proposed marriage. It was a surprise because we both swore up and down neither of us would take that walk down the aisle. Having already done it twice and failed, I was not going to subject myself to that again.

His proposal was less than romantic and stemmed from a night of drinking. A fellow chat friend and I had scheduled a meet and greet together at a hotel in Winnipeg and we booked ten rooms on the main floor. It was a weekend of drinking and gathering and everyone who came to the party had a great time. My boyfriend was my escort and proved to me that night he could be a jealous fool. We were at the bar and he kept buying me tequila shots. One of my friends pulled me aside to warn me that my date was trying to get me drunk. He had heard that when I was drinking, I tended to be less than faithful, so he was testing me. I was furious and for the first time in my life, I almost got kicked out of the bar because I was yelling at him. I could not believe that after all we had been through together he would put me through such a juvenile test.

Later that night, after hours of tearful discussion in our room, he dropped on one knee and asked me to marry him. I put my hand on his forehead and pushed him to the floor.

"Ask me again when you are sober," I responded, never thinking for a moment he was serious. The next morning, he dropped to his knee right in front of my kids and proposed again. I did not give him an answer either way. I was unsure of where my heart stood. I believed I loved him, but something also told me it was a dangerous infatuation and I should go slowly. I did not want to get married again, and if I did change my mind, it would have to be "right." It took two months for me to accept.

Once I said "yes", the hardest decision I had to make was if and when to tell my family. My mother disowned me when she heard I had married number two, but at the same time, she made me promise to call her if I get impulsive again. She'd told me she was crushed I remarried without telling her and without an invitation. But I couldn't forget the "disowning" conversation and I didn't have the heart to face her. I did not have the heart to deal with that rejection again. Besides, we were happy and I didn't want anything to destroy it. Talking to her would have just torn that all apart. So I avoided it.

There was another reason why I couldn't make that phone call. In September, my fiancé and I had run into her while grocery shopping at the local mall. We were getting a few things and I spotted her in the produce department. I couldn't just walk away without saying hello, so I wandered over to her. At first, she didn't seem to recognize me. There was no familiarity in her eyes until we'd spoken for a few minutes. I introduced her to my partner, but she showed little acknowledgement. I even had to introduce her to the two grandchildren who were with me – kids she had spent time with in the past. It was a very strange meeting. Distracted, she admitted she was shopping with my sister and had no time to talk, so I left. Yet in my heart, I knew something was not right. But I had my own problems, so left it alone.

Not having the heart to plan another wedding, I left things in the hands of my fiancé. Once I said yes, he took matters into his own hands and planned everything. We ended up getting married on December 31 in my house – the one I once shared with my first husband and the father of my children. Not in a church, nor by a priest but by a justice of the peace. But it didn't matter because we were surrounded by our closest friends and his family. My family was noticeably absent. But then, how could they be there, if I hadn't invited them?

It was a lovely wedding, small and intimate. It was the perfect way to welcome in a new year. But the night did not end on a great note. It was probably a good thing my family wasn't there after what happened around midnight. I had teased my husband that since all his friends would be there, it would be surprising if he could keep his hands off his video game system long enough to get married. He was as addicted to his video games as I was to the internet. He also had several new games and when his buddies were over, competition tended to get fierce. We ended up making a deal – he would not touch his video games and I wouldn't touch my computer for the entire night.

Shortly after midnight, the majority of our guests were gone. The kids and some of his friends were still having fun and no one wanted to go to bed. At one point, the kids wanted him to hook up the video games up in the basement so off he went. Knowing he would be gone for a bit, I logged into my regular chat room and let everyone know I'd just gotten married. As I was preparing to log off he walked into my office. My new husband went from being the happy bridegroom to a raging drunk in moments. He was pretty drunk and his behaviour was upsetting and uncalled for. He ranted and raved that my internet was more important than he was. I tried to reason with him by pointing out that he was downstairs setting up the game system anyways. I'd just logged in for a minute – not a big deal, I argued. He wouldn't listen. He kept screaming at me and would not listen to my many attempts to get his attention and most of all, get him to calm down.

At one point, he shoved me against the front door of the living room. With his hands clutched my throat painfully he screamed in my face that I'd broken my promise. For the first time, I felt fear as I stood helplessly pressed against door. Nothing I said mattered – there was no reasoning with him. This is when my son walked into the room. Seeing me crying and my husband angrily manhandling me, my son ran out back out of the room, as I yelled to him to take the phone and call the police. He scurried downstairs and hid with his sisters, and no one made the call. I finally got away, and all rationale had left my husband. I made a dash to my office and got his attention when I grabbed a hammer and smashed my brand new seventeen inch monitor. I had saved for it and it was my present to myself, so it was a big deal to smash it to pieces. He snapped out of it and realized what he had done. He sobered up instantly. He swore he would never drink again, and as long as he was with me, he kept to his word. But the damage was done – I had seen what he was capable of. In all my bad relationships, this was the only time I experienced real fear for my safety and yes, I believe he was capable of much more if given a chance or reason.

He spent the next few days apologizing profusely for his behaviour and admitted he overreacted. I forgave him and tried to make the best of it. Recognizing how threatened he actually was by my internet friends, I attempt to respect his wishes and put that lifestyle behind me. The fear he would beat me senseless if he even suspected I was chatting online was all the motivation I needed.

Determined to make things work despite this initial glitch, the January issue of the newspaper came out a week later, with a wedding announcement complete with photo of the happy couple. I did this deliberately, so my mother and siblings would know I remarried without having to pick up the phone and telling them. I did it that way also, so I wouldn't have to face them. I couldn't face hurting my mother again. I couldn't bear her condemnation. I couldn't listen to her say she hated me again. I had heard those words enough during my life.

As expected, a week after the paper hit the streets my phone rang. Unfortunately, I was not home to answer it. My mother left a message on my answering machine asking for me to call her back. I tried returning her call several times, but I was never able to reach her again. Being a coward, I didn't dare venture to her house without an invitation so I stayed away. She would have tough questions and stronger opinions. I just did not have the heart to have this battle again. It is a decision I regret every day.

CHAPTER TWENTY-FOUR

After we got married, we both seemed to focus our efforts on my family. Despite our rough start, my kids seemed to like my new husband. He was crude and rude but he was also funny and made them laugh. He spent time with them, watching movies and playing video games. He convinced me to relax some of my rules and the girls, now teenagers, enjoyed new freedom. I was not strict, but I was protective of them. Thanks to his influence, they enjoyed having their friends come over and my basement was the hub of activity.

While I enjoyed my own children, my husband was not so lucky. He had a seven-year-old son and a five-year-old daughter who he rarely saw. For months I listened to him attempt to get his ex to allow him to spend time with his kids but she either said no, or avoided his phone calls. I could understand where she was coming from because their breakup was ugly. He admitted at the end of their relationship he was bent on hurting her and he did. He admitted to sexually assaulting her on the final day they lived together. She kicked him out and since then she kept the kids away from him. I tried to put myself in her shoes and I understood how she felt, however I also saw the positive change in him since we'd gotten together. He had a full time job at the local restaurant and even went and got his driver's license. Under my influence he was growing up.

I feel strongly a father has every right to see his children. Using the only means possible, I surprised him by allowing legal aid to put a lien against my home so he could seek joint custody. He found a lawyer and the process began. I agreed to drive him to supervised visits and even extended a helping hand to his ex with babysitting. We both attended mediation and a class called "For the Sake of the Children" to ensure there would be no reason why the children could not spend time with their father. Eventually we were successful and a bi-weekly custody arrangement was reached.

My heart may have been in the right place but I did not think too far ahead. Sure he got to see his children, but it also brought a new set of challenges into our already chaotic household. Both of these children came to our home with behaviour problems. Even though my children had seen me go through two divorces, they were still fairly well adjusted and well behaved. When the two younger step-siblings came into our home, all hell broke loose. Prior to their first visit, I bought beds, dressers, clothes and toys for them. This was done so they would feel at home and limit the need to haul things back and forth. After each visit, I noticed little by little things began to disappear, until finally we caught his daughter leaving the house wearing five layers of clothing. This was how they were smuggling their things from our home to theirs. I was stunned a child that young would have figured out that if she wanted to take all her new clothing home, she had to layer them under the clothes she arrived in. In my opinion, that was not normal behaviour.

Then my son complained his things were starting to disappear. I didn't believe him at first, until we actually caught my husband's son with his pockets full of my son's toys. My son resented having to share his things with these children in the first place, then to have his trust betrayed by the theft of his favourite things, caused further animosity to grow. He had hardly anything of his own and to have the little he had stolen was heartbreaking for him. I took this all very hard. It all boiled down to respect. I respected my children's spaces and I expected the same. There was no reason for these children to steal what was generously given to them so I took it personally. I had welcomed these children and this man into my home and instead of being grateful they turned around and betrayed my trust. I couldn't understand why would they turn around and be so ungrateful.

I started to regret my decision to make a commitment to this family. My marriage was supposed to be a good thing, and instead my children were once again suffering due to my poor choice in men. Yet, I was not yet ready to let go – I had made my bed, and I was going to lie in it. However, my resentment began to build as the issues grew. I soon learned that it didn't matter how hard I tried, I was the only one who cared.

That year was very stressful. Between the issues surrounding my step-children and the added expectations on myself, I was slowly losing my grip on the situation. I was running myself ragged trying to please everyone. My husband and both my oldest daughters were working at the local restaurant. I was the only one with a vehicle, so I spent much of my time playing chauffeur. Eventually I lost my job permanently at the nursing home because I was putting my driving responsibilities first, so my only source of income was once again the newspaper. My husband's money went towards his video games and his pot smoking habit. My meagre cheque paid the bills but there was never enough extra cash so we lived from paycheck to paycheck. I owed my boss hundreds of dollars for cash advances. Soon we were pawning the little I had to ensure that my husband had marijuana and that my kids had food.

My stress level was soon at its highest and my health took another dive. I ended up in the emergency room in 2003 after suffering ongoing stomach problems. I was in constant pain and lost a significant amount of weight. It took a while and many hospital visits but eventually diagnostic surgery revealed that I was suffering from H-Pylori virus in my stomach and I had an ulcerated esophagus. Untreated, the H-Pylori could lead to cancer. I was put on an expensive medication to help my stomach heal and my treatment would take a year. It was not a cheap process, but for once I put my health first. I was useless to everyone sick and I knew it.

It was during this time, I stumbled upon the discovery that my mother was a patient of the same hospital where I had spent weeks visiting the emergency room seeking my own diagnosis. This is why I was so angry that my family did not tell me that my mother was a patient. I remember asking my brother-in-law why I was not told and he said there was no need to inform me. I know for a fact that if I had known she was hospitalized, I would have gone to see her every chance I got. After all, I had become a regular fixture in the emergency room in recent weeks and her room was only down the hall.

I was furious no one bothered to inform me she had started

'wandering' - a symptom typical of Alzheimer's and that she had walked out of the hospital unnoticed. When I confronted my brother-in-law, he did not believe I didn't know – he said it was impossible because the police had issued a press release to all media. I didn't know what he meant until I checked the newspaper. Admittedly, my life was pretty messed up. Even though I was now submitting over forty stories per issue in the *Dawson Trail Dispatch*, I never noticed the missing persons' press release printed in the October issue. It wasn't until my brother-in-law pointed it out, that I found a back issue and double checked. Sure enough, there it was in black and white. I felt so ashamed for letting my mother down – I may have been self-absorbed with my health but in my head, that was no excuse.

The day after I discovered my mother in the Bethesda Hospital, a new routine began. My mother, who I had always avoided to some extent, was suddenly near the top of my priority list. Not a day went by without me dropping in at the hospital. Even if it was just to spend fifteen precious minutes with her. We were at the hospital often anyway because my oldest daughter was having her own health problems. Eventually, it was discovered that she had an ulcer. She was only seventeen.

Sometimes when I would arrive, my Mom would run to her closet and get her coat. She always asked me to take her home. She would also tell me she had to get home to make dinner for Dad. I would gently remind her he was gone and that she needed to take care of herself for once. She would get this sad look on her face. I could tell she didn't really understand. Slowly but surely, I realized my mother would never be the same.

There were days when she would let me sit and brush her hair. It felt odd sitting on the edge of her hospital bed combing her hair, but she seemed to love it. As a child, I would sit and watch her brush her waist length locks and hope that when I grew up my hair would be just as gorgeous. It was something I never expected to be able to do.

It really bothered me that there were no personal effects in her room. I knew she was in for a long stay so I brought in pictures of myself and the children to post on the board. She'd look at them but she never really registered recognition. However, a black and white picture of me as a baby got an instant reaction. She would look at it and smile, tracing my chubby toddler face with her fingertips, while I would fight back the tears. She recognized me as a baby and the love in her eyes for that baby was so clear. For a brief moment she'd look at me as an adult, I'd see the same look of love and then it would be gone.

I could tell the first time I saw her that she had lost about twenty-years of her memory. But the harsh truth came to the surface when I finally got up the nerve to introduce her to my third husband. I was stunned when she got tears in her eyes and said, "Are you sure? You found someone to marry you? I am so happy for you."

She actually stood up and enveloped my husband with a huge hug. I know for a fact that would never have happened, ever, before this. I should have been happy about the simple gesture. It was a sign of the acceptance I had sought for thirty-five years. But instead, my insides died a little because I realized I had lost all opportunity to ever explain to my mother how I really felt. Nor would I ever be able to make her understand I loved her and I had truly forgiven her.

While some may not understand why I did not keep close contact with my mother and my siblings, I feel I have very valid reasons. I forgave Mom years ago for what I was subjected to as a child growing up. But something in her personality kept chasing me away. After my father passed away, I began looking at life differently. I didn't allow myself to be whipped by my past. There was no way I would remain a slave to my upbringing. I had finally realized what my mother said or did, didn't matter. But it mattered how I felt and how I lived my own life. With a new found strength, I finally had it in my power to protect myself from the hurts she had inflicted. Reluctantly I exercised that power. Was I wrong? I will forever ask myself that very question. One thing I know for sure was it pained me to not be able to tell her I loved her with all my heart. It was far too late for that.

Maybe chronicling my life as I remember it will help exorcise my demons once and for all. Most of all, I need to forgive myself for not allowing myself to live because of my past. I know for a fact, my past has lead to my subconscious fear about being successful. Especially in areas I know my mother would disapprove.

Looking back at my life and at the big picture, I recognize my mother suffered from some kind of mental disorder. That realization has given me the freedom to embrace life and to cut the invisible lines of control, self-doubt and fear that has been imbedded in me from the start. For as many times as my mother said I was evil and all the other nasty things she said, I know I am stronger for it. I am a survivor. And her words can only hurt me, if I let them.

I was finally free – or was I?

CHAPTER TWENTY-FIVE

I may be stubborn and some people may think I am strong, but it took hitting rock bottom to reach where I am today. When I found out my mother was ill I considered renovating my house and bringing her home with me. Thankfully, reality kicked in and I didn't pursue this. Even with my health care aide experience, I was in no condition to bring my mother into our house. Besides, we were literally full to the rafters.

It was a good thing we didn't move ahead with the plan to care for mom because when we flooded again in 2004, I would have really had problems. That summer, the heavy rains caused overland flooding and we were hit hard. I had just finished replacing everything that was destroyed from the previous summer flood. Once again, the basement was totally destroyed and until it was fixed we had to move all three girls to the second floor. We ended up with all six kids upstairs in three makeshift rooms and I lost my bedroom. My large main floor living room was then divided into half so we could have a new master bedroom.

I was constantly frustrated by what life was throwing in our direction. I was trying to put money together to replace the rugs, furniture and my daughters' clothing. We didn't have the extra money and no house insurance. Even though the municipality had declared a state of emergency, we did not qualify for assistance, not even for cleanup. There was only so much I could do myself physically and financially, yet it seemed like everyone was waiting for me to perform a miracle instead of helping. I felt like I was talking to an empty room when I begged for help around the house. There was so much that needed to be done but I was working and my time was limited. There were also physical limitations to what I could do. My ulcers were healing, but they were still bothersome so I had to be careful with some of my activities.

The more difficult things got, the more my husband immersed himself into video games and withdrew from the added problems. Eventually, he lost his job at the restaurant. Instead of looking for another job, he spent his days and nights playing video games and smoking pot. He brought the stuff into my home and soon my two oldest daughters were smoking weed. The girls were now teenagers and thought their stepfather was cool. Instead of asking me to have parties and things, they would go to him. I was tired of life and fighting for what I believed in and eventually, I just gave up. I was more than willing to put aside my responsibility in some instances because I wanted them to respect him like a stepfather. I was glad he was taking the initiative. I just wished it was in a more positive way.

Don't get me wrong. At first, things were good and I re-acquainted myself with family and friends. My husband was very funny and friendly, so they welcomed us both with open arms. In some ways, I was genuinely happy and in love. Yet, there was a dark side in our relationship that eventually led me to believing that I was once again in a situation in which I was not going to flourish.

My husband had his own issues, and at first I loved and accepted him in spite of everything. He had been raised by a single mother who was also an alcoholic. Whenever she was involved in a relationship, the children were often abused and beaten. He had been sexually molested as a boy and in turn molested his little sister. He spent time in jail for statutory rape and even worked as a call boy for a couple of years. He finally got off the streets with the help of a couple in Winnipeg who took in boys off the street. Unfortunately for him, this relationship also had a darker side. Part of the relationship was a sexual one.

About a year after our wedding, this same couple came to stay with us for a couple of days. I found out later his friend offered him money to sleep with me. What scared me was my husband actually considered accepting the offer without even talking to me. I was horrified. What man would sell his wife to another man? We had a very active sex life, and I couldn't believe he could consider sharing me with someone else. It made me feel insecure and cheap, yet I tried to suck it up – he was my husband after all – I had no rights. Yes, I know – when I was at my worst, my mother's influence still affected me.

He started to introduce other things into our bedroom. He was fascinated with sadomasochism. I was not into pain, but I tried to please him. It took him tying me to the bed once for me to say never again. As soon as the cuffs were on, I started fighting for freedom but instead of letting me go, he did whatever he wanted. I still have the scars on my wrists from where I fought my restraints until I finally broke those damn things off. I never allowed that to happen again. I did many things for him because, while I loved him, I also feared him. I knew he was capable of hurting me. He would share rape fantasies and how he wished he could get me pregnant – there was a perversion in his head that horrified me. I knew that he had sexually assaulted the mother of his children the day they split up. I was not going to let that happen to me, so I played his sick little games. While I still loved him, I began to hate and resent the control he had over me. And each time, I allowed him to do things to me, I hated myself more. For me, sex had always been a way to express my love toward my partner and he turned it into something ugly.

Despite how worthless I sometimes felt, I had learned to have respect for myself and my body thanks to my first husband. While most people I knew readily threw caution to the wind and slept with whomever they wanted without consideration, I thought better of myself. The only way I was a willing sex partner was if I was committed either by marriage or in a stable relationship. Within that relationship, I would give myself freely to my partner and enjoy an active sexual relationship, but I respected myself enough that I could not have sex without love.

I no longer felt special to him. Instead of being cherished, I felt like a mere plaything - a blow-up doll for someone else's pleasure. The more I pondered, the more it hurt and soon my mind was going to a horrible place. My mother's words that someone would never love me except for what I could give them or for what I had between my legs began playing in my head loud and clear. When I was treated like I didn't matter, it was very easy to believe that I had no value as a human being.

I guess eventually I just gave up fighting and let everyone do their own thing. It became easier to hide from reality by getting high with my husband than dealing with what was going on. I used to hate the stuff and now I was an admitted pot head. I preferred it to getting drunk. When I would drink, I would become horribly depressed – it made everything worse, but when I smoked pot, I was happy and carefree – until it wore away.

Everything about my life was so wrong. I felt like a bystander watching my family fall apart. I begged; I pleaded; I cried, but nothing got through to anyone. I felt like I was losing my mind. In a way I was, and that fall I admitted myself into the Selkirk Crisis Unit on the verge of a nervous breakdown. I guess after over twenty years of fighting a losing battle alone, I finally cracked. That day, in tears, I drove to the walk-in clinic in Steinbach and told the doctor I wanted to hurt myself – not to die, but I needed to know I mattered to someone. It was a desperate cry for help. His diagnosis was I was suffering from situational depression – I was not manic, I just had more to deal with than an average human being and I needed help. His solution was putting me on antidepressants and sending me away for a weekend. I took both gladly. I knew I needed intervention or at least to get away from my house, which at that time, I considered my prison.

So many horrible things happened in the years leading up to this crisis. Between my illness, flooding two summers in a row and the car accident, my remorse was killing me. My entire family was suffering because of my decisions. During those few days at the crisis centre I got to rest and to think. The nurses agreed I was not crazy. I was just overwhelmed and needed help to refocus. Our biggest problem at the moment was money. I was forced to look at our immediate needs and find immediate solutions. My vehicles were both uninsured, the kids were starting school without supplies and the basement was destroyed.

It was a heavy burden for me. The only person I could rely on – myself – was stumbling and failing miserably. Not only that, I was bringing down my family with me, and they did not deserve this trip. By this time I had no respect for myself. My daughters were now starting to act out by skipping school and partying until dawn. Everything was a mess. So, I was put on antidepressants and I slowly got control over myself and my home. One step at a time, I reined in my wayward children and grabbed control of my life.

The biggest project that was killing me was the house. I had to get the kids back into their own rooms. I was pointed to a government website that offered emergency assistance for situations similar to ours. I sent in an application, along with pictures of what my children were living in. Within a week I received a response. They could not help me. However, they offered me an alternative program we qualified for. I successfully applied for and received $32,000 through two government programs. This was a godsend. The money was used to clean the basement and repair things I didn't even know were a problem. With the help of an amazing contractor, my basement was cleaned and fixed, along with the roof, the bathroom and the kitchen. Extras like central air and a heat exchange system made my son's breathing easier. This was a huge project, and once it was done I felt hopeful for the first time in a long time.

It was the first big step of many big steps. It is amazing how a single ray of hope can turn into a lifeline; the first stepping stone to making some major changes in my life. It gave me strength and motivation to reach for the unattainable. Undaunted, I took on my next challenge. I found faith in myself and got back to the basics – I went back to school.

A year after admitting myself into the crisis center, I returned to high school in an adult learning environment at Red River College in Steinbach. Ten months later, I proudly graduated with my grade twelve diploma. It was a rough road getting there but worth it in the end. With every passing grade and marks in the high eighties, I learned to have faith in myself and believe I was smarter than I ever gave myself credit for. I had finally done what my mother said would be impossible for someone as stupid as me – I had finally finished school. In my mind, I had achieved the impossible dream. I also proved to myself that when I wanted to do something, I could earn it. No challenge proved to be enough to kill my determination to succeed.

I was thrilled to be able to graduate the same year as my oldest daughter. She was less enthused. Her convocation took place two days before mine. While our celebrations were focused on her, she resented the fact she had to share this experience. I however, understood why she was so upset with me. Her final year of school was difficult for her. Between going to school and working a full time job, she developed ulcers and she was sick often. Where she was once on the honour roll, she was now barely passing. It was a rough year for her.

She blamed my dysfunctional life for her illness and I carried guilt like a millstone around my neck. There was nothing else I could do because I agreed with her one hundred percent. She was seventeen years old. She should have been enjoying her final year of school, not sick with ulcers because her life was so messed up. It was a heavy cross for me to bear. The last thing I wanted was my children to suffer because of my choices.

It was time for this roller coaster of a life we were leading to stop.

CHAPTER TWENTY-SIX

Finishing school and graduating had a huge impact on my self esteem and courage. It was more than a diploma. I finally managed to prove to myself and everyone else I could accomplish what I had set out to do. After years of failure, I proved to myself I was capable of the impossible. It was like deciding to climb a mountain and having everyone tell you that it couldn't be done – and going out and proving them wrong. For the first time in years, I felt strong and able to take on the world. It was time to confront the rest of my issues head on. It was like a switch turned on in my head.

I was already on the right track but the real turning point in my life came in the fall of 2006 when I finally accepted the fact the only way I could return to life, find myself and really live was to come to grips with my past and move on.

A year earlier, I'd received a friendly phone call the pastor of Prairie Grove Church in Lorette. He'd invited me to join the Alpha program which was starting in his church. The Alpha program is designed for people wanting to investigate Christianity; new Christians, people who feel that they have never really got going as a Christian; newcomers to the church and those who want to brush up on the basics of their faith. This was not the first time I heard about the program. I met with the organizers once and wrote an article for the paper on how the Lorette churches banded together to bring the program to the community. The program is designed for people wanting to know about their faith. For me, it was an important step because I feared the church and all it stood for. I believed in God, but thanks to my upbringing and my mother's fanaticism, church and church-related activities intimidated me. I never felt like I could ever belong in a church family.

Somehow through my fog of misery I managed to recognize the need to start talking to people again. The hardest was reaching out to a community that had obviously shut me out because of my presumed lifestyle. Most people I spoke to suggested therapy, but somehow I knew I needed something more significant. Needless to say, when I got the minister's invitation, his timing was perfect. Alpha was starting in a few weeks and I was more than welcome to participate. I told him I wanted to come. I didn't have a license due to lack of money – no problem – we will get you there, he assured me.

My initial intention was to quietly listen and learn. Then I would see if I could put all my "religious" horrors aside. I attended with an open heart and an open mind. For some reason, it was the only way that I knew I would learn anything. It was the third session – "Who is Jesus?" that changed my thinking and life forever. We learned the basis of Christianity was that Jesus was forgiving and loved us no matter what we were taught or knew. No matter how awful we were, there was always hope as long as we believed in the power of forgiveness and faith.

I pondered the enormity of what I'd heard. I am unable to put into words what happened but by the end of the evening I was crying and speechless. It was beyond my comprehension that someone I didn't know loved me so much He gave His life for me. My own husband wouldn't even sacrifice his cash for my life. I knew the words in the Bible but believing them was something completely different. The hardest part for me was to believe someone I could not see loved me more than anything in the entire world – when I had suffered such rejection. I had been rejected by not one, but two mothers when a mother's love should be unconditional – and you are telling me Jesus loves me?

I went home afterwards, grabbed my laptop and locked myself in my bedroom. I didn't want to see or talk to anyone, but I felt the need to get everything out of my head and my heart. I poured out my heart in a four-page e-mail to the pastor. As I typed, it hit me I believed I had no purpose in life and that frightened me. Surely there was a reason why I had suffered throughout my life. There had to be a greater reason for it, and I was determined to find out what it was. My life could not have all been for nothing – after all, we all have a purpose in life; we just need to find it.

My heart was breaking – I felt so lost and confused, yet I knew if someone prayed it would help. So I asked him to pray for me and my family. It took a lot of courage to send that email. As I clicked send, I sobbed even harder. As I cried, I felt myself give over my pain and horror. I begged the Lord to forgive me for everything – things I remembered and things I didn't. I pleaded him to erase all the negative vibes from my life and to surround me with encouragement and love. Most of all I remember thanking Him for showing me His truth before it was too late for me and giving me tools with which I can share His love with others.

That night, I had an epiphany.

For the first time in my entire life, I believed someone loved me – all of me, no questions asked – no conditions – at no cost. As I pondered this new truth, I prayed and sobbed like never before. As I prayed, I felt something change within me. It was like a great weight lifted of my heart as thirty years of shame, guilt, fear, insecurity, uncertainty and doubt flowed out of my body with my tears. Afterwards, when I lay back on my bed exhausted, I felt an indescribable freedom – my heart was lightened.

Forgiving those who hurt me most came next. As I did that, the horrors of my childhood floated away and new memories began taking their place. I remembered the love on my mother's face when she saw my babies for the first time. The pride at my first front page headline. I remember her telling me, when I was a little girl I would one day be a great writer. Some of these memories had been hidden for decades. I have to concentrate to remember the bad stuff now – I realized that none of it really mattered anymore, and yet, I had nearly let it destroy my life.

But it didn't matter now – I had something to believe in and it gave me strength. I had direction, I had hope and I had love. The next step was to do something positive with it. Determined to change my life, for the sake of myself and my children I was not going to squander this second chance. I took the blinders off and looked at my life with new eyes. I was ready to embrace these new truths and begin living my life the way I felt I was meant to in the first place.

While I was basking in my newfound hope and strength, my husband felt threatened by my new friends at Alpha and the changes he could see going on in my head and in my heart. He admitted that he knew I was in turmoil and itching for a change. He also admitted that it scared him, because he feared he would become one of the sacrifices I would make in the end. Yet he understood and loved me with all his heart. He swore he loved me enough that if he had to go to counselling too, he would. He promised that as long as I wanted him in my life, he would support me, guide me and love me even though he himself had issues. He admitted he was part of the problem — and he would live each day we have together as if it was our last — just in case. I believed him — because I'd finally forgiven him, too, and I loved him. How could I expect someone to love and forgive me for my past if I could not do the same? But it turned out to be just words.

In some ways I still had no control over my home, so I sat and watched things through an antidepressant-induced haze. I was still taking them, even though a year had come and gone since I started. Prolonged use was affecting me physically, and I would sleep like a dead woman. They also decreased my sex drive immensely. A very sexual person, I have always enjoyed an intensely physical relationship with my partners. This part of my mother's predictions did come true. When I was emotionally secure with my lover, I gave everything in and out of the bedroom. But under the influence of antidepressants, I was genuinely not interested in having sex. At first my husband was understanding but as time went on, his attitude changed.

Eventually he would take what he wanted without any consideration towards me. One morning I woke up "knowing" that I had sex, but try as I might, I could not recall the actual act. When I asked my husband about it, he admitted that while I was sleeping, he took advantage of me. He didn't stop because he thought I would wake. But when I didn't, he just finished the job. I completely freaked out. In my mind, he had raped me. But in my skewed thinking I also believed that as my husband he had certain rights, so I couldn't complain. Seeing how distraught I was, he swore it wouldn't happen again and I let it go. A few weeks later it happened again. This time when I confronted him I reminded him of his promise while pointing out that he had violated me. Again, he apologized and swore it wouldn't happen again. Stupidly, I believed him. The third time I woke up knowing we'd had sex, but not knowing it was happening, I confronted him and it got ugly. I asked him if he intended to tell me at all. He shrugged his shoulders nonchalantly and admitted he had no intention of confessing his disrespectful behaviour because he knew I would be upset. Most people – including myself - are shocked that I didn't kick him out at this point. Many feel I should have the first time. But we were married! I still felt that as his wife, I had no say.

We stayed together for a few more months, but I was furious. In my heart I knew he'd raped me, but I was still torn between what I believed and what I was taught. It was like the guilt women sometimes feel when they get raped because they were out dancing, looking sexy and having fun. In one way, they know that they were raped and violated, and yet they question if they asked for it because of their behaviour. Until you get that settled in your head, it is hard to move on. I had yet to shake the belief that marriage meant ownership and I had to take what I got. I hated myself for being unsure and weak.

I was also still mentally and emotionally numb because of the antidepressants. In my fury and hatred of what I had committed myself to live with, I grew fearless and reckless. It wasn't until I did a three hundred-and-sixty degree turn in the middle of a dirt road with my car that I decided I needed to get off of them. I had just done a donut in the middle of the road and continued on driving like nothing happened. The usual adrenalin rush that hits after a close call didn't occur. My heart didn't even skip a beat – that scared me instantly. I realized in the minutes after the incident I had to get off the pills before they killed me or I killed someone else.

Against doctor's orders I stopped taking the antidepressants cold turkey. It was then I could see what I had done to myself. Coming off those pills was the hardest thing I ever did. First, doctors stress that you should never go off antidepressants cold turkey. I can see why. The first few days I was physically tired and all I did was sleep. After I slept off the initial affects of the medication, the emotional agony of what I had blocked out kicked in. I got furious as I started to remember the things that occurred in my numb state. Over the span of three days, everything my husband had done to me and my family over a two-year period came back to me in vivid snapshots. It was physically painful. I had no self-control as the memories flooded my mind. Bawling hysterically, I confronted my husband, screaming at him, calling him a degenerate rapist, and let him have it with both barrels. I ended up calling a friend over because I was genuinely afraid of how he would react. I was saying things I knew I would regret and I was also afraid he would hurt me in retaliation. Instead he took it all, every single word and did not deny a thing. I don't think even he realized how much damage he'd done or how it had affected me until that day. After all, I had taken it all in silence.

But I still did not walk away from the relationship. I was not ready to quit. With my newfound faith, I was determined to salvage my marriage, if it could be salvaged. He promised to seek counselling but never did. Maybe if he had, things would have been different. I see now he was not at the point that I was – while he admitted he had many issues, stemming from his own childhood and past, he still found it easier to hate his mother and blame her than to take responsibility for his own actions and make things better. He pleaded with me not to kick him out, and I would have given him more time if he had tried harder to respect me and my feelings. Alas, I knew it was impossible when after all of this, we went to a baseball tournament with my friends and I woke up with him squatting over my sleeping body masturbating. I was horrified, shocked and hurt. I ran out of the tent to where my friends where and as I told them what happened, I listened to what I was saying. It hit me like a ton of bricks. If I was listening to a friend tell me a similar story, I would be the loudest advocate telling them to pack their bags and get the heck out. Or pack his bags and kick him out. If I felt that way, then why was I allowing this to happen? No one would stand up for me, unless I stood up for myself.

I was done. I was finally able to admit that I was married to a person more messed up than I was. If he didn't care about dealing with his past, I couldn't help him anymore. It would eventually kill me to remain in that relationship. Not because of what he was doing to me, but how it was making me feel about myself. My children had to come first – I had to come first. This marriage, too, would end up in ashes.

My husband was given ample opportunity to move out. I

generously allowed him one month to find his own place and leave on his own. But he did not do it. I guess he was hoping I would change my mind over time. Instead it just made me more determined and angry. I tried to be patient but the longer he stayed, the more I worried I grew about the safety of myself and my family. Knowing the end was in sight, he really had nothing to lose at this point. It was like living with a ticking time-bomb.

I would eventually turn to my newfound church family from Alpha. I was still attending the sessions during this entire time. They were already very familiar with what I was going through. I had shared every pain, subsequent breakthrough and on-going problem. I could never have gotten through this without their support. I knew if anyone would help, it would be them.

We set a date – if he had not moved out by that date, they would show up in droves and move him out. Sure enough, the day eventually came and he was still there. Seven trucks and fifteen people showed up to help me remove him from the premises. With the help of my newfound church family he was packed and moved out within thirty minutes.

Two weeks before our fourth wedding anniversary, he was out of my house and my life.

CHAPTER TWENTY-SEVEN

Before I kicked my husband out, I was attending my second
session of Alpha. This time I took a session closer to home
because it gave me an opportunity to actually come to know
my community. This was the first time since I was a teenager and
living in Landmark that I participated in something at the church on
a regular basis.

Initially it was a chance to grow, but I eventually began making
some friends. It was nice to finally be accepted by people who had
turned their backs on our family for so many years. Not only did they
pitch in and help me move my husband out, they also celebrated with
us when God presented us with a tiny unexpected miracle.

It was production and I was working on meeting my deadline.
Production is what my editor called laying out the paper for print. I
average about forty-five articles per issue, and it is the most stressful
time of the month. It was the December issue, which is also the
biggest issue of the year and I was focussed on work. Meanwhile, my
oldest daughter came out of the bathroom and I heard her mumbling
something about wishing she would stop being sick. A light bulb
went on. I turned around and asked her, "Are you pregnant?" She
looked down at her feet, and admitted it had been awhile since her
last period. I stopped what I was doing immediately. This needed my
complete attention.

"Have you taken a pregnancy test yet?" I asked.

"No," she admitted.

"Tell you what – before everyone freaks out and assumes the

worst, let's find out for sure." I set my laptop aside and headed to Lorette and picked up a home pregnancy test from the pharmacy. Within an hour we had the results. It was positive. Doing the math, we figured out that she was about three months along.

I admit at first I was disappointed. She had graduated from school in June after struggling with her health. She barely finished school because of the ulcers she had due to our stressful and dysfunctional life. Despite my obvious issues, I raised my girls to believe they could be whatever they wanted in life, that with student aid they could get an education, and they should take their time making life decisions like getting married and having babies. I was determined they would not make the same mistakes I did in life. Instead of going to university as she planned, my daughter was suddenly faced with making adult decisions of her own.

She knew about my adoption and that I had helped my two best friends find homes for their babies when they decided to go that route, so I assured her I would support her in whatever she decided. This would be her decision, whatever it was — but she would not make it alone. Our family would walk beside her in every way possible. She had already made up her mind; she was keeping the baby, no matter what anyone said.

It was that pregnancy that brought me completely out of my stupor. I promised my daughter I would not share the entire story because it is her tale to tell. However, her pregnancy brought our crumbled and discouraged family back together. Despite the horrors our family had experienced over recent years, a baby was born that, for many reasons, should not have been — but her arrival saved all our lives. Her surprising appearance changed my daughter in many positive ways — no more parties, and crazy antics. She grew up right before our eyes. It was amazing to see.

I learned a few things from my daughter that year. Living in Landmark, the community frowned upon young, unmarried women having babies. My daughter was barely out of high school and pregnant — technically she was a statistic. And yet, she held her head up high. She worked at the local restaurant right until she gave birth. She was not proud of her situation, but she did not hide from it. I was so proud of her for doing what I could never do — carry her head up high despite the circumstances.

Thinking back to those months, I am so proud of my girl. She continued working right until days before she gave birth. She got her own apartment, admittedly in her boss's basement, but it was her own place nonetheless. I did not kick her out, but I did encourage her to find her own place because our house was full, and it was not a safe place for a newborn. After my son developed asthma due to the mold problems I did not want to take the risk of harming a helpless newborn. My grandchild deserved a fresh start.

Once again, the community that normally shunned people in similar situations reached out and helped out my daughter. A group of ladies from the local church held a baby shower and she received many wonderful baby items. I am not sure why they reached out to us like that, but it was exactly what we needed. It helped restore my faith and trust into the town that slammed the door in our family's faces for many years. By the time my granddaughter was born, things were pretty much set up for her arrival, including a gorgeous crib that was passed on to us through the church. My daughter lacked nothing as she transitioned into her new life.

My daughter's pregnancy was shared by the entire family. The baby's father was in France at the time and we were not sure if or when he would be coming back. We knew she needed the support of her family, and we were extremely close. I was thrilled to be asked to be her labour coach. Even though I had four babies, I missed out on a true birth experience. When she finally went into labour, we all descended on Bethesda Hospital, and I do mean all of us. By the time she was ready to push, there were eight women in the delivery room and one male doctor. My wee granddaughter came into the world with her two aunties in the room, two of my daughter's best friends and my ex-husband's favourite sister plus the nurses. The room was packed and loud. I remember the doctor saying afterwards that he'd never had so many people in a delivery room before, but it all served a purpose. My daughter ended up having a fairly easy delivery and I was the first to yell, "It's a girl."

Not very many grandmothers have the honour of welcoming their grandchildren into the world from the moment of their first breath. To have helped my daughter experience first-time motherhood is something I will forever cherish. Circumstances did not matter – what mattered was our unity. This was MY family and we loved and supported each other. As I held the tiny angel of my granddaughter for the first time, I realized how blessed I really was. For the first time in many years I was filled with hope. Hope for my daughter, hope for my family and hope for the future.

My children's father was soon at the hospital to meet his new granddaughter and it was such a beautiful family moment. He brought along his mother and a few aunts. I had thought this family had abandoned us with the divorce. But when we came together in this shared experience, bridges were built and hearts were healed. People who I felt had given up on us long ago, showed us more love and support than I have felt in a long time. Through their love I grew strong.

Instead of dwelling on my pathetic life, I had something new to focus on. It was fun watching my daughter learn to raise her baby. She came home to stay with us for the first couple of weeks because she was scared to be alone with her new daughter. We all participated in the baby's first few months. I hadn't felt such joy since I'd held my son when he was born.

Her story would end up having a happy ending within a few months after baby was born. My granddaughter's father finally returned home to his new family, and the pair has been together ever since. They have since added a son to their family and they are very happy. She is currently going to Red River College, through distance education, and within a few months will be graduating with a degree in Business Management. I watch their little family and I feel so much pride. My "son-in-law" could not be a better match for my daughter. The love he feels towards my daughter and their children is obvious. I could not have wished for a better life for them.

The similarities between my daughter and me are also obvious; although I am sure she would deny it. Just like I had tried before, she had her babies and continued to go to school. That is all I ever really wanted – to raise happy, well-adjusted children – and when I look at my daughter and her family, I know that in spite of my mistakes, my children are okay. There is no greater joy in a mother's heart. Our family was whole again and my heart was finally healing.

Admittedly, the hardest part of it was that I would have loved to introduce my mother to her first great-granddaughter and great-grandson, but that would never be. By the time of their births, her dementia had forced her to a place where she would not know or understand what was going on.

CHAPTER TWENTY-EIGHT

The year following my granddaughter's birth was a time of great change for our family. My second daughter graduated from high school and moved in with her boyfriend and his family. I was shocked when she packed her bags but she seemed to believe I could handle life better with less people in the house. I wish she had talked to me about this first, before she actually moved out. This was hard for me because out of all the children, we were the closest. My once-timid girl was growing up. On her own, she registered herself in beauty school where she studied to be an esthetician. What struck me about this was that she did it all herself. I was told, after the fact, she was registered, applied for student aid and was moving into Winnipeg.

As a mother, I sat on the sidelines watching her grow up and make her own way in the world. As a middle child, she was often left to her own devices. It was never deliberate – she was just low-maintenance. I was so wrapped up with life and all its drama; I failed to see her growing up before my eyes. It was a tough pill to swallow when she very quietly slipped out of the house into her own home. It hurt to realize I had missed so much and I would never get that time back.

It took a trip home to finally cement my resolve to make concrete changes in my life that would hopefully benefit everyone. That summer, my editor's mother decided to return to her roots in Fredericton, New Brunswick. He offered to load up her things and deliver them to her new home. His son was already out there, so he invited me and the two youngest on a two-week road trip. I'd always wanted to see the east coast and I jumped at the chance.

This is where I will explain about my editor. When I first walked into his office in the fall of 1997, his first reaction was "Great, the rookie." But he soon learned I had a gift for writing and he was willing to teach me to be a good reporter. While I loved to write on a personal level, writing for a newspaper was a completely different ball game. As the owner of three newspapers and a broadband company he was all business. Yet, in the decade of being my boss he has become one of my best friends. Why? Because he believed in me even when I didn't or couldn't.

He initially gained my respect because he was a single father with a son a year older than my son. I knew he could teach me so much. At first I kept him at arm's length because many people believed he was the reason my first marriage fell apart. I was normally a stay-at-home mom and the first few years of working for him I spent every production at his place for days on end. It was unusual for me to leave home and soon word around town was we were having an affair. It was never that type of relationship but he did become more than a boss to me.

He was the one who talked me down from numerous panic attacks when I would get so overwhelmed I could not think. It was my editor who wrote me advance paychecks so I could keep food on the table and the hydro connected. He even offered to pay for a hairpiece when I thought cancer treatments would make me lose my hair. He would always make me cry, but he would also find ways of giving me hope. He kicked my butt when I needed it, and he pushed me to become all I can be. When I first started with the newspaper, I was shy and timid. Now I can walk to the front of a room of strangers with my head held high and ask the questions people are afraid to ask. He taught me so much, and without his guidance I wouldn't be who I am today.

While he had already been so instrumental in my life, the trip to New Brunswick sealed the deal. It is like he knew I needed a change of scenery. The entire trip was an amazing adventure and a time for self-assessment. For both my children it was their first major road trip; an once-in-a-lifetime opportunity. It was on this trip I really began to think. Taking me away from what I considered my personal millstone, gave me a chance to look at my life through clear eyes. I was filled with regret – realizing our once, fun-filled life had become so focussed on survival, my children had missed out on many things. I also realized it was within my power to make a difference.

While it was wonderful we were on this trip, and my boss paid for the entire thing, I was ashamed of myself – it should have been me doing this for my kids. As we ate up the miles, I remembered all the times we were so broke that I would either have to go to food banks, or sell household things to survive. A real vacation was never possible for our family. We always talked about it, but the reality was when you live hand to mouth, a trip is a luxury and very far down the list of priorities. I wanted that to change.

On the way back, we took a detour into Niagara Falls. I knew this was hard for my boss for personal reasons, but it was like he knew I needed to go back to my roots. It was the first time I had been home since my honeymoon twenty-two years earlier. It meant a lot to be able to share a little of my pleasant memories with my son and daughter. I was able to show my children where I went to school and where I lived before we moved to Manitoba. It was nice to share this with the people I cared about the most.

The highlight of the trip was calling my dad's brother and his family – who still lived in Welland, Ontario. When they heard I was close, without hesitation they jumped into their car and rushed over to see me and the kids. It was during that visit I discovered some things about my dad's family. I was told they missed my father dearly after he left, and never understood why he never came home again. I was very honest about things, and told them about how life was for my father. I didn't want to hurt them but they deserved the truth. I also discovered that every year until she passed away, my grandmother sent me a birthday card and gift. I knew she sent money to my father which my mother either tore up or donated to charity. My uncle was stunned to hear that I'd never received a single card. All these years, I thought I'd been abandoned by family, yet they kept trying to connect with me. I needed to hear that. There is no worse feeling than living a life believing you'd been abandoned by those who should love you most. Reconnecting with my dad's family was what I needed most at the time. After that visit I no longer felt powerless and alone. The strength one gains from unconditional love is amazing and I was filled with it.

On the way home from that road trip I made the hardest decision of my life. No matter how many little changes I made, I had to get rid of the biggest problem in my life – my house. I don't expect anyone to understand, but there was something about that place. Maybe it was because my father-in-law had taken his own life instead of moving out of it; or maybe it was because other people had died on that property – I don't know. But there was something about it – something I cannot explain. So many bad things happened there. It was like the house fed on sadness and despair. When it was filled with happiness, things went well – but there was also so much pain within those walls. To move forward, I had to let it go.

It was not an easy decision. I loved that house – a lot of blood, sweat and tears went into that place. All four of my children were conceived and pretty much born there. They were all raised there. It was their home, more than mine. So many memories, both good and bad – and not just for me – three generations lived within those walls. But the reality was it was more than I could handle. Initially, I took great care of it. But as the years progressed and money grew tight, it began to deteriorate. It was hurting me to watch it fall apart. The only reason why I was still there in the first place was because my ex did not want it. I promised him we would stay there until our son was eighteen and then I would move out and leave it to the children. But the ongoing issues with flooding and age had worn me down. I couldn't keep fighting for a home I considered my personal prison.

First I asked my ex if he wanted it. I always try to keep my promises. After all, he was practically born there, and the house was his birthright. I offered to sign over the title and walk away without a dime, but he did not want it. I suggested he offer it to one of his family members but he never bothered. I guess he also believed the house needed new life – it was time to say goodbye. Once the decision was made, I moved ahead quickly. Within a week, I called a realtor and my house was placed on the market. Three days later I was accepting an offer to purchase.

In the end, selling the house was the smartest decision I have ever made. I took the money and bought a smaller, more manageable place about fifteen minutes from where my children grew up. I was able to pay cash for my new home. I was determined I did not want to worry about having to pay a mortgage or foreclosure. My past financial history had already proven one thing to me – I was horrible with money and the less I had to worry about the better off I was. For once, I believed I could really begin enjoying life.

The biggest surprise for myself and others around me was that I was able to handle the sale, the move and the purchase mostly by myself. For the first time I was making life-changing decisions based on my head and heart, not because of a man or a relationship. It felt wonderful and freeing. I was finally standing on my own. Things were going my way. In letting go, I was learning to live. I was no longer attempting to live up to my mother's unreasonable expectations because she was no longer sitting there casting judgement on me. She was no longer condemning my decisions and her voice was slowly slipping from my head. With every step I took consciously and subconsciously, I was slowly cutting the bonds her words and actions had created around my head and my heart.

I was living life for myself and my children. I believed in myself and my abilities. I was stronger than I ever gave myself credit. I was finally letting go of the past on my terms and it was freeing. For the first time in a very long time I felt real hope. In my heart, I knew we would make it.

CHAPTER TWENTY-NINE

I may not have lived my life the way my adoptive mother wanted but I'd like to think that now, she can see I did the best that I could based on everything I have written. On March 8, 2009, she finally got her wish; she was finally with my father again on the other side. She was seventy-six years old.

It was a Monday when I got the call. Sadly, but not surprising, it was my editor who broke the news. When he finally managed to get me on the phone I was told my brother-in-law was looking for me. I knew immediately there was only one reason why he would be trying to find me. Something had happened to my mother.

Part of my job requires that I deliver papers once a month. The Vita Nursing Home was on our list of drop-offs and each month I would peak in to see how my mom was doing. At first, I would find her sitting in the lounge and I would stop and talk to her. Other times, she would be lying in her bed stiff as a board staring at the ceiling and muttering at something or someone only she could see. She never knew who I was, but it gave me peace to see her.

I once watched a show hosted by renowned psychic named John Edwards. He claimed to speak to people who have crossed over. During one episode, he was asked by an audience member what happened to people who suffered from dementia and Alzheimer's. They wanted to know if those years were lost forever. He responded by explaining that people suffering from these diseases witness the years they missed like a movie, after they pass on to the next world. I have believed this and for some reason stored that tidbit away in my memory over the years, never knowing one day it would be applicable.

Even though she would often not even know I was there, I tried to see her every month just in case she would "see" it later. These visits always ended the same – I would lean over, brush her hair off her forehead like a mother would a child and kiss her goodbye. I'd always whisper "I love you, Mom" into her ear before I would sneak back out undetected. I was always careful because I didn't know what my sister and her husband had told staff. I knew it would infuriate my brother-in-law that I was making these secretive visits. While I needed to see Mom regularly, I didn't want to cause any problems with my siblings.

A few days before she died, I was at the nursing home to do my deliveries, but I didn't see my mother sitting in the lounge like usual. I was disappointed but since I was running late I didn't go looking for her. I had to get home in time to pick up the kids from school. While I drove through Sundown that afternoon, I was thinking about her. Before I could stop myself, I was silently whispering a prayer that her suffering would finally be over. It broke my heart knowing she was no longer there. She was just a shell, trapped in a body that no longer responded. No one deserved that, not even her. In that moment I loved her enough to recognize that. I guess God heard my heartfelt prayer. That was Thursday and she passed away on Sunday – I found out Monday afternoon.

It was my editor who broke the news. He didn't want to say anything but after my prodding he sadly confessed that my family admitted to not wanting to call me personally. I wasn't surprised at all. After the way I found out my mother was in the hospital in the first place, I had already anticipated this was exactly how I would find out. It was either that or I would read about it in the newspaper's obituary section.

Shaking, I called my brother-in-law and he confirmed what I already knew. He was all business. My mother had passed away the day before and the funeral would be later in the week. He informed me the arrangements were already made and my assistance was not needed. He even told me my attendance at the funeral was not necessary. After all, my mother had disowned me he cruelly reminded me. I was mad. How dare he tell me I shouldn't attend my own mother's funeral? He had no right at all. I don't know what angered him more - that I was coming to my mother's funeral or that I stood up to him. In no uncertain terms I told him I have every right to attend and my children – her grandchildren – would be at my side. It didn't matter, I was not going to miss saying good bye – it was my given right.

Words cannot express how I felt after I hung up the phone. There are so many things I wish I could have said to her. Instead I found comfort that my mother was finally at peace. She spent most of her life preparing her soul for this day and I hoped she found what she was looking for.

That night, as I sat down and mourned I was able to do something that had eluded me to this point. I remembered the good times with my mother. For decades I have shared the pain and heartache I suffered but never focussed on the good. The pain always overshadowed the joy. As I lay in bed that night, sleep failed me. My mind would not turn off. Suddenly, clarity hit me in a flash – I was so consumed with healing and not repeating my mistakes I had forgotten the good times. And, yes, there were many good moments.

I remembered her taking me in for tonsil surgery, how worried she was for me and her spoiling me rotten when I got home. I remember the little red patent leather shoes she surprised me with when I was about three; they were so pretty. She loved to sew for me and my sister and we always had something nice. We spent many an evening on the farm, while she taught me how to knit and crochet while she shared stories about her mom.

I remembered her many attempts to perm my hair and spending hours brushing it. How I loved sitting cross-legged on her bed, watching her brush her hair. She was the only woman I knew with hair down to her waist – it was gorgeous but no one ever knew because she always wore it in a prim bun. I think this is why I am obsessed with my hair.

She was stubborn and strong. She worked hard and taught me that hard work builds character. She loved exotic birds, gardening and taking care of the many farm animals. She taught me to cook just by watching her. I remembered walking in the fields with her getting the cows. She taught me how to make Ukrainian Easter eggs and to keep up the traditions, which I unfortunately lost along the way.

When I started writing, she was so proud of me, especially when I got the job at the paper. She thought it wonderful I had so many stories in the monthly newspaper.. I still remember her smile of pride when I showed her my first front page story.

Believe it or not, it is thanks to my mom I feel I became a better mom. Despite everything, I did not repeat the abusive aspect, but I was able to separate the good lessons and pass them onto my own children. She brought me up with real old fashioned values, which I proudly carry with me today, along with a bit of a rebel without a clue.

She taught me to value all life, that every creature was God's gift, needing to be appreciated and not squandered. She taught me to believe in God and even though things got garbled for a while, I did eventually find my own beliefs and my own way back to Him. Yes, I was lost but I did find my way back. Unfortunately, my mother's mental capacity made her unable to recognize the woman I had become. That, in spite of the hardships and the pain – and even the baggage I still carry with me – I always did try to be the best woman I knew how to be.

In the middle of the night after she passed away, I felt compelled to record these memories. I got up, typed, cried and mourned. When I was done, I felt relieved and drained, yet I celebrated, because I'd finally found the good in my mom. The side I had failed to see. I had finally remembered the things that made her happy, the things that made her the woman she was. Most of all, I remembered she did love me in her own way. Things just got messed up in her head along the way. When I look at the time frame of when the real abuse started and was at its worst, it would have been around the time she was menopausal. That, combined with her previous mental issues including depression, I don't think she really knew she was doing something wrong. She really believed she was a good parent. I may not have understood this as a child, but as a grown woman, I can see it clearly.

Emotionally spent, I closed my laptop and went into the bedroom to try to sleep again. As I walked into the room, I was suddenly engulfed with the overpowering scent of roses. It was undeniable and unmistakable. I stopped and stood there sniffing the air like a dog catching a scent thinking it was my imagination. I even picking up a few things and even smelled myself to see if there was a hint of rose in my perfume, but it wasn't me or anything in the room. Then I remembered my mom's roses. They were her pride and joy. She had dozens of varieties of the most gorgeous rose bushes, some so fragile they should never have grown in our harsh climate, but with care and love she nursed them to full glory. When they were in full bloom, she would take massive bouquets to the local churches. She was very spiritual and for her, the gift for growing beautiful roses was a way to glorify God and she did so every single chance she had.

She may have disowned me during life, but in death she sent me a sign from the other side that she was nearby and thinking about me. In the morning, I couldn't wait to tell my boyfriend what happened the night before. But I didn't have to broach the subject myself. Over coffee he recalled waking up in the middle of the night to a sensation of someone watching us. He was positive someone sat down at the foot of the bed. He was positive someone sat down at the foot of the bed but there was no one else in the room other than myself and I was fast asleep.

It took all my mental strength to attend her funeral later that week - mostly because I was not looking forward to facing my brother-in-law. After I hung up from him the day he told me my mom was gone, I called the funeral home to make sure I was given the correct funeral information. It wouldn't surprise me to find he had deliberately misled me. During that call, I found out my grandchildren had been excluded from her obituary. I made sure the funeral home corrected that obvious slight. I expected a confrontation over that at the funeral. I also knew he would not have anything nice to say to me or my children. But I am proud of my kids – they knew the history, yet they all came and stood beside me during the ordeal. We were the last family to arrive. My brother and his family were already in place and his wife welcomed me warmly. I always liked her. My sister and her husband were sitting right in front of my family but they did not even glance our way. Other than family, there were very few others at the viewing. It was awkward to say the least, but I held my head up high.

It was one thing to face my family and it was another to face my mother's dead body. I did not go up to the casket to say my goodbyes. I could not even look at her body as it lay in state. It was not that I didn't want to say goodbye, I didn't want to soil all the good memories I had just recalled. I didn't want my last mental memory to be of her lying in a casket. I leaned over to my youngest daughter and whispered to her that I was relieved I could not see Mom's body the way the casket was placed. The funeral directors had placed her casket lengthwise down the aisle with her face towards the altar. From our vantage point, I could see her hands, clutching her favourite rosary, but that was it. I should have kept my mouth shut.

Out of the blue, there was a loud bang. The front kneeler, to the first pew at the left of her casket, suddenly fell forward, crashing to the church floor. The resounding smash echoed in the almost empty church. The funeral director righted the pew and turned the casket sideways. I had no choice but to stare at her body the entire time. I giggled; thinking someone on the other side had a really good sense of humour.

The funeral was sad but hauntingly beautiful – there is something to be said for about Ukrainian funerals. Between the chancellor singing in the empty cathedral type building, to the scent of incense as the priest anointed the casket. But from where I sat, instead of mourning her loss, I was able to rejoice. Not that she had passed, but because in my heart I believed she found what she was looking for all her life – real peace and greater understanding. She was also with my father and finally at peace. I am sure my family thought I was extremely disrespectful, but even at her gravesite I couldn't be sad – she was finally free from her internal torment.

I remember thinking that when the pew fell that my mother or father was trying to tell me that I was not alone, nor would I ever be again. They may have passed over, but they would be looking over me for the rest of my life. What I didn't know at the time was how accurate that assumption was. I soon learned my mother may be on the other side, but she was not finished with me yet.

CHAPTER THIRTY

After we buried my mother, I jokingly told a friend I was now an orphan. With both my parents gone, I expected no more contact with my adoptive siblings. They had cut me out of their lives for so many years and it was too late to start fresh. My friend pointed out to me that since I was already forty years old I was too old to be an orphan. In reality, I had already lived the life of an orphan for so many years, so it should not really matter.

However the fact remained both my parents were gone and I didn't have a family anymore other than my own children. I was okay with that. I knew it would end up like this, which is why I raised my kids to love and respect each other. I take comfort in knowing while I might not have siblings to lean on; my children will always have each other. I have witnessed their love and devotion to each other many times. Their bond to each other is strong and unbreakable.

Then I received the most shocking gift that would change the way I lived and thought forever. It all started with my dog. I have always felt that Odie was unique. He was overly attached to me and has many human traits. From day one, he was jealous of anyone in my life and extremely possessive of me. My family, friends and I have joked many times, that he must have been someone in a past life, but we could never figure it out. I didn't realize how attached to him I was until he went missing a few days after my mother's funeral.

I absolutely freaked out when I went home after being at my boyfriend's for a few days to find the silly dog missing. His absence was made worse by my imagination. The night before I'd dreamt he escaped the house and wandered along the highway. In my dream, a truck came along and the occupants grabbed him and tried to take him with them. But instead he fought his capture and he got dragged along by his collar. They eventually let go and he died a horrible death tangled among their tires.

When I went home and my daughter told me that he was actually missing, I feared the worst. I had just lost my mother and to lose my dog in the same week was something I didn't want to deal with. I spent four days looking for him. I eventually found him curled up in the local dog kennel, but what I did while looking for him changed my life.

While posting online missing ads for Odie on sites like Craigslist, I decided to post an ad looking for my birth family. I don't know why I thought of it, but it seemed logical that since I was already logged in, I should expand my search. I had nothing to lose. I also did a search on Facebook, a popular social networking site, for people with the same last name as my birth mother. I found a couple possibilities listed in Edmonton. Impulsively I sent them both a note, asking if they knew my mom. That was on Friday, the day after my mother's funeral.

The following Tuesday, I woke up and checked my inbox messages. There were two replies to my earlier queries. The first was from a boy who had no clue who I was looking for, but wished me the best in my search.

The second letter took my breath away:

"You have accessed the right family. I am one of your mother's brothers. After talking to your mother she expressed that she would very much like to be in contact with you. If you would be willing to give me your phone number for her I would pass it on to her. Your birthday has been a tough day for your mother and grandmother for many years. We are glad to hear from you as we have often wondered about you."

I couldn't believe what I was reading, so I read and re-read it. I sat there for about ten minutes trying to catch my breath. I had tried looking for my family before, but it never seemed possible. My first attempt was when my third daughter was born. With her heart defect, I felt compelled to know our family health history. Instead of opening doors, I hit roadblock after roadblock. The province of Alberta was one of the last provinces in Canada to open closed adoption files. Before the law changed, a child or parent had to sign a registry. If a match was found, a reunion could be planned. But if a match wasn't made, an adoptee had no choice but to wait – sometimes forever. Then in 1995, the Alberta government opened up the files. I had signed the registry so I was automatically sent copies of my adoption file. I received copies of the original adoption documents, which included my birth mothers and father's names and brief family histories. Armed with that information, I did half-hearted searches on the internet over the years but I never found a single clue to their current location.

Until my adoptive mother died, finding my birth family was something my mother wanted me to do, but I personally, felt no reason to do so. The reality was I could not face another rejection. I had already seen so much during my life. Even the thought of it was too painful. The last thing I expected was such a positive response.

That night I penned back a quick note to my newfound uncle. I provided him the information he requested and added a little note: *"I'd love to know more. If it helps 'Mom' at all – tell her that I understand and I am good and she has four grandchildren and two great grandchildren."*

I can only imagine my birth mother's shock when she found her long lost daughter, but she also found grandchildren and great grandchildren. Two nights later the phone rang at my boyfriends' house. He answered it and handed it over to me with a huge grin. He was so happy for me. I spoke to my birth mother for the very first time, exactly two weeks to the hour of my adoptive mother's viewing, about the same time the pew fell over.

Words cannot describe how I felt hearing my birth mother's voice for the first time. There was fear, and joy, a lot of disbelief, but also some relief. The answers to so many questions were suddenly at my fingertips, all I had to do was ask. In all honestly, I didn't know where to start.

"I never thought this day would come," she started when she heard my voice for the first time. She soon succumbed to tears of joy. I tried to suppress my hope and stifled any expectations that welled up. I didn't want my birth mom to think I looked for her because I wanted something. One thing I have learned is to be realistic. I did not expect anything. Once we were done sharing the initial shock of how we found each other, she encouraged me to ask her whatever I wanted. There was one burning question I had sworn would be the only one I would ask - was she able to do what she wanted to do with her life? It was important to know giving me up had been worth the sacrifice. From the paperwork I knew she was in university, but I didn't know what she was taking.

"I finished school and I have been a teacher for almost forty years," she told me. I couldn't help but feel proud of her. It showed giving me up was not a selfish decision. In that first phone call, I found out I had a stepfather, and a sixteen year old sister. That was the most shocking - my own son was turning fifteen in a few months. My sister was old enough to be my daughter.

The greatest realization for me though, is that all my life I've believed I was unloved and rejected by two mothers. But since I found my birth family, I have discovered this belief was the farthest from the truth. I was wanted but circumstances made it impossible for my mother to keep me. Times were different then. Regardless, the one thing I hoped was that the decision had been the right one for her. I hoped that through her sacrifice she was able to continue her education and live her life. I found peace in knowing she was able to do what she wanted but I was never far from her mind.

I don't think my birth family realizes how much healing has come to me from just finding them. A friend pointed out that healing goes both ways. While I've been here dealing with my life and coming to grips with my past, my family has been in Edmonton dealing with not knowing what happened to me over the years. For all they knew, I had died years ago. My stepfather said it best when he explained that since finding me, the hole in my mother's heart is no longer hollow – the void has been filed with my presence and my love.

I believe things happen for a reason – there are no coincidences. I believe I was meant to find my family exactly the way I did and when.

That night started a series of letters and phone calls. With each contact, I discovered my birth mother's life carried many similarities to mine even though she never raised me. Starting with pictures she sent me, I can see I definitely look like my mother. I even have my grandmother's nose and streak of gray hair. Personality-wise, my birth mother loves to laugh and can be heard long before she enters a room – just like me. Even her middle name is the same as the name I was given by my adoptive mother and she wouldn't have known what it was.

My stepfather was a truck driver who drove for the same company in Winnipeg my boyfriend works for. As a matter of fact, my stepfather was part of a group of drivers my boyfriend admired. When I was younger, my step-dad also drove truck for a company in Steinbach. While I was growing up on the farm and fighting for survival, my birth mom was mere miles away as she often spent summers riding shotgun with her husband. It is hard to believe that while I was growing up thinking I was alone in the world my birth mother was actually only a few miles away. Then I giggle when I picture my teacher mom riding shotgun in a big rig, the same as I have many times over the past few years.

While I was thrilled to find my birth family and to be welcomed with open hearts and arms, it is also a very intimidating experience. I didn't want to be a disappointment to another mother. Old fears of inadequacy surfaced, but I am slowly learned to trust. I have no choice. I have nothing to lose and everything to gain. Finding unconditional love and acceptance has been my lifetime goal, and I finally had it within grasp of my love-starved heart. The door to a beautiful new future was wide-open before me and all I have to do was walk through it.

It took a lot of courage, but eventually I crossed the threshold.

CHAPTER THIRTY-ONE

Initially my birth mother and I spent time getting to know each other over the phone. During the course of many conversations, I found out the truth about my origins and about my family's life. There was no pressure, just innocent conversations and getting to know each other. Those conversations were punctuated with emails as we exchanged photographs of me while I was growing up, along with pictures of my children and grandchildren. In return, I received pictures of aunts and uncles, cousins, pictures of my mother when she was younger. The resemblance was uncanny.

It was very important for my newfound family to know I did not expect a "happy forever after" ending. I had watched too many reunion shows on Oprah and Dr. Phil to believe that just because we found each other, we would transition into a wonderful family. In reality, adoption reunions can go both ways. I was hopeful but I forced myself to remain realistic. I've been heartbroken by too much, and I couldn't do it again.

The hardest part of these conversations was telling my birth mother about my life. As I got to know her more, I could sense that finding me really helped her. There had been a hole in her soul for forty years and finally it was filled. I couldn't imagine how painful it was for her to hear how my life had turned out, but I knew the truth had to be told. It was not fair to allow her to think I had lived this wonderful life. Little by little I exposed my past and each time we would cry for what was and what could have been. I made the mistake of misinterpreting her tears as regret. But she explained to me the main reason she was crying was that she wished she was closer to me so she could pull me into her arms and make it all go away.

I could hear the pain in her voice when I told her of growing up believing I was an ugly worthless child; how I was told she gave me up because she knew I would amount to nothing. She was shocked this was what I had been told.

"That is the last thing I would ever want you to believe – you were so beautiful when I last saw you – it broke my heart to walk away," she assured me.

Even though I told her everything about my upbringing and how I was treated, I assured her I held no animosity towards her. She was not to blame for my life. She did what she had to do – she needed to get her life together. Giving me up was an unselfish decision. Maybe keeping me would have landed her on the streets, uneducated and screwed up because she had a baby. I did everything I could to assure her that I loved her and was pleased to have found her.

Despite everything I have written on these pages, I have never blamed my birth mom for my life – even before I knew the truth. How could I? She did what she was forced to do. I was a victim of circumstances. It wasn't my fault either that my adoptive mother obviously suffered from some kind of mental disorder that affected her behaviour. The more I shared with my birth mother, the more I realized this and believed in it. I was starting to let go of the needless guilt I'd carried throughout my life at not being the perfect child. She genuinely loved me and believed she was doing the right thing at the time.

After weeks of phone calls and emails, the logical next step was that we would meet in person. My forty-first birthday was around the corner and I mentioned I thought it would be neat to meet them for the first time on this particular weekend. What greater way to welcome a new mother into your life than on the day she actually gave birth to you! But I knew I couldn't afford the trip on such short notice.

Within a few days, my birth mother called me to ask if I was serious about flying to Alberta for my birthday. I was, but money was tight – I had to look out for my family first. But I assured them I would see what I could do – I was going to find a way regardless. During one of these conversations I was told to check my email.

When I did, I found an airline ticket voucher waiting for me.

On May 1, I got off the plane in Edmonton, and was pulled lovingly into my birth mother's arms for the very first time. I still remember my fear and excitement as I exited the plane. I knew my family would be waiting at the bottom of the stairs. But how emotional would it get? When I turned the corner and saw my birth mother for the first time, there was only one thing I could do. I fell into her arms and we held each other for many moments and just cried. It felt wonderful to be wrapped in her loving embrace. That is all I felt in those precious moments. Love, acceptance and joy blanketed my heart. I had finally found my way home.

From the moment she wrapped her arms around me, I felt such love and joy. In those precious first moments, the lifelong aching hole in my heart filled and it went both ways. For forty years my mother did not know what had become of me. She never saw me grow up; she never saw me get married, graduate and have my babies. In those minutes none of that mattered. We found each other and had a second chance to make up for those lost years.

Within the first few hours of my arrival, I was surprised to discover that while this woman gave birth to me and didn't raise me, I would have probably turned out the way I am today. Our similarities were uncanny and our pasts had similar parallels. Her father was similar to my mother so she could understand some of my issues. We suffered the same insecurities and meltdowns. There was an instant unexplainable connection and understanding between the two of us. There were other things – she loves to laugh and sounded like me. Emotionally we reacted the same way. By the end of my visit it was pretty creepy that I could look at her and tell if she was okay or about to collapse – she reacted exactly like me. My poor stepfather could not get over it. As for me, it was nice to not have to explain myself to anyone. There was a connection I could never explain.

I also learned how her life was greatly affected by her decision to give me up. While I was told she got rid of me because I was useless and ugly, I discovered it was the last thing she wanted to do. She told me how her father forced her to give me up. When she revealed her pregnancy, her options included keeping me and moving out or giving me up and finished school. Fearing that she would end up on the streets, she relented and signed the adoption papers. My grandfather changed his mind about the adoption afterwards, but it was too late – I'd already been placed with my new family.

"He always regretted that we gave you up but there was nothing we could do," she told me.

My mother did not tell me a lot about her life – there were some things that were obviously difficult for her to discuss. One of these things was her first marriage. After giving me up, she went to school and got her first two years of teaching education out of the way. She ended up meeting a man she later married. Their marriage ended when she landed in the emergency room. He nearly beat her to death. Unlike me, when things went sour, she packed her bags and left. When she finally left that relationship, she focussed on her teaching. She met my stepfather and they married quickly afterwards. Despite objections of her family, they've been together over thirty years. I caught myself watching them together and wishing I could have found what they have. Even after all this time, they are so close and loving; they are almost like newlyweds.

I ended up spending five amazing days with my birth family sharing stories and making up for lost time. It is kind of funny – it was the first time we'd ever met, and yet it was like I had only gone away for a few years. Everything just fit – I just melded right in like I was never gone.

One of the highlights of my visit was meeting my mother's mom – my grandmother. She was eighty-one years old and had wondered what happened to me. Once she laid eyes on me, she didn't want me to go. She could not get over my presence. It bothered me that she kept apologizing to me. When I asked her why she was sorry, she admitted she had spent the last forty years regretting not standing up to her husband about making my mother give me up. She explained that she tried to convince my grandfather to change his mind about the adoption, but he was adamant. He told her that if she wanted my mother to keep me, then she could pack her bags and leave too. She had her two sons to think about so she obeyed her husband.

"We thought of you always," she told me. Her next words made me pull her in my arms and cry. "I hope you will forgive me for not standing up to your grandfather and letting you go." There was so much love and emotion in her aged eyes. How could I deny my heart and trust to these people? The pain at this lifelong separation was evident in everyone I met but the joy at my return overshadowed it all.

I was also thrilled to meet both my uncles and their wives, along with several cousins. Considering that until a few months earlier some of them did not know I existed, I was stunned how they all welcomed me with open arms. On my actual birthday they threw me a party. I felt so blessed to be surrounded by so many welcoming people.

I didn't really understand the impact my life had upon these people until my Uncle pulled me aside at one point during the barbeque. He was the one who passed my initial email to my mother. He shared with me how his own daughter got pregnant and they considered my mother's sacrifice before making any life decisions about her baby. In the end, instead of rejecting my expecting cousin, they embraced her and the situation and helped her in every possible way.

"Your birth and the events that followed changed us all," he confided, before giving me another warm hug. "You may have been gone from our lives but you were never forgotten."

He had no idea how much I needed to hear that. It's amazing how healing that simple affirmation was. I cannot stress enough how when someone is constantly berated and made to feel insignificant and unwanted, no matter how hard someone tries, it is impossible to get rid of those inner feelings. They eat away at you; they bind you with shackles of insecurity and self-loathing. During that visit, I started putting those feeling and thoughts aside. Whatever I once believed about myself was suddenly up for debate and definitely questioned. I was not going to walk away unchanged.

Getting on the plane at the end of the first meeting was hard - I was not ready to go home. But we also knew it wouldn't be long before we would see each other again. My family was already making plans to come down during the summer to meet my children and grandchildren. In the months following that meeting I've had time to grow and re-organize my life. I had been an orphan for such a long time that it was wonderful to be welcomed into a family with open arms. I may not have been there all my life, but I was back where I started.

Sadly, despite everything I have felt and learned, I guess a part of me was still waiting for the rug to be pulled out from under my feet. While a part of me craved a mother's love and acceptance, the hardest part was putting aside my fear and insecurity to let them into my life and my heart. But time has a way of making things settle and help hearts heal.

The reality really hit that I wasn't dreaming when my birth mom, step-dad and sister showed up on my doorstep during summer holidays. They stayed in my home and spent lots of time with the youngest two children. My oldest daughter and her family came here almost every day and it was a real bonding experience. It also helped having them see how I lived my life and how my children really turned out. My adoptive mother never took the time to know her grandchildren and it mattered to me to know I had done a good job in spite of everything we had experienced.

Normally, I have a lot to say, but in this case, I could not voice what I was thinking. When they went home at the end of the week, I put my feelings into words to my birth mom in the form of a letter:

"I keep remembering what you told me when you were here – that you love me, and that you are proud of me. To hear from your lips that despite everything you know, you still think I have done okay and that I've raised my children to be good young people. I draw strength from you all.

Finding you after all these years has given me something I haven't had before – unconditional love. It amazes me that after not knowing me and what had become of me for forty years, you still accept and love me. That is real love. That is something that I have felt toward my family and children but have never felt I received from anyone.

I have realized that, over the past decade, I have lost sight of what is real and what isn't – I've been so focussed on not losing everything, that I have put my heart away and not allowed people to really love me, including my children. I've been hurt so much. Then I think of you all and how blessed I am to have you in my life. I can't imagine the agony you felt years ago but as a mother, I know how I'd feel. To be given the chance we have now is worth more than all the money in the world.

I am proud of you, Mom, for being the wonderful woman you are. I need you to understand that I am really not used to having a mother to confide in. A mother's eyes have always condemned me. I don't see that in your face and it's something I have to learn to accept. I guess a part of me is waiting for it all to be taken away from me again, so I am afraid to let go to you too, for fear that I will lose you again – love has always come at such high cost.

I want you to be proud of me. I know that your love will help me break down these walls. I have no right to ask you for anything, but I am taking a chance here and begging that you help me learn and accept this gift that I have been given. It's not too late for either of us. I know I am not making it easy, but I would like to learn how. I hope you have the strength Mom. I want you in my life – your love, your wisdom, your patience, and your understanding. Love always, your daughter forever."

I have finally learned that by opening my mind and heart to the possibilities laid out before me, I can finally close the book of my past and embrace the future. The gaping hole in my heart is no longer empty. I have come home and it is a welcoming place. It is time for me to live, love and celebrate.

CHAPTER THIRTY-TWO

Initially I thought this story was complete once I had found my birth family and picked up the many pieces of my life. I found God. I had found love and acceptance. I found peace and forgiveness. I finally felt whole and complete. This was huge after spending a lifetime running around like a hamster in a wheel. Then something happened that I never believed possible. Anyone who watches shows like Medium or Ghost Whisperer will understand this more than others. I am sure many will think I am cracked for what I am about to share. But this story would not be complete without including this once in a lifetime experience.

Not long after my mother died, my second oldest daughter pointed me in the direction of a website for the Spirits Conference, hosted by Muddy Waters Tours. She was personally fascinated by the aspect of spirits because she had her own very real experiences. I have seen and heard enough from her that I have no doubts that she has a similar gift of her own; she just has not developed it.

The conference was fairly new to Winnipeg and designed to bring together people interested in certain aspects of spirituality and the afterlife. The keynote speaker was Donna Elliot, an infamous Canadian medium, who returned to Winnipeg for a month to do spiritual readings. My interest was piqued, so I emailed her in hopes that I would be able to score a ticket to the event as a reporter. I wanted to cover it but I was also personally curious. I was told the conference was sold out but I would be on the list should a new event be scheduled.

While waiting for an invitation, I did some random internet searches and eventually found Donna's personal website. I emailed her a quick note telling her who I was and that I would enjoy sitting down with her and possibly even do a reading. She does smoke readings using a candle and a piece of paper and she interprets the smoke markings that are left on the paper.

I was shocked to receive a personal response from her a few months later. She was coming to Winnipeg and she wanted to meet me. My phone number was attached to my initial email and within a day or two she personally called to confirm. At the time, we spoke for some length about her gift and my idea for writing an article and she promised on her next trip to Winnipeg she would look me up. I got an email from her a few months later saying she was still interesting in meeting me. I figured if anything, I would interview her for a newspaper article and maybe even for material for a book, so a meeting was set up. I never admitted it out loud, but I was secretly hoping someone on the other side was looking for me. But I was not going to admit it out loud because the whole idea of mediums and spirits was against everything I was taught and believed.

On March 22, 2010, we agreed to meet at my boyfriend's apartment so she wouldn't have to travel out of town. I was nervous – I really believed in these gifts. I also believed that anything could happen. I had heard bad things about events like this and I was terrified about what (or who) we might stir up. She was late, which added to my anxiety. I was beginning to think she was not going to come when she called, explaining she was ill and just leaving the doctors. I found out later that few years ago, she'd been diagnosed with Stage Four cancer and told she would not live. She rallied back and survived but was recently experiencing pain again. She had spent the morning receiving a treatment she needed to help her with the pain and swelling. She should have cancelled on me, but she refused to. She explained that for some reason she "needed" to meet with me.

When she finally arrived the three of us – Donna, my boyfriend and I – adjourned to the living room. She sat across the room from us and I started with some simple interview-type questions. She told me about what she does - she speaks to the dead through smoke readings and other ways. She talked about several investigations she'd participated in where she's found restless spirits and had even recently solved the mystery of room 212 from the Fort Garry Hotel. She told us how a smoke reading revealed to her that a bride who had gone missing on her wedding night from that very room had been murdered by her new father-in-law. Her body was never recovered. It was an interesting interview and I was totally engrossed.

For the most part, I listened and took notes. A few questions came to mind but I was scared to ask. I felt that by opening my mouth I was inviting something or someone in. But she was very easy to talk to. I remember asking how one knew if a spirit was present. I was thinking of the night my mother passed and I was overwhelmed by the scent of roses, but I didn't speak a word. Donna's reply included manifestations of scents or visions. She also said that we can sense spirits through temperature – it either gets hot or cold.

The urge to turn the interview into a more personal experience was strong. I wanted to know if she shared the same belief John Edwards did. I needed to know what happened to people who suffered from dementia or Alzheimer's after they pass over. I never got to ask. She started explaining that people who are mentally ill or physically crippled are "perfect" on the other side. I was surprised when she answered my unspoken question. Without explanation, I was suddenly overwhelmed by intense emotion and I had to leave the room. I made a less then gracious escape to the washroom to compose myself.

When I returned, I sensed they had been talking about me in my absence. I apologized for my hasty retreat and sat back down on the couch beside my boyfriend. Donna was looking directly at me when I sat down.

"Your mother was just here," my boyfriend stated. I looked at him. His words did not register. "My grandmother was too."

"Really?" I asked. He quickly explained how after I left, Donna started telling him about a woman who was in the room. He knew it was his grandmother because Donna said she was pointing to her leg, which had a visible gap missing in the calf. His grandmother had passed away years ago from galloping cancer. They had removed a portion of her calf and he'd been fascinated with her scar as a child. He was quite excited that she had popped in to say "hello".

I'd barely settled down when Donna turned her focus on me.

"You mother wants to know if you got the necklace." Excuse me? Necklace? What necklace? It didn't register what was happening yet. My mind searched memories for anything about a necklace and I came up blank. It didn't ring a bell, so I shrugged it off. Almost immediately I became painfully aware that my skin felt like it was on fire. My body erupted in a prickly heat so uncomfortable that I wanted to strip. It was distracting me. I didn't know how to respond. The medium continued, breaking the silence.

"What is with the single rose?" Donna asked. I had to think, single rose? I thought of my mother's love for roses, I had two rose tattoos but she just shook her head "no".

"She says you kissed it", she continued.

It was then my boyfriend started elbowing me. "The funeral," he whispered so only I could hear. I was still puzzled. I looked at him then it hit me like a ton of bricks. I remember standing at the gravesite during her funeral and the funeral director plucked some roses out of the spray on her casket. He handed each of us one, my sister, brother and all our family members. I took mine and brought it to my lips and unconsciously kissed it as gently as I kissed my mother's cheek. The moment was hard to forget because I chided myself for being frivolous enough to kiss a rose – plus my mother would have hated the gesture. My family even spoke about it on the way home from the funeral.

"She says she saw you kiss the rose." Donna stated emphatically. I felt like she had kicked me in the stomach. I lost control of the emotions I had swallowed earlier. I started crying. It hit me the interview was officially over and this was really happening. Clutching my boyfriend's hand, I silently wiped away my tears.

"You mother wants you to know that every time she said you were horrible, worthless, useless and wouldn't amount to anything she didn't mean it - she said it because she was being mean," she continued. "She didn't mean it - she says she is sorry, she now sees the damage she has done; she loves you and is proud of you."

At this point, I was bawling uncontrollably. There was nothing I could do. The words the medium used were exactly my mother's words, spoken as I heard them many years ago. I had blocked them out in my mind – I recalled daily what she was trying to tell me, but her exact words have always eluded me – until that afternoon. It all came back in a flash.

"Your mother says that she is going to make it up to you - she isn't done with you yet," the medium concluded. Stunned, I looked around. I was crying, my boyfriend was crying and even Donna was crying. She suddenly looked tired and ready to leave. When she was done, and my mother was gone – I noticed my body temperature had returned to normal and I felt like I was coming out of a daze. It took me awhile to digest what had just happened. I am grateful for my witness; otherwise I would doubt it even happened.

I marvel at how far I have come since that day.

This woman, a complete stranger - a medium – with no clue to my past somehow found the most tragic part of my life and exposed it unexpectedly. Those deadly words have been in my head for thirty years. Every time I have failed at something I felt I was living up to my mother's predictions. Every relationship, friendship and even my children – I have beaten myself up and when I failed, I would say, "My mother was right". They were toxic to me and the foundation of all my self esteem issues. Anyone who knows me will attest to that – I have repeated what she'd said many times, to many people long before this happened.

As for the necklace - I remember what she was talking about now. When I was a baby, I was given a little gold chain with a tiny gold cross - my mother put it on me when I was baptized. It was given to me by my godmother. My mother had always promised to give it to me when I was grown but never did. I am assuming that it is in the hands of my sister who still has most of my mother's personal items.

Considering how religious my mother was and how terrified she was about the supernatural, I find it ironic she would come to me this way; that she would use a medium to get her message across. I cannot help but look back and wonder. I really believe that she reached beyond the grave to bring me the one thing that I always needed from her. I was her "unfinished business".

She said she wasn't done with me – is that why this year has played out the way it has? I think about it. My mother passed away March 8th; I found my birth mother within days and spoke to her exactly two weeks after burying my adoptive mom. That gave me a new lease on life and helped me find the truth about my past and my life. It gave me a self acceptance I never expected. I found healing and love.

Then suddenly, I felt driven – and I do mean driven - to write my life story and I was able to pen this book. A book that has caused my head to ache and my soul to bleed as I searched my heart for memories long suppressed. In the aftermath, I sat back and felt true relief and healing. Reading about my life from the outside looking in, I see myself very differently. I made choices along the way that people will judge, but I made many of those choices because I didn't have other options. I see my triumphs and I see my failures. I have found forgiveness for myself and others. Most of all, I don't hate myself anymore.

I find it ironic that recently I found out my mother had indeed disowned me in her will. It was not just words. My brother and his family received a small portion and my sister and brother-in-law received the rest – my name wasn't even mentioned in the entire document. It hurt to see the proof in black and white – but I realized something on the way home from consulting a lawyer on the matter. I was relieved. Admittedly, the money would have been nice and I had solid grounds to fight it just because I was written out of it completely. And by rights, I should have - when you look at the big picture, my children and I have struggled more than any of us ever deserved. Even a small token would have helped. But I realized, in the end, I have something much more precious. I have my life back. In the end, I found who and what I was always meant to be and for me, that is the greatest gift my mother could ever have given me. It is now time to close the book on this part of my life and start a new book.

Through this process, I have learned that I am strong because I know my weaknesses; I'm alive because I'm a fighter; I am wise because I've been foolish; I laugh because I've known sadness and I love because I know what it is like to be hated. In the end, I have been truly blessed.

EPILOGUE

There is no denying that things have vastly improved in my life over the past two years since I penned the first draft of this book at the beginning of 2010. I have a family, I have a home, I have two jobs I love, I wrote a book (which you are reading), I am cancer-free and I am genuinely happy in my heart. I have discovered who I am and what I want to be and most of all – I have found peace, acceptance and love. I have found confidence in myself and abilities - something that is still alien to me.

I believe I needed to write this book so that I could see the big picture; once it was complete its "job" was done and it was no longer as important for me to get it published. However, I think someone is "steering" this project in the direction I need to go. I've had several "signs" over the past year that make it blatantly obvious this project had to be completed.

The first came in the form of running into my grade 9 teacher, who I wrote about earlier in this book. He was the only teacher who seemed to care about me and encourage me. When my editor asked if there was a teacher or someone I would want at my book launch, this teacher stood out. I got the twinge to get back to work, but I ignored it.

Not long later, feeling discouraged about the printing, I mentioned to someone I was done, but I was going to burn my manuscript and it would be gone forever. People kept asking me, "when is your book coming out?" and it was frustrating trying to explain that it was taking longer than expected, because of how emotional this project was. A few days later, fate (or coincidence) stepped in again. I ran into the boy who helped me run away from home the first time. He'd helped me escape my home, gave me safe place to stay, and he was there during those first few weeks that I finally fought back for my life. I ended up breaking his heart and disappearing from his life, but he was remembered in the story of my life (and book) as my very first "hero". It had been about twenty years since we'd last crossed paths. I drove away from our accidental reunion thinking "someone is trying to tell me to finish my book."

Exactly three days later, I was covering an event in Niverville. I pushed to be able to get access to take pictures of Emerson Drive – normally I avoid events with huge crowds but I was unexplainably driven to attend. When we arrived at the concert, we were passing through the gates when the first person I ran into was my old foster uncle, the same one who introduced me to my first husband. Again, it had been several years since we'd seen each other. I looked at my companion, who already knew how I felt about all the "signs" and said "Don't say a thing." We had actually been discussing it on the way to the fair. As we were getting ready to leave after the concert, I heard someone calling my name. What now, I thought.

Looking around, I spotted a woman walking quickly towards me. I recognized her instantly. When we were both teenagers, she used to spend two weeks every summer at my foster home as part of the annual riding camps. I nearly fainted. She rushed up to me and demanded to know my previous last name. Misunderstanding, I rattled off my former married name. "No, what was your maiden name?" I told her.

"That's what I thought". I looked at her confused.

"I live in your old house". *Excuse me?* I was taken aback.

"I live on your parent's old farm." Her next set of words blew me away. "This is going to sound strange but I think we have a ghostly visitor". I gasped. After the episode with my mother and the medium, I have often wondered. I stuttered while she assured me that once in awhile there is a peculiar odor filtering through the house. She described it as a mixture of rotting flesh and barn smell. I knew it was my dad – he had died in that house and while he was alive, he had an ulcer caused by varicose veins on his leg that sometimes smelt really bad.

Needless to say, it took a few minutes to gather my thoughts -

they were EVERYWHERE at that point. I had already spoken to my editor about going to the farm and possibly doing a video montage showing where things took place, so that readers would know it was real - and to help market this book. My son had already agreed to tape it for me. We were also talking about how we should drop in with hopes the new owners would let us walk through the farm. And here was a woman from my past - who again, is part of my book, coming to me, out of the blue and telling me she lives exactly where my life once fell apart. I went home wondering "what the heck is going on". I also had an open invitation to come by and walk through (and film) the old homestead (and catch up with an old friend) anytime.

The most significant sign came as a result of a tragic event. A friend and I were in Lorette on September 13, 2011 when we spotted a group of people trying to catch something on the road. Getting close, I recognized it was a wild loon, obviously lost and confused. My partner and I collected it and took it to a local wild life sanctuary. As we left, I remember laughing about how either someone was trying to tell me to get back to the book or it was a warning. My mother loved loons and if she was sending me signs, a bird or roses would be something she would use. I shouldn't have joked about it. The next day, I got the call my only brother was in the hospital. Within three days he passed away from colon cancer. He fell gravely ill one week and the next he was gone. He slipped into a coma on Monday and passed away without ever knowing what he had.

When I received the call he was hospitalized I left work nearly immediately. I rushed to my sister-in-laws side, because that is what family does. I knew if it was me in her shoes I would not want to face it alone. I knew my family and I knew she'd be at his side, strong for her boys, but there would be no one there for her.

I feel like I was given a gift as I sat at my brother's side when he drew his last breath. I will never forget counting down his heartbeats until the final flutter and then there was nothing but a flat-line. After my experience with the medium a few years ago, I was confident my mom was waiting for him with open arms and the words "I am sorry" on her lips. I knew that finally, after 55 years of heartache and pain, he was free and knew the truth.

At my side was my sister – the same sibling I assumed hated me all my life. What a turning point. We ended up working on the funeral together and had a chance to talk. It was the first time in my entire life, my sister admitted we were all abused. That is all I have ever wanted - someone to finally acknowledge that what I experienced was real, not just the shattered memories of an abused child. It hurts me to know that after I left home, while I always assumed she was the ``glory child`` my sisters life was far from easy. The woman I sat with planning the funeral and afterwards was not the sister I remembered and yet, she was. My daughters commented after the funeral the coolest part of the entire day was watching my sister and I giggle together while we talked - just like sisters. They`d never seen that before and never thought they would see it.

The conversation I had with my sister was so wonderful, I felt comfortable sharing my Donna story with her. She didn't laugh at me, nor turn down her nose like I expected. I told her about who owns the farm and, the many `signs` I've had since Mom passed away. She seemed to accept it (or she was humoring me). Until a few days later - at the funeral, we were getting ready to say good bye when she pulled out a little white box out of her purse. My heart stopped. I knew what it was before opening the box. It was my necklace - THE necklace that my mother asked about through Donna. Now, thanks to my sister, it is back around my neck where it belongs. My sister found it the night before my brother`s funeral while looking for something in my mom`s things.

A door was opened that day and my sister and I have been communicating through email and she is always in my thoughts. I hope that one day we will be able to move forward. The past is the past and I see things clearer now.

Unfortunately, dealing with my brother's passing and then the holidays, the publication of this book stalled once again. And once again, I seriously contemplated destroying it and moving on. However an unexpected email from an old bully from thirty years ago turned my attitude around. In a heartfelt apology, he thanked me for changing his life. Taking it for what it was, I attempted to tell him how things turned out but in the end I was okay. I think I sounded a little more messed up but I hope he will understand when he reads this story, that he was the catalyst to the completion of "Finding Gloria". It took a lot of courage for him to hunt me down. I had forgotten all about him. But he never forgot me. Over the years, I've been the face to his examples on how bullying can affect the victims. Without knowing, I was a teacher.

That is the purpose of this book – to teach readers that the human spirit can overcome anything. My life is far from perfect and I still have my daily struggles with self worth and self esteem. But it is way better than it used to be. I recognize I am a work in progress and one day, I will be a masterpiece.

PHOTO ALBUM

Cover Artwork inspired by artwork by the author's oldest daughter

My birth mother posing for a picture about a year before I was born.

My adoptive parents on their wedding day back in 1954.

My adoptive mother is all smiles as feeds me for the first time after bringing me home.

My adoptive brother and sister on the day I came home from the agency.

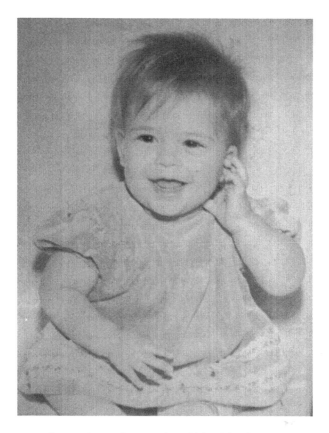

I was about six months old in this picture.

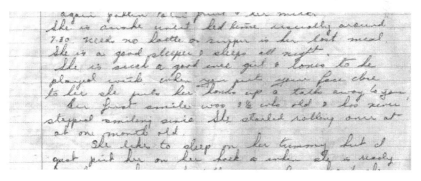

For the first few months of my life I was in foster care. My foster mother wrote this letter for my adoptive parents so they would know my likes and dislikes.

I was just learning to walk when this picture was taken outside my Baba's house in Welland, Ontario.

Our house on Montrose Road in Niagara Falls, Ontario.

Kindergarten   Grade 2   Grade 3

When I was little I adored Winnie the Pooh. I finally received one for Christmas. Unfortunately it disappeared during one of my mother's rages.

Playing with my cousin during Christmas at Baba's house.

The way our family lived changed completely when my mother embraced the apocalyptic prophecies of Veronica Leuken from Bayside, New York.

The dairy farm south of Steinbach where I found out I was adopted. In the far left (white building) is the implement shed where I spent an entire summer living in a derelict van. In the forefront is one of my mother's garden plots where I spent days weeding in the searing heat.

Shortly after I ran away from home, I celebrated my 16th birthday. For the first time in my life I was allowed a birthday party. The boy to my immediate left was my boyfriend at the time. His brother was my first hero because of the role he played both times I ran away.

After moving to Oakbank with my foster family, I lived close to my mother's favorite church in Cooks Creek. I convinced my foster sister (right) and other friends to come along. The girl in the middle is now the owner of my family's farm south of Steinbach.

About a year after I ran away, I was able to return to public school. This is my grade 11 picture from Transcona Collegiate. (1985)

I was barely eighteen when my children's father and I got married in October 1986.

The old homestead in Silberfeld back in 1942.

We purchased the family homestead in Silberfeld, south of Landmark where my husband grew up. We spent eleven years living there together, raising our family of four. (1997)

Barely nineteen, I embraced new motherhood.

The oldest two daughters loved to be silly.

During the summer we loved to camp in St. Malo.

This family picture was taken in the fall of 2001.
My oldest daughter was still hurting after a car accident we were in three months earlier.

My children and I at Christmas in 2007.

After my eleven year marriage ended I fled to Premont, Texas where I spent a month doing ride-alongs on the ambulance. (1998)

Left: When I returned from Texas, I went to school and for a few years I worked as a medical responder for De Salaberry EMS. (1999)

Right: I proudly accepted my Health Care Assistant diploma from Red River Community College in 2002.

In 2005, I went back to school at Red River Community College in Steinbach where I took the High School Diploma Program and graduated with honors. A psychology class helped me recognize that my adoptive mother suffered from a mental illness and an English class gave me the foundation for my memoir *Finding Gloria*.

As a reporter I get to interview interesting people including Manitoba Premier Greg Selinger.

I've also had to take on challenges like repelling down this cliff north of West Hawk Lake or participating in ATV derbies.

At the 10ᵗʰ Anniversary of the Royal Canadian Sea Cadets Dawson in Lorette I was given the honor of inspecting the troops. Afterwards I was presented with a plaque for all the work I've done promoting the program in the *Dawson Trail Dispatch*.

It wasn't until I got into foster care that I was finally able to learn how to ride horses. Soon I was spending hours riding alone or with friends.

When I was a little girl, I would hide in the back field and play baseball by myself for hours using a stone and a pipe. While I coached my daughter's teams and even created a T-Ball league in Landmark, it wasn't until I was 40 I finally had to courage to join a team.

It took over two decades to feel comfortable getting on a motorcycle after I was involved in a tragic accident back when I was sixteen.

Many people have come and gone throughout my life, except my two best friends. We have stuck together through thick and thin since junior high.

In 2007 I returned to Niagara Falls and showed my two youngest children where I grew up.

I also had a chance to see my adoptive uncle and aunt (my father's only brother) while visiting Niagara Falls. It was our first meeting in twenty-one years.

The newest loves of my life – my two grandchildren

In May 2009 I finally connected with my birth mother and my maternal grandmother. Unfortunately this weekend would be the only chance I had to spend time with my grandmother. She passed away a year and a half later.

My half sister was thrilled to welcome me into the family on my 41st birthday.

A few months after our reunion, my birth mother came to Manitoba to meet my family. We took a four generation photo with my mother, my oldest daughter, my granddaughter and myself.

Adoptee finds family on Facebook: Reunion brings healing in two provinces

Adoption reunion stories are always a hit on shows like Oprah or Dr. Phil, but as an Ile des Chênes woman recently learned, they are even better when they happen close to home.

Marianne Curtis found out she was adopted when she was around 11 years old and it was not a pleasant surprise.

"There are things that happened and were said as I was growing up that made me really believe that being adopted was the worst thing that could ever happen to a child," explained Marianne. "I grew up believing that I was rejected by two mothers."

Conditions eventually became unbearable and at 15 years of age, Marianne packed a pillowcase and fled the little farm south of Steinbach. A few years later, her adoptive mother handed over her adoption papers and encouraged her to look for her birth family.

"I remember her telling me that maybe by looking for my family I would find the answers that I always sought, but out of respect and my love for her I didn't do anything with them at the time," Marianne added.

Eventually when her third child was born with a heart defect, Marianne changed her mind and signed the Alberta Adoption Registry. At the time adoption files were closed and only non-identifying information was released. Her search ended abruptly until the province changed their laws in 1995 and files were opened. She was sent a very detailed package in the mail, including her real name and the name of her mother.

"I did several half-hearted searches on the internet over the years but found nothing. Eventually I believed that finding anyone in my family would never happen," Marianne noted.

That all changed in the middle of March, a few weeks after her adoptive mother passed away.

"My dog went missing days after my mother died and I wasn't handling it very well – I posted ads, posters, anything that would help me find him faster," Marianne explained. "On an impulse I figured since I was already in 'looking' mode I would try one more time – I had nothing to lose."

A quick search on Facebook revealed three possible family members in Edmonton, so she quickly fired of a note to each. A few days later she received a note from her birth mother's brother.

"His note floored me – what caught me was how he told me that every year on my birthday for 40 years, my mother has remembered me in some way – she had never forgotten me and wanted to talk to me immediately," she recalled.

Two weeks to the hour of her adoptive mom's viewing, Marianne spoke to her birth mother Caroline Walsh for the first time.

"The first thing I asked her was if the decision to give me up was the right one for her," Marianne shared. "She told me that yes, she finished school and had made a good life – she's been a Grade 3 teacher for 30 years – that meant a lot to me."

Over the next few weeks, Marianne and her newfound family spent hours on the phone getting to know each other. She also has a 16-year-old sister and a stepfather.

"It is like we have lived parallel lives, yet two provinces apart – I am definitely my mother's daughter," laughed Marianne. "There are so many crazy similarities – I'd even met my step-dad before without even knowing it when he used to drive for Big Freight."

Right from the start things just "fit" and Marianne joked that it would be nice meet everyone for the first time for her birthday, and that is exactly what happened, thanks to her maternal grandmother.

On May 1, two days before her 41st birthday, Marianne got off the plane in Edmonton and was embraced by her birth mom for the first time.

"It was very emotional, and yet, so comfortable – I felt like I was coming home for the first time in my entire life," recalled Marianne. "I fit right in."

Along with meeting her family came the answers to many questions and healing.

"I wanted to keep her so much, and kissing her goodbye was the hardest thing I've ever had to do in my life – but I never ever forgot her," explained Carol.

"Unfortunately at the time, with circumstances being as they were, there was no way that I could have kept her without us ending up on the streets – I did what I thought was the best for her because I loved her and always have."

Carol admits that it was difficult to hear that things did not turn out as well as she had hoped for her daughter, but she is excited to have another chance.

"All these years there has been a huge hole in my heart but it is no longer empty," Carol shared. "I never thought this would happen – I lost Marianne once, and I am not going to lose her again."

Unlike many reunion stories, this one has a happy ending. Marianne is currently excitedly planning a reunion at the end of July when her mother, step-dad and sister will travel to Manitoba to meet her four children and two grandchildren.

"I can't believe I am a great-grandma," Carol laughs. "But I wouldn't have it any other way."

**as published in the Dawson Trail Dispatch .

ABOUT THE AUTHOR

Since the fall of 1997, Marianne Curtis has been writing for the Dawson Trail Dispatch. She has since published over 7,000 articles in the monthly publication.

While she prefers investigative pieces, Ms. Curtis does not limit her expertise. Over the years she has covered hardcore news, political issues, public interest groups, community events, sports and entertainment. She also does her own photography.

When Ms. Curtis is not writing for the newspaper, she enjoys spending time with her family, gardening and with her many friends.

Contact Information
Email: mariannecurtis.author@gmail.com
Website: mariannecurtis.wordpress.com
Facebook: Marianne.Curtis
Twitter: writerchick68